As of late 2013 there exists an iPad/iPhone application available at the App Store that uses the science-based approach described in this book to make forecasts for stock prices. It is a powerful, user-friendly, and well-documented program capable of making price forecasts with improved accuracy further into the future. Its uniqueness is that it treats stocks like species and the stock market as an ecosystem.

There exist four versions of this application ranging from the full iPad version selling for $49.99 to the light iPhone version selling for $0.99. They all produce price forecasts with quoted uncertainties corresponding to a 95% confidence level.

WATCH A SHORT VIDEO DEMO HERE:
https://www.youtube.com/watch?v=Tqb0ykBHadQ

NATURAL LAWS IN THE SERVICE OF THE DECISION MAKER

How to Use Science-Based Methodologies to See More Clearly further into the Future

―――――――――――――――

THEODORE MODIS

Growth Dynamics
Lugano, Switzerland

LIBRARY OF CONGRESS
Registration Number: TXu 1-851-456
ISBN: 978-2-9700216-8-1

Produced by GROWTH DYNAMICS
Via Selva 8, 6900 Massagno, Lugano, Switzerland
Tel. 41-91-9212054
http://www.growth-dynamics.com

Contents

PROLOGUE   7

PART I: THEORY AND PRACTICE

1. INTRODUCTION   13
   1.1 Invariants   14
      Car Accidents   15
      Car Average Speed/Mileage   17
      Software to Hardware   18
      Do All Animals Die at the Same Age?   19
   1.2 Case Study   21
      In-Hospital Infections   21

2. NATURAL GROWTH IN COMPETITION   23
   2.1 The S-Curve of Cumulative Growth   25
   2.2 The Law of Natural Growth   27
      Controls on Rabbit Populations   29
      When Can We Use S-Curves?   33
   2.3 Case Studies   34
      Sales of the DEC Minicomputer VAX 11/750   34
      World Gold Production   36
   2.4 Backcasting and the Early Catching-up Effect   37
   2.5 Deviations from S-curves   39
   2.6 S-Curves with Variable Ceiling   41
   2.7 S-Curves and Economies of Scale   45

3. SEASONS OF GROWTH   49
   3.1 Growth from Chaos and Chaos from Growth   54
   3.2 Case Studies   56
      The Concord   56
      DEC's 64-Bit PC   57
      The Possibility of Microsoft's Breakup in Early 2000   58
   3.3 A Large-Scale Historical Example   59
   3.4 A Second Lease on Life   62
   3.5 Where Are You on the Curve?   64
   3.6 Downward-Pointing S-Curves   67
   3.7 Intuitive Use of S-Curves   68

4. SUBSTITUTIONS   71
   4.1 One-to-One Substitutions   72
   4.2 Case Study   80

DEC Microvax II Substituted for the Minicomputer Vax 11/750   80
4.3 Successive Substitutions   82
4.4 Case Studies   84
     Where Has the Energy Picture Gone Wrong?   84
     Semiconductor Market Trends   89

5.   CASCADES OF S-CURVES   93
    5.1 Just-in-Time Replacement   93
    5.2 Fractals of S-Curves   96
    5.3 Case Studies   101
     The MicroVAX Family of DEC Minicomputers   101
     Microsoft Windows Operating Systems   104
     The Stages of Human Growth   105

6.   EVENT ENHANCEMENT   109
    6.1 Case Studies   112
     HLB International   112
     HRM FI Conference   116

7.   LIFE CYCLE OF SERVICES   121
    7.1 Case Study   128
     The Minicomputer VAX 11/780   128

8.   VOLTERRA-LOTKA   131
    8.1 More than One Species in the Niche   132
    8.2 Attacker's Advantage, Defender's Counterattack   133
    8.3 Competition management   136
    8.4 Advertising and Image Building   139
    8.5 Case Studies   143
     A Major European Beer Producer   143
     Nobel Laureates   145

PART II: METHODS AND TOOLS

9.   COMPLETING THE PANOPLY   153
    9.1 Where Are You on the Curve?   154
     Using Data from Company Records and Annual Reports   155
    9.2 Instinct versus Rationale   160
    9.3 Could You Take Aim at an Apple on Your Son's Head?   165
    9.4 Strategy Advice Depending on the Position in the Season   166
    9.5 Case Studies   170
     Appleton Papers   170
     Prudential   178
     NEOSET   184
     QUALCOMM   187

10. EXCEL-BASED TOOLS 191
  10.1 Using the EXCEL SOLVER to Fit Curves on Data 191
    The Use of Chi Square 193
  10.2 How to Fit S-Curves 195
    The Software Package "A Second Lease on Life" 198
  10.3 How to Fit S-Curves with a Variable Ceiling 200
    Example: US Nobel Laureates 201
  10.4 How to Fit the Volterra-Lotka Equations 204
    Example: Nobel Laureates as a 2-Species Niche 205

EPILOGUE 209

APPENDIXES 213
  A.1 Estimation of the Uncertainties in S-Curve Fits 213
  A.2 Deviation between S-Curve and Corresponding Exponential 215
  A.3 Mathematical Formulations 217
    The Logistic Life Cycle 217
    The Chaos Equation 218
    Price Elasticity 219
    Learning and Economies of Scale 220
    S-Curves with Variable Ceiling 221
    The Life Cycle of Services 222
    Volterra-Lotka Equations for More than Two Species 224
    Finding Good Starting Values for the Solver in Volterra-Lotka
      Applications 224

NOTES AND SOURCES 227

ACKNOWLEDGMENTS 235

INDEX 237

PROLOGUE

Natural laws have always been the basis of my thinking. I was trained as a physicist and for many years carried out research in particle accelerator laboratories. Some of these laws have persisted at the center of my thinking playing a prominent role guiding me ever since I left an academic career to work first as a management consultant at Digital Equipment Corporation and later as futurist and strategist. *Fundamental* concepts, such things as equilibrium, competition, feedback, and survival of the fittest, are notions encountered in the marketplace daily.

Equilibrium is typically what happens when supply meets demand. The right price falls out as a byproduct of this phenomenon. *Feedback* can be responsible for oscillations, for example, when demand signals for a newly launched product are overinterpreted. *Competition* intensifies as the market niche becomes saturated; this coincides with the downturn on the product's sales life cycle. *Survival of the fittest* determines who among the prey will survive the predator. The market is full of competitors acting in one or the other capacity.

My first attempt to apply ideas from the natural sciences to the marketplace was to treat products like species, with the focus on the notions of life cycles, market penetration, and product substitution. This approach was extended to families of products, technologies, markets, and similar growth processes that are subject to competition. Then, it was possible to focus on the various stages of the product or technology life cycle and finally to understand intercompany competition and the strategies that will sustain growth over prolonged periods.

Certain events appear to occur in an irregular sequence of nonrepeating patterns. Such a picture, which corresponds to the scientific notion of *chaos*, may seem to be useless in preparing for the future. But chaos in business, like many other phenomena, appears to be *seasonal*. In particular, chaos is associated with low-growth business seasons. Once a business gets into a high-growth period, events become more orderly. Moreover, *good business seasons alternate with bad business seasons, implying that chaos eventually leads to order and vice versa.* There is "harmony" in this swing from chaos to order and back, which can be utilized in preparing for future events.

When facing up to a seasonal change in business our actions must be adapted to the economic climate to ensure survival. Low-growth, seemingly chaotic days demand horizontal structures, entrepreneurship, and innovation. Early growth periods need investment. Rapid growth responds to a more "vertical" approach. In other words, there is a season for leaders and a season for entrepreneurs, a time for specialists, and, surprisingly, a time for bureaucrats. Reengineering, total quality, and benchmarking all have a time when they are best—like oranges in winter and watermelons in summer. Creativity and innovation are not the first priority at all times, just as total quality must take second place while searching for new directions.

Seeing events and actions to be taken as a function of time is key to a successful strategy. The seasonal dimension can be imposed on all business activity. Birth implies death. A business life cycle has different stages, each governed by its own rules. Those who follow these rules will grow in harmony and along the path of least resistance.

Among the pieces of information needed are:

- What is the remaining growth potential?
- Where in the growth process is your business? What "season" is it in?
- What is the timeframe for the growth, decay, and rebirth of your business?
- What should you trust more your instinct or your rationale in a given situation?
- What is your competitive role in the marketplace?
- What is the right image and the most effective advertising message?
- Should you differentiate or counterattack?

This book will enable the consultant to guide his/her clients in answering these questions. It complements my books *Predictions* and *Conquering Uncertainty*, and a series of articles that can be downloaded from my website.[1,2,3] The reader is encouraged to consult these additional sources of information, which nevertheless do not constitute a prerequisite for being able to fully take advantage of what is offered here.

The first part of the book, Theory and Practice, presents the theory behind the natural laws considered and illustrates how they can be applied in real-life situations. Attention is drawn to strengths and weaknesses as the case may be. The second part, Methods and Tools, demonstrates how to proceed in general with a customer engagement from the very beginning. Detail technical advice is given on how to fit S-curves and how to employ the Volterra-Lotka equations using EXCEL. There are also instructions on how to use other software from Growth Dynamics such as *Where Are You on the Curve and What to Do about It*. All along case studies illustrate the approach describing real engagements.

For the science-friendly reader the Appendix includes rigorous mathematical formulations for the natural laws invoked in Part I and for the Excel-based curve-fitting procedures described in Part II. The reader will find in this book research results that have never been published before. For example, the mathematical constructs in the Appendix describing the use of least squares to pinpoint accurate starting values—effectively a first solution —for the fitting procedures, and the numerical solutions of the Volterra-Lotka equations and the S-curves with variable ceiling.

It is not expected that all readers who go through Part I will continue to Part II; only those who want to "get their hands dirty" will. Even fewer individuals are likely to tackle the Appendix; only those who need scientific justification for their own conviction or to defend the approach against challengers will. But I invite everyone to read the Epilogue. After all busy professionals often limit themselves to reading only abstracts and conclusions.

PART ONE:
THEORY AND PRACTICE

1 – INTRODUCTION

I worked as an experimental physicist at CERN for more than 10 years. Throughout this time I sadly witnessed my role as an investigator diminish while experiments became bigger and bigger, it took longer and longer to obtain results, and there was less and less excitement in my work. Therefore I looked around for alternatives and seized the opportunity to work as a forecaster for the second largest computer manufacturer at the time, Digital Equipment Corporation (DEC). Not knowing anything about forecasting I approached the subject as a physicist, that is, from first principles; I went to the biology library to learn about competition. This brought me to Cesare Marchetti a physicist working at the International Institute of Advanced Systems Analysis (IIASA) in Laxemburg, outside Vienna. He had been using natural laws and in particular the S-shaped pattern of growth in competition (S-curve) to better understand and forecast growth processes in the widest range of applications. As soon as I was charged officially with a forecasting project, I took the first plane for Vienna to see Marchetti at IIASA.

He received me in his office buried behind piles of paper. Later I discovered that most of the documents contained numbers, the data sources serving him very much like scrapbooks serve artists. He welcomed me warmly, we uncovered a chair for me, and I went straight to the point. I showed him my first attempts at determining the life cycles of computers. I had dozens of questions. He answered laconically, simply indicating the direction in which I should go to search for my own conclusions. "Look at all computers together," he said. "Small and big ones are all competing together. They are filling the same niche. You must study how they substitute for one another. I've seen cars, trains, and other human creations go through this process."

My discussion with Marchetti lasted for hours. During lunch he kept tossing out universal constants—what he called *invariants*—as if to add spice to our meal. Did I know that human beings around the world are happiest when they are on the move for an average of about seventy minutes per day? Prolonged deviation from this norm is met with discomfort, unpleasantness, and rejection. To obscure the fact that one is moving for longer periods, trains feature games, reading lounges, bar parlors and other pastime activities. Airlines show movies during long flights. On the other hand, lack of movement is equally objectionable. Confinement makes prisoners pace their cell in order to meet their daily quota of travel time.

Did I know, Marchetti asked, that during these seventy minutes of travel time, people like to spend no more and no less than 15% of their income on the means of travel? To translate this into biological terms, one must think of income as the social equivalent for energy. And did I know that these two conditions are satisfied in such a way as to maximize the distance traveled? Poor people walk, those better off drive, while the rich fly. From African Zulus to sophisticated New Yorkers, they are all trying to get as far as possible within the seventy minutes and the 15% budget allocation. Affluence and success result in a bigger radius of action. Jets did not shorten travel time, they simply increased the distance traveled.

Maximizing range, Marchetti said, is one of the fundamental things that all organisms have been striving for from the most primitive forms to mankind. Expanding in space as far as possible is what reproducing unicellular amoebas are after, as well as what the conquest of the West and space explorations were all about. In his opinion, every other rationalization tends to be poetry.

Without realizing it Marchetti had initiated me to a subject that was meant to become my *raison d'être*. In the beginning I was driven by my eagerness to check for myself the validity of the things he was telling me. Later I indulged in exploring further and building on these ideas. I collected data on the use of cars, average car speed, average annual car mileage, accidents, etc. I was not surprised when I got confirmation of Marhcetti's claims that the average car speed in the United States hardly changed since Henry Ford's time and that the number of deaths due to car accidents has been auto-regulated since the appearance of the automobile.

1.1 – INVARIANTS

The simplest possible law dictates that something does not change—an *invariant*, in scientific terms. Invariants are, of course, the easiest things to forecast. They reflect states of equilibrium maintained by natural regulating mechanisms. In ecosystems such equilibrium is called *homeostasis* and refers to the harmonious coexistence of predator and prey in a world where species rarely become extinct for natural reasons.

States of equilibrium can also be found in many aspects of social living. Whenever the level of a hardship or a menace increases beyond the tolerable threshold, corrective mechanisms are automatically triggered to lower it. On the other hand, if the threat accidentally falls below the tolerated level, society becomes blasé about the issue, and the corresponding indicators begin creeping up again with time.

Invariants have the tendency to hide behind headlines. For example, the number of deaths due to motor vehicle accidents becomes alarming when reported for a big country like the United States over a three-day weekend, which is what journalists do. However, when averaged over a year and divided by one hundred thousand of population, it becomes so stable over time and geography that it emerges as rather reassuring!

Car Accidents

Car safety has been a passionate subject frequently appearing in headlines. At some point in time cars had been compared to murder weapons. Still today close to two hundred thousand people worldwide die from car accidents every year, and up to ten times as many suffer injuries. Efforts are continually made to render cars safer and drivers more cautious. How successful have such efforts been? Can this rate be significantly reduced as we move toward a more advanced society?

To answer these questions, we must look at the history of car accidents, but in order to search for a fundamental law we must have accurate data and an appropriate indicator. Deaths are recorded and interpreted with less ambiguity than other accidents. Moreover, the car as a public menace is a threat to society, which may "feel" the pain and react accordingly. Consequently, the number of deaths per one hundred thousand inhabitants per year becomes a better indicator than accidents per mile, or per car, or per hour of driving.

The data shown in Figure 1.1.1 are for the United States starting at the beginning of the 20th century.[1] What we observe is that deaths caused by car accidents grew along an S-shaped pattern with the appearance of cars until the mid 1920s, when they reached about 24 per 100,000 per year. From then onward they seem to have stabilized, even though the number of cars continued to grow. A homeostatic mechanism seems to emerge when this limit is reached, resulting in an oscillating pattern around the equilibrium position. The peaks may have produced public outcries for safety, while the valleys could have contributed to the relaxation of speed limits and safety regulations. What is remarkable is that for over 60 years there has been a persistent self-regulation on car safety despite major increases in car numbers and performance, and important changes in speed limits, safety technology, driving legislation, and education. Why the number of deaths is maintained constant and how can society detect excursions away from this level? Is it conceivable that someday car safety will improve so much that car accidents will be reduced to zero? American society has tolerated this level of accidents for more than half a century. A Rand analyst has described it as follows: "I am sure that there is, in effect, a desirable level of automobile accidents—desirable, that is, from a broad point of view, in the sense that it is a necessary concomitant of things of greater value to society."[2] Abolishing cars from the roads would certainly eliminate car accidents, but at the same time it would introduce more serious hardship to citizens.

An invariant (a homeostatic level) can be thought of as a state of well-being. It has its roots in nature, which develops ways of maintaining it. Individuals may come forward from time to time as advocates of an apparently well-justified cause. What they do not suspect is that they may be acting as agents to deeply rooted forces maintaining a balance that would have been maintained in any case. An example is Ralph Nader's crusade for car safety, *Unsafe at Any Speed*, published in the 1960s, by which time the number of fatal car accidents had already demonstrated a forty-year-long period of relative stability.[3] But examining Figure 1.1.1 more closely, we see that the 1960s show a small peak in accidents, which must have been what prompted Nader to blow the whistle. Had he not done it, someone else would have. Alternatively, a timely social mechanism might have produced the same result; for example, an "accidental" discovery of an effective new car-safety feature.

DEADLY CAR ACCIDENTS

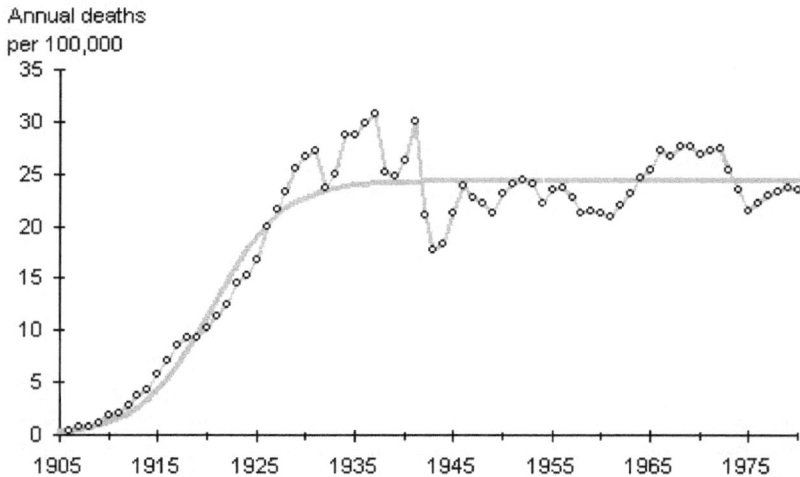

Figure 1.1.1. Following an initial growth phase that lasted until the mid 1920s the annual number of deaths from motor-vehicle accidents per 100,000 population has stabilized at a ceiling of 24 around which it has been fluctuating ever since. The peak in the late 1960s provoked a public outcry that resulted in legislation making seat belts mandatory.

More recent data show a systematic decline in the annual number of victims from car accidents but this is due to the fact that the airplane has been steadily replacing the automobile as a means of transportation. Despite the fact that the automobile still commands a dominant share of the transportation market today, Americans have in fact been giving up, slowly but steadily, their beloved automobile, and the fatal accidents that go with it.

Car Average Speed / Mileage

From the appearance of the automobile in America drivers seem to have adhered to an average speed of 30 miles per hour. All road and car-performance improvements during the 20th century served merely to counterbalance the time lost in traffic jams and at traffic lights.

At an average speed of 30 miles per hour, a traveling time of one hour and ten minutes a day, the natural invariant for the daily displacement, translates to about 35 miles. This daily quota for car mileage is indeed corroborated from data on car statistics. For more than half of the 20th century, yearly mileage in the United States has been narrowly confined to around 9,500 miles, despite the great advances in car speed and acceleration over this period, see Figure 1.1.2. It turns out to be 36.4 miles per working day, in good agreement with the daily displacement quota of 35 miles.

ANNUAL CAR MILEAGE IN THE US

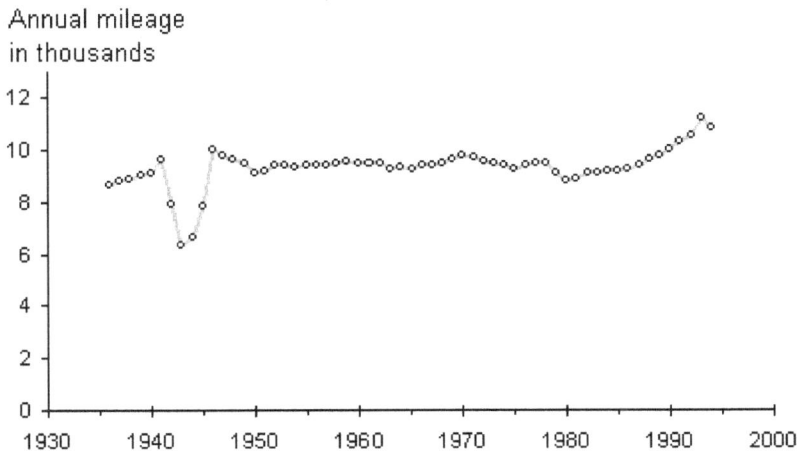

Figure 1.1.2. For more than 60 years car mileage has been confined to around 9,500. Notice the significant deviation introduced by "abnormal" events such as WWII.[4]

The average car speed of 30 miles an hour can be combined with the 70 minutes available for daily displacement to yield the size of our cities. The average distance covered per day is the natural limiting factor in defining the size of urban areas. Communities grow around their transport systems. If it takes more than 70 minutes to get from one point to another, the two points should not reasonably belong to the same community. Cars permitted towns to expand. When people only traveled on foot, at three miles per hour, towns consisted of villages not much larger than three miles in diameter.

There was a factor of ten in speed between foot and car transport, and cities such Los Angeles attest to the 30-miles-in-diameter size. Airplanes expanded the limits of urban areas further, and it is possible today to work in one city and live in another. Air shuttle services have effectively transformed pairs or groups of cities in the United States, e.g., Boston and New York, into one large "town."

Software to Hardware

Invariants characterize a natural equilibrium, a state of well-being. A physiological example is that the average person sleeps during one third of the day-night cycle. It therefore seems reasonable that a balance should exist between the amount of physical and intellectual work carried out during a day. In the world of computers, software can be likened to intellect and hardware to body, and their relative importance seems to be emerging as an invariant that contradicts the best judgment of some information-technology experts.

From the discovery of the wheel to the birth of the transistor, history is punctuated with milestones marking the appearance of machines that relieved humans from repetitive burdens. Industrialization featured mostly muscle-surrogate inventions, but that did not significantly decrease the number of working hours. Allowing eight hours for sleep and another as much for personal matters, the time available for work revolves around eight hours per day across many cultures. Human nature is such that working much more or much less than that is poorly tolerated; cases of depression may be more frequent among people who have little to do. (This also links the two invariants for displacement, namely 70 minutes per day and 15% of one's energy, considering that energy expenditure takes place mostly during working hours and that 15% of 8 hours is 72 minutes).

Soon after the introduction of computers, the need for software gave rise to a thriving new industry, because a computer is useless until programmed to do a task. The fast growth of successful software companies at some point in time had triggered speculation among computer manufacturers that someday computers might be given away free; all revenue would be made from services and software. This meant that the computer industry's major effort would ultimately become the production of software.

Such a trend actually began to develop. In the 1970s, large research institutions built computer-support departments heavily staffed with programmers. Some of them devoted their youth and talent to writing thousands of lines of Fortran to offer scientists the possibility of making graphs, histograms, and computer-generated drawings. But graphic capabilities were progressively transferred to the hardware. Today video terminals provide graphic capabilities without even bothering the central processing unit of the computer with such menial tasks. Meanwhile, those programmers who spent time with graphics routines moved on to higher challenges, such as increasing manyfold a computer's performance through parallel processing techniques. But these techniques were also fully incorporated into the hardware later.

A study carried out for the years 1981 to 1988 showed that the hardware-to-software ratio of society's expenditures was stable over this time at around 25%. This could be a general phenomenon implying that in Western society the natural equilibrium level wants this ratio to be about 3 to 1. The ratio reflects a homeostasis between human work (software) and machine work (hardware) in the information technology industry.

Do All Animals Die at the Same Age?

The notion that all animals die at the same age sounds implausible if you measure age in years and months, but becomes rather logical if you count the number of heartbeats. Isaac Asimov has pointed out that most mammals living free in nature (not in homes and zoos) have accumulated about one billion heartbeats on the average when they die. It is only the rate of the heartbeat that differs from animal to animal. Small ones, like mice, live about three years, but their heartbeat is very rapid. Middle-size ones, rabbits, dogs, sheep, and so forth, have a slower heartbeat and live between 12 and 20 years. Elephants live more than 50 years, but have a slow heartbeat. Asimov remarked, "Whatever the size, ... the mammalian heart seems to be good for a billion beats and no more."[5]

For hundreds of thousands of years humans had a life expectancy between 25 and 30 years. With the normal rate of 72 heartbeats per minute, they conformed nicely to the one billion invariant. Only during the last few hundred years has human life expectancy significantly surpassed this number, largely due to reduced rates in infant mortality from improved medical care and living conditions. Today's humans reach three times the mammals' quota, positioning *Homo sapiens* well above the animal world. Are we finally making progress in our evolution as a species?

"On the contrary, we are regressing!" exclaims Marchetti in his usual playing-the-Devil's-advocate style. Life expectancy at birth increased primarily because infant mortality decreased. But what also increased at the same time was the availability and acceptability of safe and legal abortions, resulting in a rise of prenatal mortality, thus canceling a fair amount of the life expectancy gains. The end result, he says, claiming to have seen the data that substantiate it, is that life expectancy at conception is still not much above 40.

If there is any truth in this, we are back—or close enough—to the one-billion-heartbeat invariant, but with an important difference. Low infant mortality rates result in the birth of many individuals who may be ill suited to survive a natural selection process favoring the fittest. At the same time, abortions are blind. They eliminate lives with no respect to their chance of survival. A selection at random is no selection at all, and the overall effect for the species is a degrading one.

With life expectancy defined at conception, the one-billion-heartbeat invariant seems to still be roughly in effect for humans. From now onward there can be no significant further gains in infant mortality rates because they are already quite low. Moreover, the overall death rate has practically stopped decreasing. All this argues for bleak forecasts about life-expectancy growth. There may be a message for us coded in the one-billion-heartbeat invariant. According to the Bible we are now reaching the upper limit in life expectancy:[6]

> Seventy years is all we have—eighty years, if we are strong; yet all they bring us is trouble and sorrow; life is soon over, and we are gone. (Psalm 90:10).

On the other hand, an invariant turning into a variable is nothing un-usual. A frequent discovery in physics is that something thought of as a constant is, in fact, a limited manifestation of a simple law, which in turn is a special case of a more complicated law, and so on. When the complexity becomes unmanageable, physicists turn toward unification, searching for a general law that will describe a multitude of diverse phenomena, each hitherto abiding by elaborate custom-made rules. In other words, they look for a new invariant on a higher abstraction level. For example, the acceleration of gravity, 10m/sec/sec, had been perceived as a constant from the early falling-apple days until Newton showed that the rate decreases with altitude. Later Einstein's relativity theory revealed more complicated equations for the falling apple. Today, besides apples, there are hundreds of elementary particles, all behaving according to rules made to measure. The physicists' dream in the meantime has become the Grand Unification wherein the behavior of apples, as well as particles, stars, galaxies, and light, all can be described by the same set of equations.

To predict the future we must first find out the constraints which have to be met, the invariants and other natural laws that have influenced or governed in the past and will, in the highest degree of probability, continue to do so in the future. There are many mathematical equations that can describe such certainties, but I have found that much of their essence is often captured visually through the shapes associated with these equations, which accurately depict the past and provide reliable forecasts for the future.

1.2 – CASE STUDY

In-Hospital Infections

In 1995 I was invited to address medical doctors attending their annual meeting at the 9ème Entretiens de Beaulieu in Geneva. The topic for my talk had been imposed as "Can There Be Health without Medicine?" undoubtedly because of my book *Predictions*, in which heavy and sometimes unorthodox use of the laws of natural growth and competition give rise to surprising conclusions. The gist of my talk is summarized in the abstract of the article that was subsequently published in the medical journal *Médecine et Hygiène*:[7]

> The concept of competition and its formulations is exploited quantitatively to describe the struggle between diseases as they try to claim a larger number of victims. Constrained by society's self-healing and autoregulating mechanisms, "old" diseases fade with time in favor of "young" ones which grow. The evolution of a disease's ability to claim victims is a natural-growth process and as such it can be forecasted. Victory over a disease does not have to depend on the discovery of a miracle drug. Most often effective medication against a disease is the consolidation of learning accumulated over a prolonged period of time. That is why vaccines usually become established when a disease is already in the phasing-out stage. From this standpoint, we should not expect a

vaccine for AIDS before the number of AIDS victims starts declining. Nevertheless, society has already confined AIDS to a "microniche".

Following my talk there was a lively discussion on the action of natural laws and in particular invariants. The next speaker talked about in-hospital infections and how difficult it proved lowering them below the level of 25% despite coordinated efforts on many fronts: hygiene, organization, isolation, decontamination, etc. At the end he concluded that it might be counterproductive to insist trying to lower infections further because this level may represent an invariant, a "desirable" homeostatic level in the same sense as deaths from car accidents, that is, concomitant of things of greater value to the hospital, such as being able to treat many different diseases simultaneously. Obviously if the hospital admitted patients who suffered from only one disease, e.g. cirrhosis of the liver, or tuberculosis, in-hospital infections could be reduced to a negligible rate. The price for being able to treat all diseases in one place is a certain quota of in-hospital infections.

IN CLOSING

Invariants may be tricky to uncover but often reveal secrets. In the bigger picture invariants may be found to represent parts of more sophisticated laws such as natural growth and competitive substitutions, which we will examine more closely in the following chapters. For now, we should retain that an invariant represents homeostatic equilibrium of opposing forces and a state of well-being. The challenge each time is to search for the benefit hidden behind the conservation. In other words, what is that for which the invariant in question behaves like price, as was the number car-accident deaths per population for the use of cars, and in-hospital infections for the ability to treat all diseases in one place. Sometimes this may prove very difficult to unveil, for example, what is the benefit(s) for which the invariants of Figure 1.1.2 act as "prices"?

2 – NATURAL GROWTH IN COMPETITION

Invariants are the simplest possible natural laws that exist for long periods of time, without a beginning, middle, or an end, and which could be visualized as a straight horizontal line. However, there are natural laws with increasing complexity having a beginning and an end but with an invariant overall form. Such is the law of natural growth over a span of time wherein a beginning is linked with growth and a decline with death. Coming into and out of existence is often called a life cycle, and its popular pictorial symbol is a bell-shaped curve shown in Figure 2.1.

Originally used in biology, the bell curve illustrates that anything with life grows at a rate which goes over a peak halfway through the growth process. A sunflower seedling, for example, reaches a final height of about eight feet in 70 days. The growth rate reaches a maximum around 35 days. If Figure 2.1 were to represent the rate of growth, it would have a time scale in days, so that "Birth" appears at zero days, "Growth" at around 20 days, "Maturity" at 35, "Decline" at around 50, and "Death" at 70 days, beyond which no more growth is expected. If, on the other hand, Figure 2.1 were to represent the "life cycle" of a pianist's career—expressed in terms of the number of concerts given annually—an approximate time scale would indicate: "Birth" at around 20 years of age, "Growth" at 30, "Maturity" at 45, "Decline" at 60, and "Death" around 70. The bell-shaped curve would qualify the pianist as promising young performer at 20, gaining popularity at 30, world renowned at 45, and in decline at 60.

A LIFE CYCLE

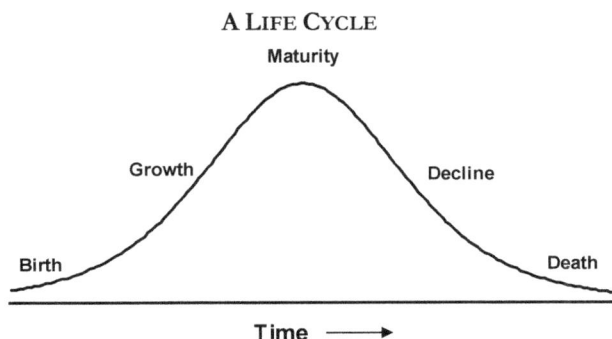

Figure 2.1 This bell-shaped curve is used across disciplines as a template for the cycle of life.

A natural-growth life cycle is remarkably similar to the bell-shaped distribution curve usually referred to as "normal", or otherwise called a Gaussian that has been overused by hard and soft sciences to describe all kinds of distributions. Examples range from people's intelligence (I.Q. index), height, weight, and so forth, to the velocities of molecules in a gas, and the ratio of red to black outcomes at casino roulette wheels.

The Gaussian bell-shaped curve is obtained through an elegant mathematical derivation and resembles very much these distributions with which people are often concerned. Therefore the tendency is to put Gaussian labels on most of the variables on which people get their measuring sticks. In reality, however, there are not many phenomena that obey a Gaussian distribution precisely.

The logistic life cycle is so close to a Gaussian curve that they could easily be interchanged. No psychologist, statistician, or even physicist would ever have come to a different conclusion had he or she replaced one for the other in a statistical analysis. What is ironic is that the Gaussian distribution is called "normal" while there is no natural law behind it. It should rather have been called "mathematical" and the name "normal" reserved for the S-curve law that is so fundamental in its principles.

The concept of a life cycle has been borrowed by psychologists, historians, businessmen, and others to describe the growth of a process, a product, a company, a country, a planet. In all cases it represents the rate

THE NORMAL DISTRIBUTION IS VERY SIMILAR TO THE NATURAL LIFE CYCLE

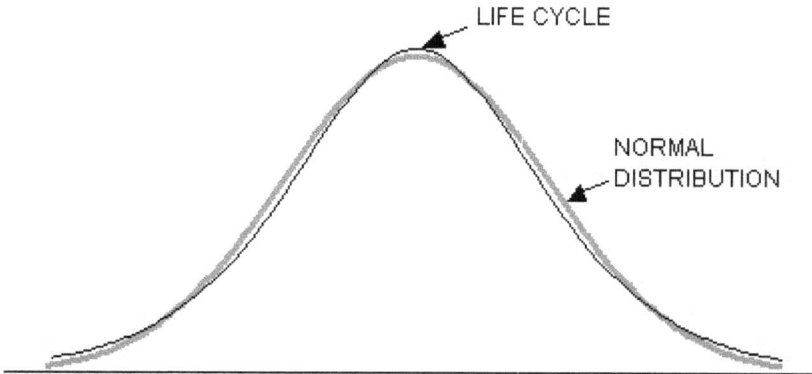

Figure 2.2. Comparison of the Gaussian distribution—usually referred to as *normal*—and a natural life cycle. The two curves have been normalized to cover the same area.

of growth, which is zero before the beginning and it becomes zero again at the end. The bell-shaped curve of Figure 2.1 has become a visual symbol for natural growth and serves most often only qualitatively. However, it can also be of quantitative use.

2.1 – THE S-CURVE OF CUMULATIVE GROWTH

As one moves along the life-cycle curve passing through the various stages, the cumulative number of the units represented by the bell curve grows in such a way that it traces the shape of an S, shown at the lower part of Figure 2.1.1. The S-shaped curve (or S-curve) can therefore become a visual symbol for cumulative growth. For example, while the rate of growth of a sunflower seedling traces a bell-shaped curve, the overall size of the plant produces and S-curve going roughly from six inches at seven days to eight feet in seventy days. Halfway through, when the growth rate is fastest, the plant's height is around four feet, which is half its final height.

As for the other example mentioned earlier, the career of a pianist, the rate at which he gives concerts over the lifetime of his career traces a bell-shaped curve, but the cumulative number of concerts he has given up to a certain time traces an S-curve.

A last example is the launching of a new product. The life cycle of the product can be measured by the number of units sold per month and follows a bell-shaped curve, while the cumulative number of units sold up until any given month follows an S-curve. In mathematical terms the S-curve is the integral of the life-cycle curve and therefore it represents point by point the area under the life-cycle curve.

Just as an S-curve can be obtained from a life cycle by measuring the cumulative rate of growth over time, one can calculate a life cycle from the S-curve through successive subtractions. For example, monitoring a plant's growth over the days by plotting its height on graph paper produces and overall S-curve. If one is interested in the life cycle of the process, one must subtract from each day's measurement the previous day's, thus producing a set of numbers representing growth per day, which will follow the bell-shaped curve of the natural life cycle.

An S-curve and the associated life cycle are two different ways of looking at the same growth process. The S-curve represents the size of the growth and points out (anticipates) the growth potential, the level of the final ceiling, how much could one expect to accomplish. The bell-shaped life-cycle curve represents the rate of growth and is more helpful when it

THE PATTERNS OF NATURAL GROWTH IN COMPETITION

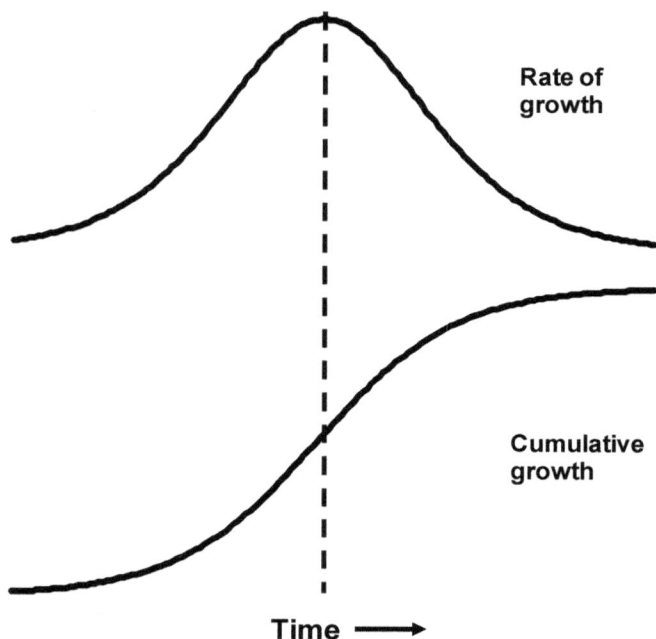

Figure 2.1.1 While the rate of growth follows a bell-shaped curve, the cumulative growth traces out an S-curve. The S-curve is the integral of the bell-shaped curve; at every point in time the latter represents the area under the former.

comes to appreciating the growth phase you are traversing, and how far you are from the end. The S-shaped curve reminds us of the fact that competitive growth is capped. The bell-shaped curve reminds us that whatever gets born eventually dies. From an intuitive point of view, an S-curve promises a certain amount of growth that can be accomplished, whereas a bell-curve heralds the coming end of the process as a whole. Both curves possess predictive power.

. At the ceiling (homeostasis) the level remains invariant and therefore it is trivial to forecast. But there is predictability also during the rapid-growth phase (rheostasis). You can easily project the trajectory of a fast-moving train. A bicycle is stable only when in motion and the faster it is going the more stable it is, the easier it is to project its trajectory

But the predictive power associated with these curves is mainly associated to their symmetry. A rapid rise will be followed by an equally rapid decline. Popular wisdom incorporated in such proverbs as "Easy come, easy go" and "Early ripe, early rot", reflects the fact that to a first approximation any life cycle will be symmetric. Many companies that rose rapidly declined equally rapidly. An example is the People's Express experiment in air travel, which went up and down in a few years. Another example, of longer time scale, is DEC, which impressed the information technology industry equally with its rise as with its decline. IBM's life cycle could also be symmetric, but it is very slow moving; it may take more than 150 years to go from beginning to end.

2.2 – THE LAW OF NATURAL GROWTH

The law describing natural growth has been cast into mathematical equations called growth functions. The simplest mathematical function that produces an S-curve is called a *logistic* and is the solution of the following differential equation that describes natural growth in competition:

$$\frac{\mathrm{d}X}{\mathrm{d}t} = \alpha X(M - X) \qquad\qquad 2.2.1$$

where X is the size of the population and α and M are constants, the latter representing the size of the niche (the ceiling of the S-curve).

This law has been derived by simple reasoning. It says in words that the rate of growth is proportional to both the amount of growth already accomplished X and the amount of growth remaining to be accomplished $(M\text{-}X)$. If either one of these quantities is small, the rate of growth will be small. This is the case at the beginning and at the end of the process. The rate is greatest in the middle, where both the growth accomplished and the growth remaining are sizable. Furthermore, growth remaining to be accomplished implies a limit, a saturation level, a finite market size. This ceiling of growth is assumed to be constant throughout the growth process. Such an assumption is necessary in order to be able to solve Equation 2.2.1 analytically, but it is also a good approximation to many natural-growth processes, for example, plant growth, in which the final height is genetically pre-coded. For those processes where the niche capacity M may be increasing during the growth phase a more elaborate approach to solve the equation is described in Section 10.3.

The solution of Equation 2.2.1 is:

$$X(t) = \frac{M}{1 + e^{-\alpha(t - t_o)}} \qquad\qquad 2.2.2$$

where t_0 is the time when the growth process is half-way complete.[*]

It is a remarkably simple and fundamental law. It has been used by biologists to describe the growth under competition of a species population, for example, the number of rabbits in a fenced off grass field. It has also been used in medicine to describe the diffusion of epidemic diseases. J. C. Fisher and R. H. Pry refer to the logistic function as a diffusion model and use it to quantify the spreading of new technologies into society.[1] One can immediately see how ideas or rumors may spread according to this law. Whether it is ideas, rumors, technologies, or diseases, the rate of new occurrences will always be proportional to how many people have it and to how many don't yet have it.

The analogy has also been pushed to include the competitive growth of inanimate populations such as the sales of a new successful product. In the early phases, sales go up in proportion to the number of units already sold. As the word spreads, each unit sold brings in more new customers. Sales grow exponentially. It is this early exponential growth that gives rise to the first bend of the S-curve. Business looks good. Growth is the same percentage every year and hasty planners prepare their budgets that way. Growth, however, cannot be exponential. Explosions are exponential. Growth follows S-curves. It is proportional to the amount of the market niche still unfilled. As the niche fills up, growth slows down and goes into the second bend of the S-curve, the flattening out. Finally we reach zero growth and the end of the life cycle; the growth process in question comes to an end. The bell curve depicting the rate of natural growth goes back to zero, while the S-curve of cumulative growth reaches its ceiling.

What is hidden under the graceful shape of the S-curve is the fact that natural growth obeys a strict law, which is seeded with knowledge of the final ceiling, the amount of growth remaining to be accomplished. Therefore, accurate measurements of the growth process before it is completed can be used to determine the law quantitatively, thus revealing the final size (the value of the ceiling) ahead of time. This is why the S-curve approach possesses predictive power.

---

[*] Equation 2.2.2 has a 3rd parameter t_o which is an integration constant.

The S-curve has also being referred to as a learning curve in psychology as well as in industry. For example, the evolution of an infant's vocabulary has been shown to follow an S-curve that reaches a ceiling of about 2500 words by age six.[2]. Acquiring vocabulary can be thought of as a competitive process where words in the combined active vocabulary of the two parents compete for the infant's attention. The words most frequently used will be learned first, but the rate of learning will eventually slow down because there are fewer words left to learn. This ceiling of 2500 words defines the size of the home-vocabulary "niche," all the words available at home. Later, of course, schooling enriches the child's vocabulary, but this is a new process, starting another cycle, following probably a similar type of curve to reach a higher plateau.

Equations 2.2.1 and 2.2.2, graphed in the two patterns of Figure 2.1.1, display an asymptotic behavior, that is, they approach zero, the level of the ceiling continuously but reach it only in time - ∞, + ∞ respectively. On the other hand the fact that growth is proportional to the amount of growth already achieved renders the beginning of every natural-growth process very difficult in practice (theoretically impossible because zero growth achieved yields a null rate for growth and so things cannot be started!) This demystifies the known difficulty associated with beginnings. An ancient Greek proverb on achievement equates the beginning with half of the whole! The consequences on learning are enlightening. Theoretically speaking learning cannot begin without outside intervention. The work of teachers becomes indispensable in this context. The teacher is the custodian of knowledge and oriental schools of thought preclude search for esoteric knowledge and personal development without a teacher.

This theoretical difficulty getting growth started touches upon philosophical questions akin to the *genesis* because of the requirement that some external discontinuous intervention from a potent wise entity is necessary in order to get something going from nothing.

Controls on Rabbit Populations

There is an inherent element of competition in logistic growth—competition for space, food, or any resource that may be the limiting factor. This competition is responsible for the final slowing down of growth. A species population grows through natural multiplication. Besides feeding, rabbits do little else but multiply. The food on their range is limited, however, with a capacity for feeding only a certain number of rabbits. As the population approaches this number, the growth rate has to slow down. How does this happen? Perhaps by means of increased kit mortality, diseases, lethal fights between overcrowded rabbits, or even other more subtle forms of behavior that rabbits may act out unsuspectingly. Nature imposes population controls as needed, and in a competitive environment, only the fittest survive.

At the ceiling, we may witness oscillations as the rabbit population explores the possibility to go further and overshoots the niche capacity only to fall back later giving the grass a chance to grow back and feed more rabbits. At this point we may talk of a homeostasis, a stable state of equilibrium between the number of rabbits and the amount of grass, see Figure 2.2.1. More often than not invariants result from S-curves that have reached their ceiling. That was typically the case with deadly car accident discussed earlier in Section 1.1. Of course, such oscillations cannot happen if we are dealing with a cumulative variable.

Since the growth of a rabbit population follows an S-curve from the beginning, one may conclude that these natural controls are so sophisticated that they take effect from the very first rabbit couple on the range. The same mathematical function describes the process from beginning to end. The function can be determined, in principle, after only a few early measurements on the rabbit population. Theoretically, therefore, as soon as this function is defined, the fate of the growth of the rabbit population is sealed.

INVARIANTS FROM S-CURVES

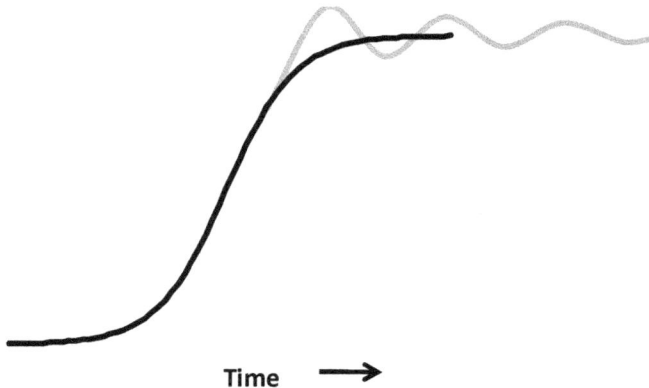

Time ⟶

Figure 2.2.1 Populations approaching a ceiling may break into oscillations, a trial-and-error attempt to overshoot the capacity of their niche.

I became suspicious the first time I was confronted with this notion. I could not explain how the first rabbit couple would have to behave "in accordance" with a final limitation it had not yet felt. My doubts were resolved when I realized that the early part of an S-curve is practically indistinguishable from an exponential. In fact, early rabbits behave as if there are no controls. If the average rabbit litter is taken as two, then we observe the rabbit population go through the successive stages of 2, 4, 8, 16, 32, 64, ..., 2^n in an exponential growth. There is a population explosion up to the time when a sizable part of the niche is occupied. It is only after this time that limited food resources begin imposing constraints on the number of surviving rabbits. That is why trying to determine the final ceiling from very early measurements may produce enormous errors.

In addition, all measurements are subject to fluctuations. Special conditions such as bad weather or a full moon may perturb the reproductive process. Similarly for the analogous case of product sales, the numbers are subject to political events, truck-driver strikes, or stock-market plunges. Small fluctuations on a few early measurements, if that is all we use, can make a huge difference on the estimate of the final niche capacity.

That is why the S-curve can be meaningfully determined only if the growth process has proceeded sufficiently to deviate from the early exponential pattern, namely the penetration level toward the final ceiling must be at least 15%.[*] It is advisable to determine the curve from many measurements and not just from a few early ones. This way we diminish the impact of rare events, and measurement errors will largely average out. The correct procedure is a fit described in detail in Section 10.2. The process involves the minimization of the square of the differences between theoretical S-curve and data (in mathematical jargon a Chi Square) in order to search through trial and error for the S-curve which passes as close as possible to as many data points as possible. The curve chosen will provide us with information outside the data range, and in particular with the value and the time of onset of the final ceiling.

Critics of S-curves have always raised the question of uncertainties as the most serious argument against forecasts of this kind. Obviously the more good-quality measurements available, the more reliable the determination of the final ceiling. But I would not dismiss the method for fear of making a mistake. Alain Debecker and I carried out a most extensive study of the uncertainties to be expected as a function of the number of data points, their measurement errors, and how much of the S-curve they cover. We did this in the physicist's tradition through a

---

[*] See Appendix A.2 for a detailed table on the deviation between an S-curve and the exponential it reduces to for very small times.

computer program simulating historical data along S-curves smeared with random deviations, and covering a variety of conditions. The subsequent fits aimed to recover the original S-curve. The results were published, and a summary of them is given in Appendix A.1, but the rule of thumb is as follows:[3]

> If the measurements cover about half of the life cycle of the growth process in question and the error per point is not bigger than 10%, nine times out of ten the final niche capacity will turn out to be less than 20% away from the forecasted one.

The results of our study were both demystifying and reassuring. The predictive power of S-curves is neither magical nor worthless. Bringing this approach to industry could be of great use in estimating the remaining market niche of well-established products within quoted uncertainties.

A frequent point of confusion is whether one should fit an S-curve to the raw data or to the cumulative number. Both the S-curve and the life-cycle curve of Figure 2.1.1 begin with an exponential trend. Confronted with historical data that are still growing exponentially, which picture is appropriate? An S-curve fitted on the raw data and an S-curve fitted on the cumulative data will result in dramatically different forecasts.[4]

It is essential here to exercise wise judgment. What is the species and what is the niche that it is growing into? To the frustration of business-school teachers there is no universal answer. When forecasting the sales of a new specific product it is rather obvious that one should fit the cumulative sales because the product's market niche is expected to eventually fill up and sales will drop to zero. It is also obvious that one should not fit the cumulative number concerning forecasts on the evolution of Internet users or of the Earth's population as these numbers are not expected to begin decreasing anytime in the near future. But if we are trying to forecast the evolution of a company, should we fit the evolution of its annual growth pattern (be it measured by revenue, unit sales, employees, etc.) or of the cumulative annual numbers from the beginning of the company's existence?

The question that needs to be answered is whether this particular company's existence is a transient phenomenon (like a fad or an epidemic, if on a large timeframe) or whether the company is here to stay with us "forever" like the Internet or the building up of a smoking habit. In the former case, we should fit an S-curve to the cumulative revenue; in the latter we should fit it to the company's raw numbers as quoted per unit of time. The forecasts obtained in the two cases are progressively more different the further in the future we project them.

Needless to say life is not simple. If products are not sufficiently differentiated, they are sharing the niche with others, in which case the combined populations must be considered. Furthermore, the fitting procedure as described in Section 10.2 allows for weights to be assigned to the different data points. The wise user can thus put more emphasis on some points than on others as deemed appropriate. The end result is value added by the person who is doing the fit. This methodology does not automatically produce identical results by all users. Like any powerful tool, it can create marvels in the hands of the knowledgeable, but it may prove deceptive to the inexperienced. The forecaster's involvement is crucial because he or she plays a decisive role. The forlorn hope of marketers and artificial-intelligence designers for a push-button solution whereby everyone will be able to trivially obtain the same forecast without the need to exercise judgment is a utopia. The forecaster's ultimate test is the goodness of his or her forecasts not the elegance or the easiness of the method used.

When Can We Use S-Curves?

The indispensable ingredients for natural growth are the ability of a "species" to multiply and a finite niche capacity. Of course it is understood that we are dealing with a well-defined species, which is not something obvious. In generalizing the concept of a species we may run into difficulties deciding what constitutes one. For example, the Soviet Union constituted a species more defensibly than the USA. After their revolution the Bolsheviks inherited a multinational empire that was created by the Tsarist expansion over four centuries. But this mosaic of cultures did not change appreciably during the lifetime of the Soviet Union, which was isolated from the outside world. The USSR was a rather stable "species" that came into existence at a well-defined moment and occupied a well-defined niche in absence of excessive mutations. In contrast, the USA took 150 years to take shape, and different-culture people never ceased to poor in it and continue to do so even today. As a consequence, the evolution of the USSR can be described better by an S-curve than that of the USA.

In general, a forecaster must have good reasons to believe that an S-curve fit is appropriate. Logistic growth is natural growth in competition. Therefore besides a species capable of multiplying there should also be competition for a limited resource. Alternatively, an *a posteriori* argument for using an S-curve can be made if a good fit has been achieved. If the data do fit well a large section of an S-curve, then one can argue for logistic growth just because "if it walks like a duck and quacks like a duck, it must be a duck." Still, one will gain confidence if one can identify a well-defined species "genetically" stable that is competing for a limited resource.

There have been S-shaped patterns (sigmoid functions) associated with many models and mathematical formulations other than the logistic function described by Equation 2.2.2. Examples are the Gompertz function, the Bass model, and the integral of the Gaussian life cycle.[5,6,7] Many of them also employ only three parameters and could be successfully used instead of logistic S-curves in most situations. But the logistic formulation is the simplest one and it stems from a natural law as fundamental as the survival of the fittest.

2.3 – CASE STUDIES

Sales of the DEC Minicomputer VAX 11/750

The first computer product I was officially asked to study in mid-1985 was one of Digital's early successful minicomputers, the VAX 11/750, which turned out to be a showcase. The cumulative number of units sold is shown at the top of Figure 2.3.1. An S-curve passes quite closely to all twenty-eight quarterly data points. In the lower graph we see the product's life cycle, the number of units sold each trimester. The bell-shaped curve is the life cycle as deduced from the smooth curve at the top.

When I produced this graph I concluded that the product was phasing out, something which most marketers opposed vehemently at the time. They told me of plans to advertise and repackage the product with free software in order to boost sales. They also spoke of seasonal effects, which could explain some of the recent low sales.

The actual data during the following three years turned out to be in agreement with my projections. To me this came as evidence that promotion, price, and competition were conditions present throughout a product's life cycle and would not change the course of a natural phasing-out process established in the presence of these conditions. The promotional programs that marketers put in place were not significantly different from those of the past and therefore did not produce a modification of the predicted trajectory. When I confronted DEC marketers with the ineffectiveness of their actions they offered the following explanation. The phasing out of the VAX 11/750 had been precipitated prematurely by the launching of MicroVAX II, a computer as powerful but at one-third the price. But this argument of "cannibalization" was irrational. The VAX 11/750 had been a well-positioned product with a well-defined market niche. MicroVAX II was launched in mid-1986 by which time the VAX11/750 had been well on its way out. Had DEC delayed the launching of the new product, its competitors would have stepped in to fill the gap created by the phasing-out product. Inadvertently DEC's marketers had launched MicroVAX II just in time!

A SUCCESSFUL COMPUTER PRODUCT FILLING ITS NICHE LIKE A SPECIES

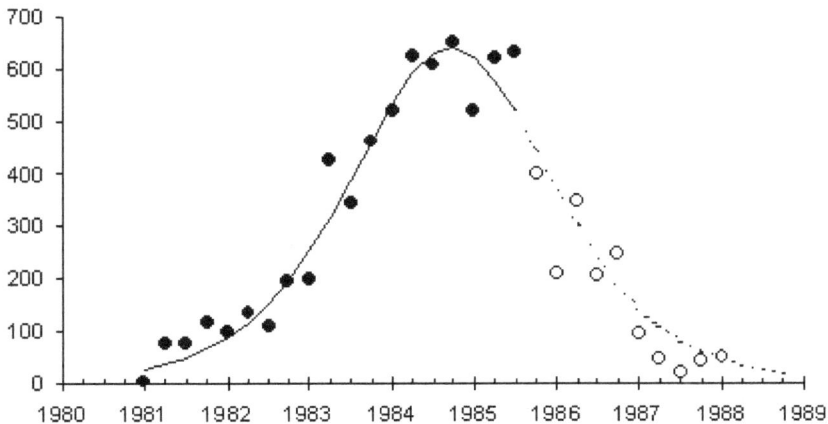

Figure 2.3.1 At the top, growth of cumulative sales in Europe for DEC's mini-computer VAX 11/750. The S-curve is a fit carried out in 1985. The dotted line was my forecast at the time; the little circles show the subsequent sales. The product's life cycle at the bottom has been calculated from the figure at the top.

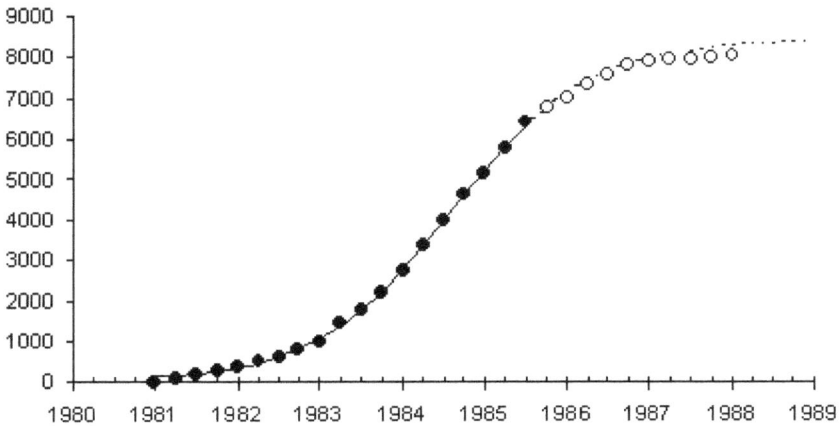

World Gold Production

In mid-2009 a firm advising investors asked me to study the production of gold and its impact on the gold price. Gold production qualifies as a competitive process not only because there is a finite amount of gold in the earth and the more we extract the less there remains to be extracted (a limited resource), but also because the need for gold in society may be finite. New materials are substituting for gold in many uses.

I began by collecting data on worldwide production of gold, which has been well documented, particularly from 1900 onward (yearly data).[8] Treating gold as a "species" filling (or emptying) a finite niche I fitted an S-curve on the cumulative data. In Figure 2.3.2 we see that indeed cumulative gold production has followed an S-curve rather closely for more than 150 years. The life-cycle picture that depicts annual rates of growth is calculated from the graph in Figure 2.3.2 and is shown in Figure 2.3.3. There is a variation around the bell-shaped trend that seems rather regular. If we graph the ratio data to trend, we can better evidence this variation as cyclical with a period of 27-28 years, which is also interesting for another reason. It is half the Kondratieff cycle and it has been argued that wars, which generally impact demand on gold, resonate with such a frequency.[9]

The rest of my analysis included correlations between the cyclical variations on gold production and variations on the gold price. A negative correlation between production and price was established, at least for the second half of the 20th century, which permitted forecasts for the price of gold.

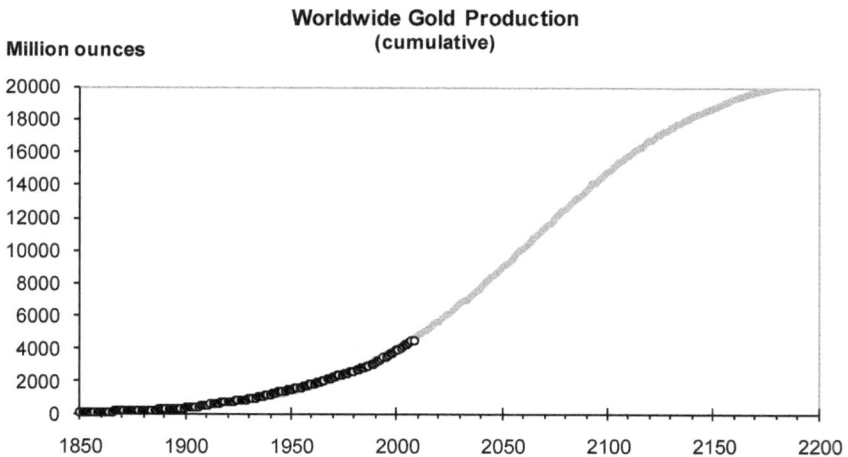

Worldwide Gold Production (cumulative)

Figure 2.3.2. Data and S-curve fit on yearly data points. Before 1900, the data are reported only every five years so for this graph yearly estimates have been interpolated.

Million ounces

Worldwide Gold Production - Life Cycle
(annually)

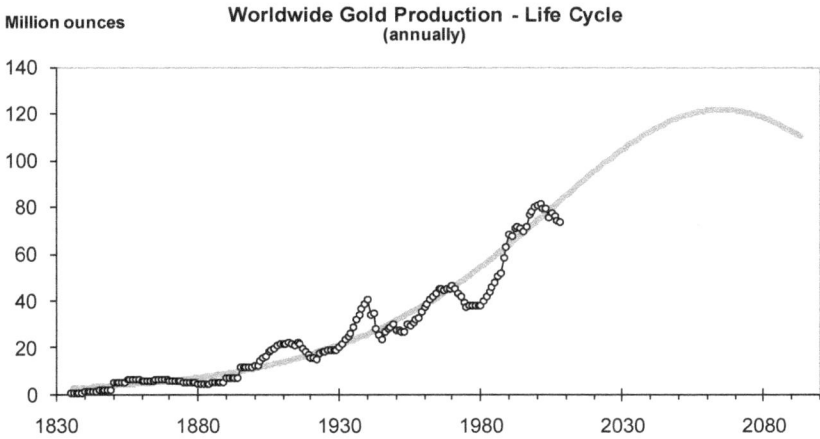

Figure 2.3.3 The life cycles (rates of growth) corresponding to the curves of Figure 2.3.2.

2.4 – BACKCASTING AND THE EARLY CATCHING-UP EFFECT

Following a successful S-curve fit the values of the three parameters of the logistic function—four if there is a pedestal—are determined and therefore we can evaluate the function for any time in the future (forecasting) or in the past (backcasting). The latter occurs when there is a negative pedestal, that is, when we are missing data up front on the early phase of the growth process. Backcasting may be less frequently asked for but it can shed new light in our understanding of the growth process. A case in point is the construction of particle accelerators discussed in my book *Predictions*.

During the 20th century physicists built laboratories of progressively larger dimensions called particle accelerators or atom smashers, which proliferated after World War II to produce a population whose growth has followed an S-shaped pattern, see Figure 2.4.1. The historical data consist of the number of particle accelerators coming into operation worldwide. The S-curve fitted on them approached a ceiling in 1990.

In this dataset each accelerator counts as one even if the size of the device varied significantly over the years. The early setups were of modest dimensions. The Cosmotron of Brookhaven National Laboratory, where preliminary work for the discovery of the antiproton was carried out in the 1950s, was housed inside one big hall. At CERN, the ring of the electron accelerator LEP was completed in 1989. It measured eighteen miles in circumference, lied deep underground, and passed under suburbs of

THE ERA OF PARTICLE ACCELERATORS

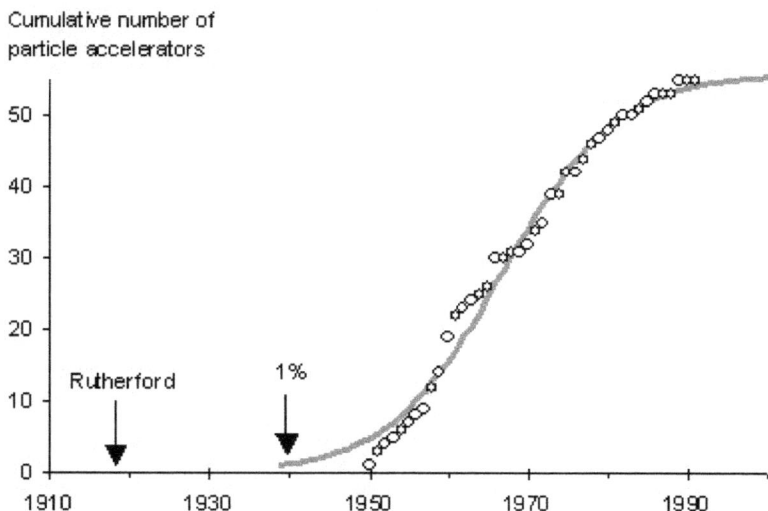

Figure 2.4.1 The data on particle accelerators coming into operation worldwide were fitted with an S-curve whose nominal beginning points at War World II rather than Rutherford's famous experiment.

Geneva, several French villages, and the nearby mountains. A later proposal for an accelerator in Texas, the Superconducting Super Collider (SSC), involving an underground tunnel with a circumference of almost fifty-four miles was rejected by the US government. The rejection came as confirmation that the "dinosaur's" size became too large for survival.

One may think that accelerators like the Cosmotron and LEP, being so different in size, should not both count as one in defining the population. On the other hand, building the Cosmotron with the knowhow of the early 1950s was no lesser a feat than the ring of LEP in the late 1980s.

The reason the size of accelerators has grown to practically absurd dimensions is that we have progressively exhausted the utility of the fundamental principle of electron accelerators: the radio-frequency electromagnetic cavity used for acceleration. Every new horizon of particle physics research requires higher particle energies, more acceleration, and more radio-frequency cavities. In the end, it is purely the size, with the associated expenses, which renders the process obsolete. By and large the era of high-energy physics particle research as we have known has come to a close.

An unexpected finding in Figure 2.4.1 was that the nominal beginning of the curve (the 1% of maximum level) points at the outbreak of World

War II. But physicists have traditionally attributed the beginning of matter's exploration via particles to Rutherford's famous experiment in 1919 when he first used particles from a radioactive source to study the structure of the atom. According to the S-curve this beginning was closer to 1939 but "technicalities" during the war years delayed the actual construction of laboratory sites for about ten years. The data do in fact show an early catching-up effect—a faster than normal rate of growth up front—a phenomenon often witnessed upon sudden release of pent-up demand.

Seen in retrospect, Rutherford's seed was given a chance to sprout thanks to the intense activity on nuclear research during the war years. One may even want to see the subsequent demonstration of overwhelming power in nuclear energy as the potent fertilizer that made accelerators grow to gigantic dimensions.

2.5 – DEVIATIONS FROM S-CURVES

There are many reasons why the evolution of a natural-growth process may deviate from an S-shaped pattern. We saw earlier how World War II interfered with the car-mileage invariant (Section 1.1) and the beginning of the particle accelerator curve (Section 2.4). Other "unnatural" events may include earthquakes and any other significant phenomena that never occurred before during the historical window considered. In general when the unnatural event subsides, a return to the S-curve course is expected.

Also concerning a person's creativity or productivity our data horizon may be spanning the cascade of two S-curves; for example, a childbearing cycle for a woman succeeded by a book-writing one. Or the case of a niche-within-a-niche, for example, the works of a moviemaker who branches out to make television serials; the overall number of his creations is not likely to follow a single smooth curve. It is also possible to have double-barreled life, for example, when a medical career progresses in parallel with an artistic one.

Below is the case of Robert Schumann whose life work followed an S-curve but was punctuated by a nervous breakdown and a suicide attempt. Figure 2.5.1 shows the cumulative publication of Schumann's compositions.[10] They oscillate somewhat around the fitted trend. The overall curve is segmented into three periods by his major nervous breakdown in 1845 and his attempted suicide in 1854. Both of these events interfered with the natural evolution of his work, yet one can distinguish a smaller S-curve for each period.

ROBERT SCHUMANN (1810-1856)

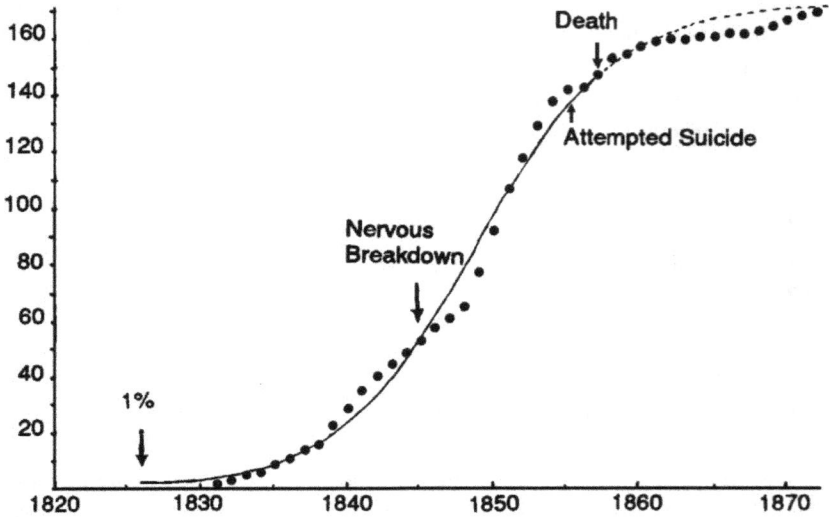

Figure 2.5.1   The publication of Schumann's compositions. The fitted curve begins around 1826 and aims at a ceiling of 173. Schumann's publications reached 170, sixteen years after his death

According to the nominal beginning of the process, Schumann must have received his vocation as a composer in 1826, at the age of sixteen. To corroborate this I turned to biographies and I found that music did not play an important part in Schumann's early life. During his childhood he was not musically inclined but was forced to take piano lessons as a part of his general education. It was not until the age of thirteen that he started enjoying piano practice and taking an interest in choral music. Soon, however, he was sent to law school. He changed universities, trying in vain to study law. It was only when he became twenty that he summoned up enough courage to declare openly that he wanted to give up law and devote himself to music. One year later he was publishing musical compositions.

His composing was erratic. It ceased entirely or accelerated quickly following outbreaks of his mental illness. The publication of his works follows a more natural course, however. Society smoothed out his irregular composing pattern. His attempted suicide with the ensuing death make only a small dent in the evolution of his published work. And his publications kept appearing after his death, closely following the curve that had been established to a large extent during his lifetime. As far as the public was concerned, Schumann remained alive, composing, slowing down progressively, and finally stopping in 1872 at the more appropriate age of sixty-two.

Schumann's career is a case where an early forecast by the S-curve approach would have produced erroneous results in spite of the fact that the data may have been validated, well-documented, and error-free. By considering publication dates instead of composition dates we have succeeded in obtaining a more regular pattern, but still not regular enough to ensure reliable predictions. Decidedly, there are people whose lives do not follow a natural course and consequently are unpredictable.

2.6 – S-CURVES WITH VARIABLE CEILING

The S-curve we determine by fitting data has a tendency to flatten toward a ceiling *as early and as low* as it is possible within the constraints of the fitting procedure. All fitting programs will yield logistic fits that are generally biased toward a low ceiling. Uncertainties on the data points accentuate this bias by permitting larger margins for the determination of the S-curve parameters. In fact the larger the fluctuations on the data the greater this bias may be.

To compensate for this bias I usually make several fits with different weights on the data points.[*] I then keep the answer that gives the highest ceiling for the S-curve (most often obtained by weighting heavily the recent historical data points, see Section 10.2). This generally compensates for the bias toward a low ceiling but the procedure must be used wisely. It can be that this bias is unjustifiably blamed for, as was the case of US Nobel laureates described below.

It was Marchetti who first suggested that the competition for Nobel-Prize awards can be described by logistic-growth curves.[11] Following his example I tried to study the evolution of the number of Nobel Prizes won by the United States.

Winning a Nobel Prize is a competitive process because Nobel Prizes are desirable and at the same time they constitute a "limited resource" with a restrained number of them being awarded each year. By definition, the best-fit candidates win. Obviously, a peace Nobel Prize is very different from a prize in Physics. Moreover, some prizes may be shared among as many as three individuals whereas others are given to only one

---

[*] In the fitting procedure the weights of the data points are generally defined as inversely proportional to their uncertainties $1/\sigma_i$, see The Use of Chi Square, Section 10.1.

individual. Nevertheless for my study I counted each laureate as one independently of what discipline he or she was in and independently of how many colleagues shared the prize. The justification for this is that we are counting individuals with exceptional contributions to the benefit of mankind and on the average relative underachievements are compensated for by relative overachievements.

My first attempt to fit an S-curve to the cumulative number of US Nobel laureates in 1988 concluded that the US Nobel niche was already more than half full and implied a diminishing annual number of prizes for Americans from then onward.[12] Ten years later I confronted those forecasts with more recent data in my book *Predictions – 10 Years Later*.[13] The agreement was not very good. The forecasts fell below the actual data and despite the fact that there was agreement within the uncertainties expected for a 90% confidence level the discrepancy did not go unnoticed. A technical note published in *Technological Forecasting & Social Change* in 2004 highlighted the inaccuracy of my forecasts and cast doubt in the use of S-curves to forecast US Nobel laureates.[14] On my part, I refit the updated data sample with a new S-curve pointing to a higher ceiling. I also began wondering whether there was evidence here for the known bias of S-curves to underestimate the final niche size despite my compensatory procedures. The new forecast again indicated an imminent decline in the annual number of American Nobel laureates.

Years later while preparing a yet another edition for my book— *Predictions – 20 Years Later*—I once again confronted my forecasts with recent data. The situation turned out to be the same as ten years earlier, namely the forecasts again underestimated reality and despite agreement with the result of ten years earlier within the uncertainties expected for a 90% confidence level there was now clear disagreement between recent actual numbers and the original forecasts of twenty years earlier. The situation was reminiscent of the celebrated Michele-parameter episode in experimental physics where a measurement repeated many times over the period of fifty years kept reporting an ever-increasing value always compatible with the previous measurement but finally ending up in violent disagreement with the very first measurement.

One explanation for the S-curve ceiling to be constantly increasing is the fact that the US population itself has also been increasing over the same historical period. An increasing population provides an increasing "niche" for Nobel-Prize winners. In fact, Equation 2.2.1 in Section 2.2 can be analytically solved only if M is a constant. A logistic S-shaped pattern for the US Nobel-laureate population is presumptuous and probably wrong if M increases with time.

An obvious way to account for the growing American population would be to study the number of laureates *per capita* thus rendering *M* time-independent and Equation 2.2.1 solvable. So I repeated the previous analysis now for Nobel Laureates normalized to population and obtained different results with better-quality fits and consistency this time, namely the values of *M* for all three periods were within the expected uncertainties of ± 20% from each other. Yet, there was still some tendency for *M* to increase, if within the estimated uncertainties of the results, and I also obtained counterintuitive forecasts for a dramatic decline of American Nobel laureates and/or a major increase of the American population by the second half of the 21st century.[15]

The tendency of *M* to still grow with time suggested that considering US Nobel laureates *per capita* did not fully account for the increase of the "niche" size over time. In fact, the niche of individuals qualified for Nobel-Prize candidature in America could be increasing faster than the average population. After all, in my study I classified laureates with double nationality as nationals of the nation where the research for which they were being distinguished was accomplished. America, as a rule, welcomes research scientists from all over the world while it thwarts immigration by the uneducated. It could very well be that the population sample capable of producing Nobel laureates in America is growing faster than the rest of the population.

The need then arises for solving Equation 2.2.1 in Section 2.2 with *M* a function of time, which can be done only numerically.[16] The corresponding fitting procedure is described in Section 10.3 but the results are plotted in Figure 2.6.1. With data up to 1988, we see my original S-curve fit as well as a fit with an S-curve of variable ceiling. The actual numbers during the following 20 years—depicted with little circles—confirm the suspicion that indeed we are dealing here with a niche that is growing faster than the population. The results also include forecasts that remain rather flat for the next few decades. We will get confirmation of this forecast in Chapter 8 when we come back to this subject via the more sophisticated Volterra-Lotka approach to competition.

US NOBEL LAUREATES PER CAPITA

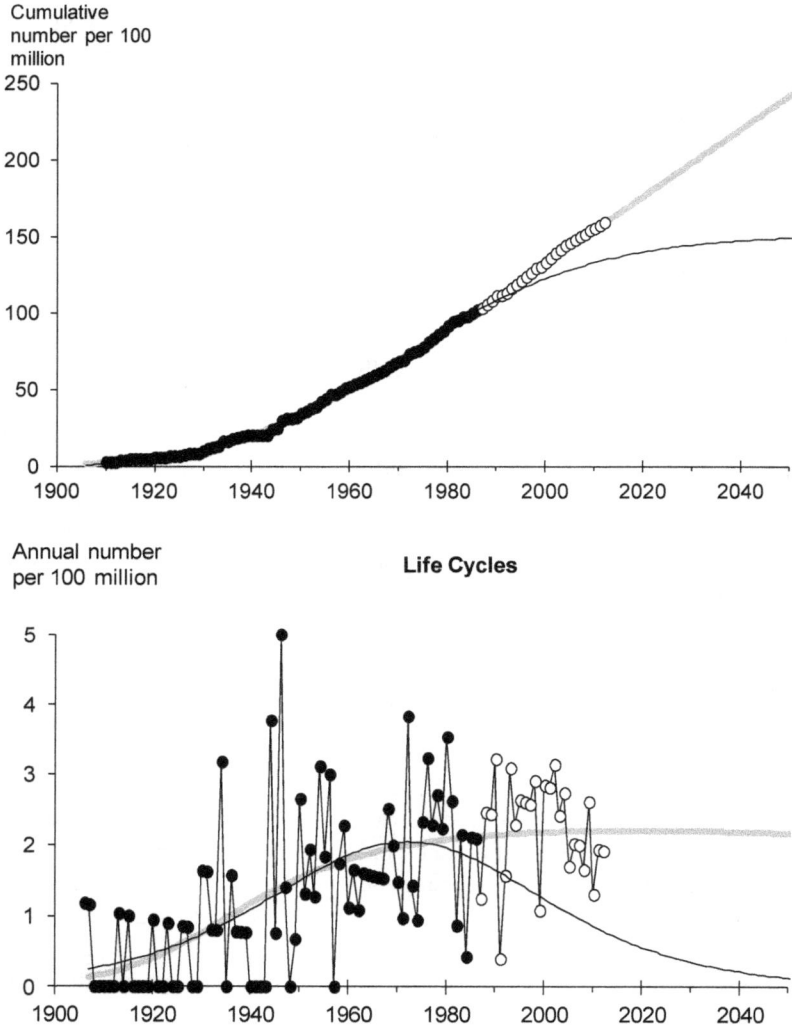

Figure 2.6.1   At the top we see the cumulative number of US Nobel Laureates per capita. The thin black line is an S-curve fit and the thick gray line a fit to an S-curve with variable (increasing with time) ceiling. The fits were performed on data up to 1988 (black dots). The little circles denote more recent data. Below we see the life cycles that correspond to the curves at the top.

2.7 – S-CURVES AND ECONOMIES OF SCALE

Most industrial knowledge has been acquired on the job. As a consequence, such knowledge is characterized by unquestionable validity but also by a lack of analytical formulation. Unquestionable truths are intriguing because they signal an underlying law. In my search for guidelines for successful business decisions, I found that mathematical manipulations of the logistic-growth function yield pairs of relationships between price and time, performance and time, or price and performance. While I was carrying out those manipulations I stumbled onto a new derivation for a fundamental piece of industrial knowledge: the economies of scale.

Economies of scale mean that the more units you produce of a product, the less each unit costs. Production costs decrease with volume for a variety of reasons: automation, sharing overhead, reducing material costs through wholesale prices, and general process optimization resulting from production experience. A major part of the cost reduction can be attributed to learning in some way or another.

Business schools teach economies of scale qualitatively by the volume curve, which shows that costs per unit decrease as a function of the volume of units produced. The usual theoretical argument is that costs are typically proportional to the area (surface) of whatever is being produced and consequently increase slower than the volume. The curve looks like a hyperbola, or a decaying exponential, reaching a minimum final value when the costs can be reduced no further. But this kind of curve could be our familiar S-curve in disguise!

The mathematical expression of the S-curve is the logistic-growth function. This function is a simple fraction that has a constant in the numerator and a constant plus a decreasing exponential in the denominator, see earlier Equation 2.2.2 in Section 2.2. It is exactly the inverse of an economies-of-scale expression (costs per unit being equal to a constant plus a decreasing exponential). In other words, the volume curve can be well approximated by the inverse of the S-shaped learning curve (see Section A.3 for the explicit mathematics). Businesspersons using volume curves for decades may have been dealing with S-curves without realizing it. The moral of the story is that learning alone can account for the reduction of costs with volume.

The truth probably involves both phenomena: learning and the fact that costs increase like a surface—that is, slower than the volume. But I am convinced that learning will play a progressively more important role. In the manufacturing of microprocessors, for example, the surface-to-volume argument for the definition of costs breaks down. The argument will break down further with such future pillars of the world economy as services, telecommunications, and the Internet. Learning is fundamental because it is linked to natural growth in competition.

IN CLOSING

What I have learned from my experience with S-curves can be summarized by two realizations. The first is that many phenomena go through a life cycle: birth, growth, maturity, decline, and death. Time frames vary, making some phenomena look like revolutions and others like natural evolutions. The element in common is how the change takes place; for example, the slow and steady way things march to an end is not unlike the way they came into existence. The end of a cycle does not mean a return to the beginning, however. The phases of natural growth proceed along S-curves, cascading from one to the next, in a pattern that reinvokes much of the past but leads to a higher level.

My second realization concerns predictability. There is a promise implicit in a process of natural growth, which is guaranteed by nature: The growth cycle will not stop halfway through—no ecological niche in nature was ever left half full under natural conditions. The catchall phrase *natural conditions* has been misunderstood more often than not.

> "You mean that is what's going to happen if we do nothing?" was the typical reaction of marketers when I presented to them my logistic forecasts.
>
> "No," I would reply, "that is what is going to happen if you keep doing the same type of actions that you have been doing."
>
> "What if the competition comes up with a powerful new product?"
>
> "How many times has the competition come up with powerful new products during our historical window?" I would challenge them.
>
> "Many times," was the invariable answer.
>
> "Then the launching of powerful new products by competitors is a natural condition."
>
> In fact, natural conditions include all the types of events that have taken place during the historical window covered by the data. In contrast, if there is a nuclear war, or other never-seen-before incident, then one has a valid reason to doubt the forecast.

Whenever I come across a fair fraction of a growth process—in nature, society, business, or my private life—I try to visualize the full life cycle. If I have the first half as given, I can predict the future; if I am faced with the second half, I can deduce the past. I have made peace with my arrogance and have grown to accept that a certain amount of predetermination is associated with *natural* processes, as if by definition from the word *natural*. It is natural, for example, that you do not have the option of making a sharp turn when driving on the highway at 60 miles an hour. At the same time, there are periods—after growth subsides or before it picks up—when there is much choice. You can choose any direction, when you first get in your car.

The logistic function is intimately associated with the law of natural growth. Both bell-shaped and the S-shaped curves are seeded with a parameter describing the ceiling, the capacity of the niche in process of being filled. The important difference between them, from the statistical analysis point of view, is that the S-curve, which often depicts a cumulative rate of growth, is much less sensitive to fluctuations because one year's low is compensated for by another year's high. Therefore, the S-curve representation of a natural growth process provides a more reliable way to forecast the level of the ceiling. From an intuitive point of view, an S-curve promises the amount of growth that can be accomplished while a bell-curve heralds the coming end of the process as a whole.

3 – SEASONS OF GROWTH

Business, like the weather, goes through seasons, and so do the correct management policies. Products, companies, and entire industries experience weather-like variations as do agricultural crops; they go through seasons in a cyclical way. Summer is the high-growth period around the midpoint of the cycle. Winters are the low-growth periods one finds at the end and at the beginning of the cyclical process. Between winter and summer comes spring, characterized by a progressively rising growth rate. Fall is the time between summer and winter, when the rate of growth continuously declines.

Borrowing images from biology to fit the marketplace is not new. Companies resemble living organisms. They are born; mature; get married; have daughters; become aggressive, sleepy, or exhausted; grow old; and eventually die or become prey to a voracious predator. As early as the turn of the 20th century, enlightened economists and broad-minded physicists applied scientific notions such as periodic harmonic motion and Darwin's survival of the fittest to human products. In 1918 Alfred J. Lotka successfully predicted the size of the American railway network, via the logistic-growth function.[1] At about the same time (1926), the Russian economist Nikolai D. Kondratieff was establishing evidence for a long economic wave with a period of 50 to 60 years. This claim scored high points in popularity when the stock market crashed in 1987 and continued to score high with the persisting depression-like economy that, as had happened 58 years earlier, followed the 1987 crash.

Periodic swings of the economy reflect successive large-timeframe S-curve growth steps. Such waves are echoed in the preachings of management consulting gurus, who may pass easily from thesis to antithesis, and do not stop short of giving contradicting messages. It is not rare to see a company investing in business process reengineering and total quality—zero defects—at the same time? It is not trivial how to reconciled the benefits of leadership with those of empowerment and self-managed teams. Advocates of centralized control and vertical integration became rather quiet in the 1990s. Instead we heard about business units, core competencies, and horizontal corporations. These changes did not reflect conceptual breakthroughs in the theory of doing business. They were simply reactions to the economic climate and its seasonal variation.

Throughout history, periods of bureaucracy and control interspersed by waves of innovation and entrepreneurship. Notorious bureaucracies, such as the Roman Empire and the British civil service, were preceded and followed by entrepreneurial eras, such as crusades and revolutions (both social and industrial). The way to do business has followed suit. Many have addressed the question of how organizational behavior evolves over time. But it was Niccolo Machiavelli—early in the 16th century—who first pointed out the importance of adaptation. He wrote in *The Prince*:

> I believe also that he will be successful who directs his actions according to the spirit of the times, and that he whose actions do not accord with the times will not be successful.

Many management theorists divide the growth cycle—typically a product's sales cycle—into segments. Theorists generally consider four periods according to the phase of growth: start-up, rapid growth, maturation, and decline. Their treatment is invariably qualitative, and the four phases are not necessarily of equal duration or precise definition.

Here I present the business cycle somewhat differently, using the four seasons as a metaphor. Winter reflects the critical growth period encountered during the beginning and the end of a natural growth process. Products experience two winters in their lifetime. The first winter is while they are struggling for a foothold in the marketplace, and the second one when they are exiting and the follow-up product is fighting for succession. By definition, the end of the first winter signals that the growth process has survived "infant mortality"—that is, it has realized around 7% of its growth potential.

The seasons metaphor has more than poetic justification. The advantage over more traditional segmentations is that our familiarity with the mechanisms associated with nature's four seasons can shed light on and guide us through decisions on business and social issues. For example, the low creativity observed during summer is only partially due to the heat. New undertakings are disfavored mainly because summer living is easy and there is no reason to look for change. In contrast, animals (for example, foxes and sparrows) are known to become entrepreneurial in the winter. There is wisdom encoded in nature's seasonal patterns and behaviors. These can be studied and transferred to whatever situation depicts a succession of season-like stages.

Like the four seasons, the segments into which we divide the cycle must be of equal length. The time scale may vary widely depending on what growth process we are looking at. For a product, a season may last six months or a year. For an industry, a season may be five to ten tears.

For the world economy cycling through 50- to 60-year waves, a season may be fifteen years long.

A product's first winter coincides with the incumbent product's second winter. Consequently this timing also implies that the new product must be launched during the fall season of the product it is replacing (no wonder farmers sow in autumn). Winter then becomes the time of selection, when wanton death eliminates the weak and the unfit. Spring corresponds to "adolescence", the formative years. Spring is also the time for research and development of future replacements.

Most product managers have intuitive knowledge of this product-succession sequence. They know, for example, that the new product is promoted most heavily while the old product phases out—to be precise, during the last 20% of its life cycle, that is, its second winter. They also know that research and development for the new product must parallel capacity buildup for the old product, which is approaching maximum rate of sales and profitability.

Figure 3.1 shows one business cycle, namely one S-curve growth step straddled between the end of the previous one and the beginning of the next one. The season assignment is such that summer occurs between 30% and 70% penetration of the S-curve and straddles the maximum rate of growth.

"Seasons" can be defined not only for products but for anything that grows in competition: markets, technologies, industries, and so on. It is generally true that spring is concerned with the *what* and fall with the *how*. That is why at the industry level product innovation occurs in spring and process innovation in fall. At the same time, at the economy level, technology and finances dominate in spring, and social and political forces dominate in fall. Spring is the time for investments. It is also the time for learning and continuous improvement. Specialists are in demand. Not so in winter. Sometime in the early 1990s I explained to a Geneva bank director that winter is the time to fire bureaucrats and hire Leonardo da Vincis—that is, cross-disciplinary, well-rounded men and women who stand a better chance than specialists to come up with revolutionary ideas for new profitable business. "Fire bureaucrats is exactly what we need to do, sir", he exclaimed. "Could you please tell us how to do it?" To my surprise, I heard two months later that the man had been fired.

But often what naturally happens is what should happen. As strange as it may sound, seeing your specialists progressively evolve into bureaucrats may be a good sign. It is one indication that summer is setting in. The word *bureaucrats* carries a negative connotation, but if we call them *process agents* instead, we realize that they provide an important function during times of high growth and prosperity. It is during summer that enterprises

ASSIGNING SEASONS TO THE LIFE CYCLE

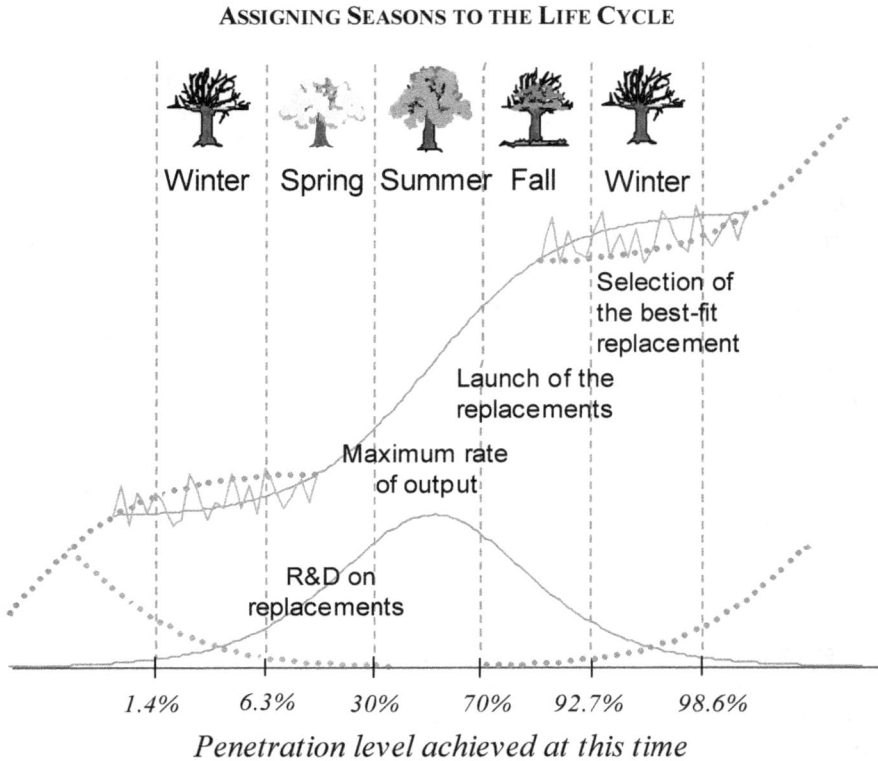

Winter Spring Summer Fall Winter

Selection of
the best-fit
replacement

Launch of the
replacements

Maximum rate
of output

R&D on
replacements

1.4%   6.3%   30%   70%   92.7%   98.6%

Penetration level achieved at this time

Figure 3.1 Segmentation of a business cycle into four seasons. The growth levels at the delimiting positions satisfy the following two conditions: (1) all seasons have the same duration, and (2) the early winter of the replacement overlaps with the late winter of the incumbent. Low-growth periods are accompanied by large and chaotic fluctuations.

become successful, centralized, conservative (no one tampers with something that works well), and in need of clockwork operations. Fine-tuning and zero defects (the original aspiration of total quality management) are particularly appropriate for a summer season. But then, what about benchmarking, continuous improvement, and BPR (business process reengineering)?

Being second best hardly yields a competitive advantage. But positive feedback theories, that produce rapid fluctuations resembling chaos, argue that early gains for two simultaneously launched competitors eventually tilt the balance in favor of the "lucky" one and not necessarily the better one.[2] Early gains do not presuppose excellence.

When videocassette recorders were first introduced, the market was split between VHS and Beta. The two market shares fluctuated early on because of circumstances, luck, or marketing tactics. But soon early returns tilted the unstable situation toward VHS despite claims that Beta was technically superior. There are many such examples. Connoisseurs of personal computers value Apple products more highly than PCs, but the market-share gains of the latter have biased standardization in their favor.

Such manifestations of positive-feedback mechanisms have long been understood. During the nineteenth century Alfred Marshall—professor of political economy in Bristol, England—wrote that whatever firm first gets a good start will corner the market. To get a good early start, a product must appeal to the masses rather than to the elite, and that argues for postponing sophistication and refinements for a later season. New products are launched in the fall, but excellence is only excellent in the summer.

It is worth looking in more detail at each season's characteristics and how they can help us on everyday work decisions. There are advantages and disadvantages to each season. In my book *Conquering Uncertainty* I have devoted a chapter describing the characteristics of each season. One must keep in mind that these characteristics are meant to be in *relative* terms—that is, whatever happens in one season is with respect to what

HIGHLIGHTS OF SEASONAL RECOMMENDATIONS

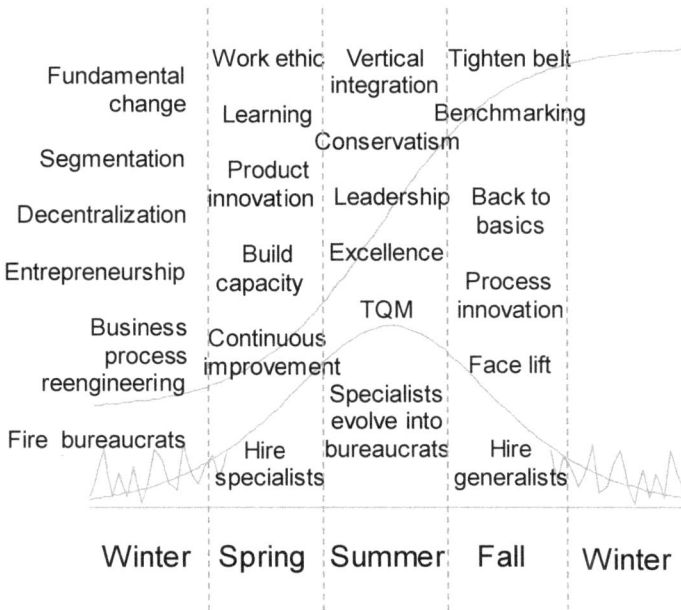

| | Winter | Spring | Summer | Fall | Winter |

Figure 3.2 General guidelines for what is appropriate in a given season.

happened during the previous seasons. For example, to say that competition becomes lowest in spring does not mean it is negligible. It simply means that competition is relatively lower in spring than during the other seasons. Figure 3.2 lists some highlights for each season. It also sketches the chaotic fluctuations that accompany winters, which is an intrinsic characteristic of natural growth.[3]

3.1 – GROWTH FROM CHAOS AND CHAOS FROM GROWTH

Theory makers like to tear down and rebuild the work of their predecessors. In the 1990s chaos scientists have argued that equilibrium and orderly growth are only the tip of the iceberg. The true richness of our world comes from the noisy, apparently random behavior encountered in the unpredictable patterns of currency movements and market reactions. In his best-selling *Chaos*, James Gleick explains that chaos scientists are not interested in steady growth processes. They concentrate on the fluctuations that become prominent whenever the growth rate drops to zero. Through fractals* popularized via beautiful computer-generated pictures, chaos scientists have succeeded in extracting some order out of randomness. They want to believe that their theory contains all one needs to know about markets. But practicing professionals remain skeptical.

Extreme swings of the pendulum typically straddle a wise intermediate position. The fact is that order and randomness coexist at all times, merely shifting their role as protagonist. During a high-growth period—summer season—the direction of growth is well defined, order dominates, and the fluctuations play a minimal role. But in a period of a general stagnation—winter season—the fluctuations are all we see; in fact, they become very prominent, giving rise to a state of chaos. This state of chaos reflects the random trial-and-error search that people and organizations undertake to reestablish new growth paths.

Sustained growth is not a steady and uniform process. It consists of successive S-shaped steps, each of which represents a well-defined amount of growth. Every step is associated with a market niche that opened following a technological breakthrough, a major innovation, or some other fundamental change. Growth steps are punctuated by periods of chaos. Both theoretical and practical evidence exists for the chaotic fluctuations sketched freehand in Figures 3.1 and 3.2.

---

* Fractals are irregular patterns that reveal an identical structure when zooming in and out. They are a consequence of a different geometry that has structure at multiple levels.

The relative order associated with the summer season of the growth process and the chaos associated with the winter season can be theoretically proved by using the fact that everything in nature is discrete. When the analytical mathematical expression of the S-curve is cast into a discrete formulation, instabilities emerge at both ends of the growth process.[4] In Figure 3.1.1 we see the onset of chaos, for a certain combination of the parameters values. At this point, chaos is not yet fully installed, but there is an important oscillation in the beginning and at the end of the growth process. In real-life situations we cannot see the early oscillation completely, because negative values have no physical meaning. We see, however, a precursor followed by an accelerated growth rate, an overshoot of the ceiling, and finally erratic fluctuations. These features correspond to real phenomena. Accelerated growth is a catching-up effect, usually attributed to pent-up demand. The overshoot is a typical introduction into the steady state. As for the precursor, it is often considered a fiasco, unfairly so.

The first two case studies below tell us that fiascoes and failures should not always be taken at face value. They may be heralds of new markets, particularly if other well-established growth processes corroborate such an interpretation.

MAKING AN S-CURVE DISCRETE

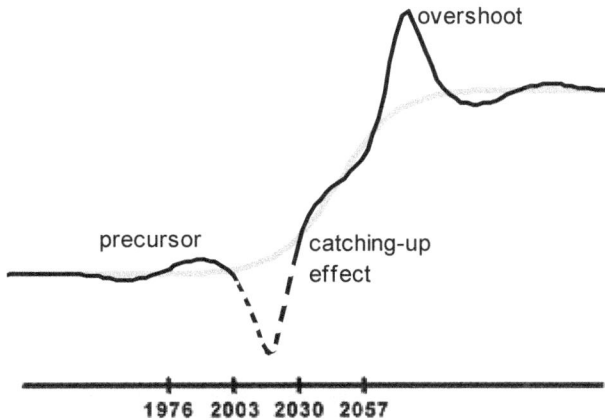

Figure 3.1.1. One of the first patterns we obtain by putting an S-curve in a discrete mathematical form. The deviations from the familiar S-curve demonstrate the precursor, the early catching-up effect, and the overshoot. The dates on the horizontal axis mark milestones for supersonic travel with the precursor designating the Concord, see text.

3.2 – CASE STUDIES

The Concord

Following the crash of the Concord outside Paris in July 2000, I received many suggestions/requests for a topic in my monthly newsletter concerning the future of supersonic passenger transport.

We saw in Section 1.1 that the daily displacement invariant of seventy minutes combined with the speed of our transport defines the size of our cities. A supersonic airplane of the future of average speed, say 3,000 miles per hour, would render the whole Western world as one town. In his book Megatrends, John Naisbitt claimed that Marshall McLuhan's "world village" was realized when communication satellites linked the world together informationally. This is not really the case. Information exchange is a necessary but not a sufficient condition. It is true that empires in antiquity broke up when they grew so large that it took more than two weeks to transmit a message from one end to the other. But it is also true that communications media are poor substitutes for personal contact. The sufficient condition for a "world village" is that it should take not much more than one hour to physically reach any location in it.

Expanding in space as far as possible is of primordial importance for all species. Accordingly supersonic travel and the realization of "world village" become inevitable some time in the future. But there are constraints. Productivity (that is, the product speed times payload) cannot be compromised. As with the standard of living, decrease is not an option for a new way of life. The productivity of a new-technology aircraft must increase. This was not the case with the Concord whose productivity significantly fell short of the productivity of the Boeing 747 introduced around the same time. The Concord's payload was too small. It should be able to carry around 250 passengers to match the productivity of wide-body aircraft. And even with 100 passengers the time the Concord gained flying, it lost refueling. This explains its commercial failure but not the end of supersonic travel.

Aviation know-how has already achieved maturity today, and simple technological advances cannot produce factors of ten improvements. A new technology, fundamentally different, is required—for example, airplanes fueled with liquid hydrogen. The new competitor must possess an indisputable competitive advantage. The scrapping of the supersonic transport project (SST) back in 1971 by the Senate displeased the Nixon Administration but may have been symptomatic of fundamental, if unconscious, reasoning. The comment by then Senator Henry M. Jackson,

"This is a vote against science and technology," can be seen today as simplistic and insensitive to rising popular wisdom.

Supersonic aircraft technology will have to rely on a richer fuel, such as liquid natural gas or liquid hydrogen (more on this when we will discuss the substitution between primary energies in Section 4.4). This fuel will permit high productivity, namely, supersonic speeds as well as relatively high carrying capacity, but probably narrow fuselage (single corridor). Last but not least, the hydrogen fuel will do marvels for the environment. We leave for later the arguments that the most appropriate energy source and realistic way of producing and liquefying hydrogen in such quantities today is via nuclear energy.

The Concorde enjoyed much publicity and popularity. It made a cultural dent and demonstrated the public's appreciation and need for high-speed travel. Its lifetime was limited for technical reasons. But it constitutes a precursor in the supersonic-travel growth process. The time scale in Figure 3.1.1 has been chosen accordingly. Following the Concorde there may be another 27 years or so with no commercial supersonic planes. However, once a new-fuel technology becomes available (probably based on hydrogen or natural gas in liquid form), growth in supersonic travel will be rapid because of pent-up demand. It may lead into a supersonic "craze" (overshoot) around 2060 and finally stabilize at a lower level toward the end of the 21st century.

The necessity for uniting the world combined with the fact that supersonic aviation technology has proceeded to beyond infant mortality, as demonstrated by the Concord, the Russian Tupolev Tu-144, and a host of military aircraft guarantee that this growth process will continue to completion.

DEC's 64-bit PC

In 1993 DEC launched a personal computer model built with the company's new and powerful 64-bit Alpha microprocessor. But despite high expectations and the product's outstanding performance, sales disappointed even the pessimists. Two years later, the product was considered a failure. A variety of explanations were given—such as the lack of compatibility with software applications—and DEC went back to building personal computers with the traditional 32-bit Intel chips.

But in the light of Figure 3.1.1 (not with the particular time labels), DEC should have pursued the Alpha PC business line, treating the first unsuccessful model as a precursor rather than as a failure. The 64-bit technology had demonstrated that it had survived infant mortality by becoming well established in larger computers. It was reasonable to expect that the technology would eventually downsize to personal computers, by which time demand would accelerate (the catching-up effect) and favor the manufacturers that would be ready with that product.

The Possibility of Microsoft's Breakup in Early 2000

In early 2000 and following rumors that Microsoft was getting too big for certain antitrust watchdogs I was asked to evaluate the eventuality of the company's break-up.

We can study Microsoft's growth pattern assuming it is a "species" filling a well-defined niche in the market. We can fit an S-shaped curve to it cumulative revenue (corrected for inflation) and then deduce an overall life cycle for Microsoft's growth process. Figure 3.2.1 shows the results.

In February 2000 Microsoft found itself in a late spring season. Even at the most pessimistic case (see lower intermittent line in the drawing) the earliest turning point (beginning of a fall season) would be around 2005. In other words, the evolution of Microsoft was *naturally* endowed with still more growth in the years ahead. Late spring is the least likely time for a company to break up. The typical segmentation period is late fall/early winter. This did not mean that a break up of Microsoft was to be excluded. But it said that stopping Microsoft's growth at that time amounted to one of those "abnormal", rarely observed, and difficult to

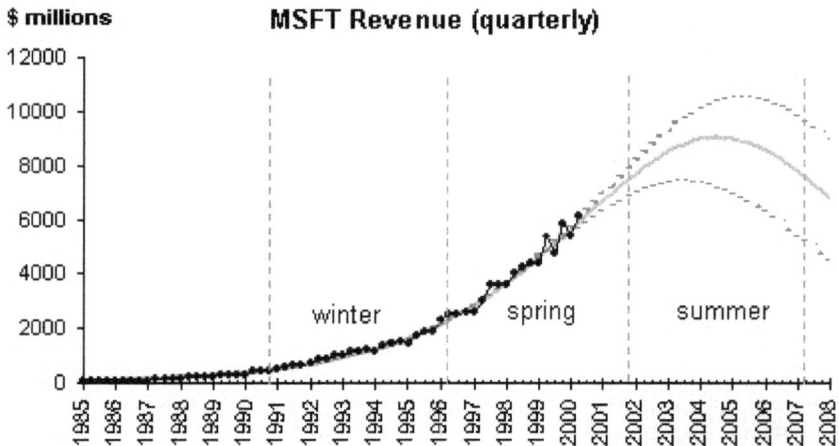

Figure 3.2.1. The solid gray line is not a fit to the data. It has been calculated from an S-curve fit on the cumulative data. The intermittent lines indicated the 90% confidence level (what is likely to happen 9 times out of 10).

achieve interventions. Let us not forget that the Department of Justice had launched an antitrust suit against IBM in 1968 to finally drop it fourteen years later. IBM was traversing a long summer season during that period.

The forecast for Microsoft's revenue as spelled out by the thick gray line proved quite accurate for the following 4-5 year after which it fell progressively short of the actual company performance. In contrast to nature "species" in the marketplace undergo easy and frequent "mutations": reorganizations, mergers, acquisitions, and the like. Therefore forecasts need to be regularly updated, particularly if they concern revenues or prices. Even when corrected for inflation, prices are not good indicators of lasting value. Inflation and currency fluctuations due to speculation or politico-economic circumstances can have a large unpredictable effect on monetary indicators. Extreme swings have been observed. For example, Van Gogh died poor, although each of his paintings is worth a fortune today. The number of art works he produced has not changed since his death; counted in dollars, however, it has increased tremendously.

The wise user of S-curves had better stick to physical variables such as dimensions, weight, energy, and number of units sold, whenever possible.

3.3 – A LARGE-SCALE HISTORICAL EXAMPLE

An example of seasonal growth in a large timeframe is the world economy, as evidenced by the evolution of energy consumption. Per capita energy consumption worldwide is seven times greater today than it was 150 years ago. This increase took place, not in a steady, uniform rate, or even in a random fashion, but in two well-defined steps. The first step ended around 1920 with a period of stagnation that lasted for about two decades. The second energy-consumption step was completed around 1975, and we have just witnessed the beginning of a third step. There can be little doubt that this indicator has significant growth potential, considering the insatiable appetite for energy in the West and the dire need for industrial growth in the developing world.

Energy consumption correlates in an unambiguous way with industrial development and economic prosperity. The profile of the energy curve over time eloquently points out two chaotic low-growth periods, one centered on the mid-1930s and another one around 1990. These economic depressions echo Kondratieff's economic cycle mentioned earlier.

Many economists today dispute the existence of long economic waves, perhaps because most proponents of long waves have relied on monetary and econometric indicators—labels unreliable for assigning lasting value. Figure 3.3.1 provides evidence for a long cycle based on a physical indicator namely per capita energy consumption expressed in tons of coal-equivalent. I have studied and documented in my book *Predictions* other cyclical phenomena resonating with this energy-consumption cycle. For each human endeavor considered—production, consumption, manu-facturing, construction, creativity, productivity, criminality, and the like—I used data expressed in their proper units, not by their prices. Through all these observations I was able to determine this cycle's period to be equal to fifty-six years, give or take two years.

Per Capita Annual Energy Consumption Worldwide

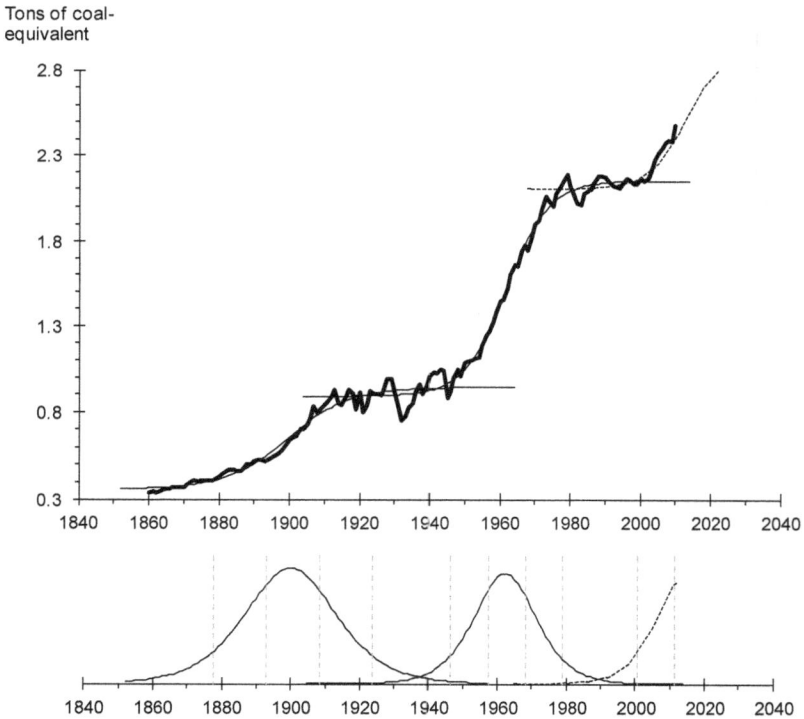

Figure 3.3.1. The per-capita annual energy consumption worldwide: data, fits, and a scenario for the future. In the lower part we see the life cycles that correspond to the S-curves and a delimitation of their seasons as defined in the beginning of this chapter. The average season length is 15 years yielding a cycle with a period of 60 years.

Several theoretical explanations have been offered for the origin of a long economic wave. In the 1930s, Joseph. A. Schumpeter at Harvard put forth socioeconomic theories, such as the rapid growth of leading sectors and the clustering of technological innovations. More recently, Jay Forrester at MIT was able to reproduce the same long wave with his sophisticated system-dynamics model, which studied major shifts in private-sector incentives for investing in capital plant, borrowing, and savings. Finally, in *Predictions*, I offer two more hypotheses for the existence of such a long wave. One has to do with periodic changes of the climate, the other relates to the mean life span of a person's commercially active career.

But let us go back to the energy consumption picture with its two low-growth periods around the 1930s and the 1990s. The two growth cycles are not quite the same in duration and the overlap results in rather long winters. During these winters the chaotic state is manifested through bottom-up, bursting cultural forces that lead to segmentation, decentralization, and horizontal markets. Leadership becomes ineffective. In contrast, during the high-growth period, top-down vision-driven forces tend to unify and integrate, vertically or otherwise.

Predictably, the two chaotic states are associated with periods of low economic growth but also periods of discovery and innovation. Difficult times make people inventive. A host of important innovations in the 1930s set the pace for a recovery that led to the high-growth period of the 1950s and the 1960s. To mention a few such innovations: television (1936), Kodachrome (1935), synthetic rubber (1932), wrinkle-free fabrics (1932), helicopters (1936), rockets (1935), automatic transmissions (1939), power steering (1930), magnetic tape recording (1937), diesel locomotives (1934), ballpoint pens (1938), radar (1934), Plexiglas (1935), fluorescent lighting (1934), and nylon perlon (1938). By analogy, the 1990s incubated a multitude of industry-generating innovations that triggered a recovery and another economic summer scheduled for early 21st century. Examples of well-positioned candidates for such industries are: portable computers, cellular telephones, optical fibers, optical disks, tomography, high-bandwidth communication networks, all-invading intelligent micro-processors, space shuttle, biosciences, gene technology, robotics, and high-temperature superconductivity.[5]

The depressed world economy of the 1990s was responsible for the widespread breaking up of large enterprises into smaller ones. In contrast, industries that despite the world economic climate found themselves in a high-growth season—for example, the telecom industry—prospered from corporate alliances, mergers, acquisitions, and other unifying mechanisms.

Because different business seasons dictate distinctly different behavior, successful strategic actions become telltale signals for the season the company is in. When we read that chemical empires in continental Europe, such as Bayer and Hoechst of Germany and Rhone-Poulenc of France, spun off fibers, bulk and specialty chemicals, pharmaceuticals, and agriculture into legally independent subsidiaries, we could have concluded that the European chemical industry was in difficulty, even if we were not knowledgeable about this industry. By contrast, the announcement of impressive long-range plans by MCI Communications Corporation insinuated a healthy balance sheet. Long-range strategies are characteristic of a summer business season.

The association of segmentation with low growth and unification with high growth is a general phenomenon that extends beyond the world of business. An example is the politicization process in Europe. When communism collapsed in the mid-1990s, the Eastern countries found themselves drifting into a state of chaos. Appropriately, they were torn apart by bottom-up forces, decentralizing, segmenting, subdividing, searching for identity and political system, and in general, exploring all directions including extreme ones, such as private police units in Moscow and murderous belligerencies in former Yugoslavia. Bottom-up forces make leadership unstable. Exceptional leaders like Mikhail Gorbachev, Eduard Shevardnadze, and Boris Yeltsin proved rather ineffective in controlling the strong and turbulent cultural forces.

In contrast, Western European countries have undergone a considerable political development and enjoy a certain maturity as a result. Mediocre leaders have no difficulty surviving there. The name of the political game is unity hence the European Union.

3.4 – A SECOND LEASE ON LIFE

The predetermination ingrained in S-curve forecasts is often disturbing. Invariably these questions arise: Is there no way to avoid the announced end of life? Is there no way to find oneself in spring again? Well, Alfred Hitchcock achieved this when he moved from cinema to television.

Figure 3.4.1 shows the number of films for which Hitchcock could claim credit at any time during his career. As a child Hitchcock manifested interest in theatrical plays, but as a teenager, he went to the cinema frequently and soon began visiting movie studios. At the age of 20 he took a modest job as a designer of titles for the silent movies of the time, pretending—something that he maintained even later—that he had no ambition to assume more responsibility. This is in contradiction to his insistence on learning everything there was to learn about filmmaking and volunteering to try out his hand at any new assignment. In fact, the lower

HITCHCOCK'S TWO NICHES IN CINEMA

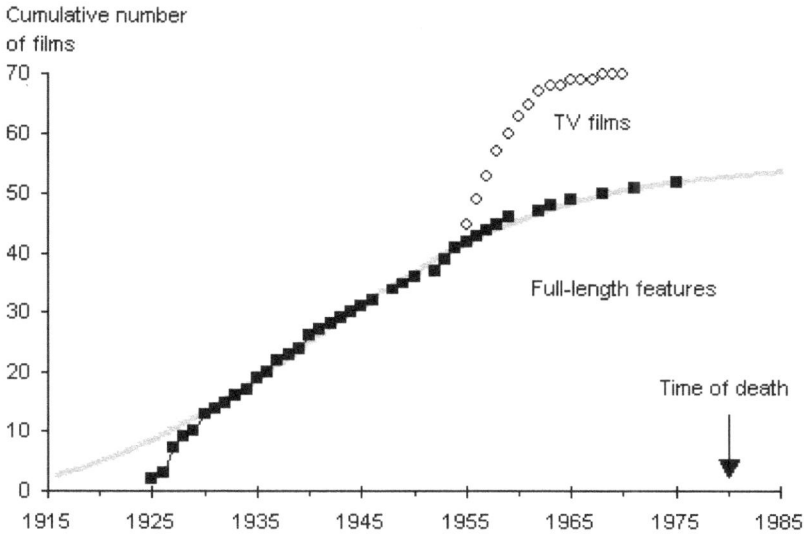

Figure 3.4.1. The squares indicate full-length films, and the circles indicate the sum of both full-length and shorter television films. The fit (gray line) is only to the full-length films. A smaller curve is outlined by the television films and seems to have its beginning in Hitchcock's film works.

part of the curve fitted to the data of his full-length films seems to originate well before 1925, when his first movie appeared. This means that his impulse for direction was deeply rooted. When he finally started his career as a film director at 26, he produced prodigiously during the first 6 years, as if he were trying to "catch up"—not unlike many others discussed in *Predictions* whose early careers display this sudden release of pent-up productivity.

We see in Figure 3.4.1 that from 1930 onwards the cumulative number of Hitchcock's full-length features grows smoothly to reach 52 by 1975. But the rate of growth is progressively lower after the mid-1950s. It is not by accident that in 1955 he was persuaded to make television films for the celebrated series *Alfred Hitchcock Presents*. The open circles on the graph represent the sum of both full-length and shorter television films. A shorter S-curve can be clearly outlined on top of the long one. This second niche contains 20 films; the process of filling it up starts in 1955 and flattens out, approaching natural completion, by 1962.

The evolution of Hitchcock's work just before he embarked on the television adventure contains a suggestive signal, a slowing-down leading smoothly into the subsequent television activity. Statistically speaking, the small deviation of the data points around 1951 has no real significance. It coincides, however, with the period that the US film industry felt most strongly the competition from the growing popularity of television. It also coincides with the time Hitchcock's main-feature career entered a period of declining growth—fall season. The television series put Hitchcock in spring again. It provided him with new potential for creativity and another high-growth period for his career. He was fortunate in his timing. New career cycles, like agricultural crops, must be seeded during the fall of the previous cycle.

There are many examples of individuals who had two and three or more cascading careers with an S-curve describing each one of them. Typically, women launch a new activity once the fertility curve ends in the early forties. Likewise, athletes and other careers strongly dependent on physical condition often embark on more intellectual pursuits (coaching, writing, and the like). Two conditions must be satisfied for a successful career renewal. One is timing—that is, the seeds must be put down during the fall season of the previous career. The other condition is that the new activity must be sufficiently differentiated so as to constitute a new "species". That is where Mozart failed.

Mozart's curve was rather complete when he died—see *Predictions* for a full discussion—which argues that he had exhausted his creative potential. This is in sharp contrast to the popular belief that the world has been deprived of many musical masterpieces by his "premature" death. But when Mozart entered his fall season in 1785 he composed the *Dissonant Quartet K465*, which can be considered as his attempt to branch out into a new niche for musical composition. The timing was right considering he had just entered a fall season. But the new "species" was perhaps not sufficiently differentiated, and certainly not gifted for survival (it was rejected by being too far ahead of its time.) Mozart would have had a better chance at a second lease on life perhaps as a musicologist, a music critique, or even a writer.

3.5 – WHERE ARE YOU ON THE CURVE?

Before setting any strategy we need to ask the following question: "Where are we on the curve?" The timeframe can vary. If we are addressing an entire life, or a company's existence from beginning to end, it is probably decades. If we are concerned with a product's life cycle, or a business season, it may be years or months, and there will be many cycles before the company or the technology responsible ceases to exist.

In Chapter 9 we will discuss a number of techniques for quantitatively estimating one's position on the curve. They are incorporated in the software package *Where Are You on the Curve and What to Do about It* from Growth Dynamics. Here we will see one simple but powerful intuitive approach for determining the cycle phase one is in. It is based on the fact that the prospects for growth affect one's emotional disposition— subconsciously—and thus become intuitively accessible.

The method utilizes the concepts of calculus. The S-shaped overall pattern is very sensitive to the rate of change of the rate of growth. Mathematically, this corresponds to the second derivative—in other words, the prospects for growth. To better understand the concept of the second derivative, think of traveling by car. Let us begin by saying that the total distance you cover as a function of time looks like an S-curve. (This does not mean that you swerve around but that your trip has a well-defined beginning and end.) The first derivative—the rate at which the distance changes—is the car speed. When the speed is high, much distance

DIFFERENT WAYS OF LOOKING AT NATURAL GROWTH

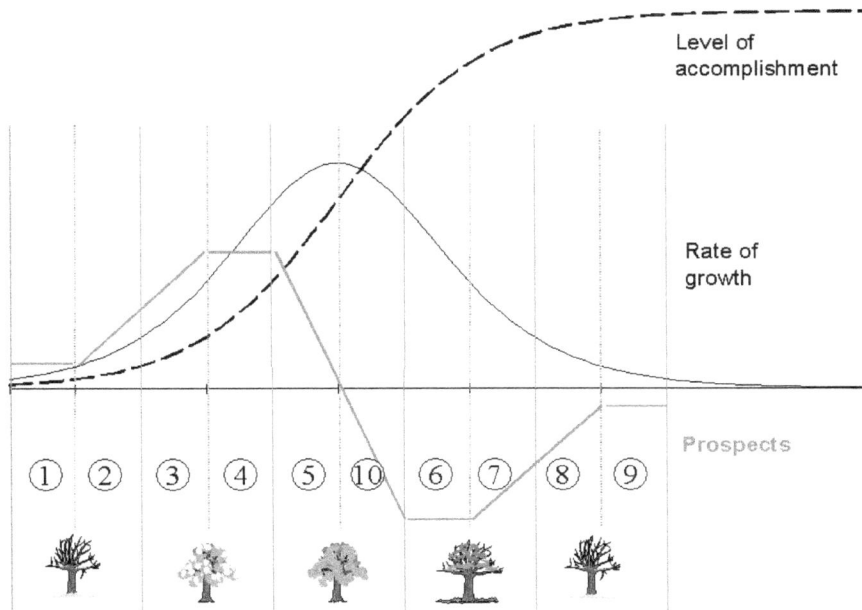

Figure 3.5.1. Three curves describing a natural-growth process: The S-curve and its two derivatives (the 2nd derivative—gray line—has been approximated with straight-line segments.) The circled numbers correspond to the numbers of the questionnaire; they point out a position in a season.

is covered in a short time. The speed curve is typically bell-shaped—that is, low in the beginning and at the end, but high in the middle of the trip. The second derivative is the acceleration, the rate at which the speed changes.

The acceleration is directly proportional to the force exerted by the car. The more powerful the car, the higher a speed it can attain in a short time. This curve goes up and down and up, since you start at zero, you accelerate, and later decelerate in order to stop. Figure 3.5.1 shows the three curves mathematically calculated. Without loss of generality, the second derivative has been approximated with straight-line segments to map into the seasons.

A more relevant example is found in product sales. As we saw, the cumulative number of products sold—the filling of the market niche—is described by an S-curve. Sales per quarter represent the first derivative. They comprise the product's life cycle and follow a bell-shaped curve. In this case, the second derivative is the company's investment in its product. Investment is positive during the product's early days and negative—returns instead of investment—during the product's later life.

Similarly in the stock market, the share price during a growth cycle is described by an S-shaped curve. The returns on investments (ROI) per unit of time are given by the bell-shaped curve. The second derivative reflects the prospects for growth, something like the analysts' rating of AAA, A+, A, A−, three stars, two stars, and so on.

For any growth process, we need to identify the quantity that corresponds to its second derivative—that is, the rate of the rate of growth, or the prospects for growth. Here are some examples:

S-shaped curve	Bell-shaped curve (1st derivative)	Up and down and up (2nd derivative)
Distance	Speed	Acceleration (force)
Cumulative sales of product	Sales by quarter	Investments on product
Size of organism	Rate of growth	Growth prospects
Stock price	ROI	Stock rating
Knowledge	Learning	Rate of progress
State of the economy (GNP, $ per capita, etc.)	Rate of economic development	Value of money (opposite of inflation)

You can pinpoint your position in the growth cycle by answering the questionnaire below that addresses your emotional world. The questionnaire determines the position on the cycle with an accuracy of half a season. As you respond, think of the prospects for the future and the direction in which they are moving. Or simply whether you feel good or bad, optimistic or pessimistic toward the future—all with regard to a product, an activity, a company, a career, or whatever else may be in your mind. But remember, the activity you choose must grow under conditions of natural competition—that is, the law of survival of the fittest.

When the employees or stockholders of a company complete such a questionnaire on their company as a whole, they reveal more than their perception and mood. They give a better determination of the company's position in the business cycle than the opinions of its management team. We can try it right now. Check one box in the questionnaire below.

What are the prospects for the future?
(compare to last season)

POSITIVE	NEGATIVE	
1-☐ Very low and stable	Very negative and stable	6-☐
2-☐ Low and rising	Very negative but rising	7-☐
3-☐ High and rising	Little negative and rising	8-☐
4-☐ Very high and rather stable	Little negative and stable	9-☐
5-☐ Deteriorating	Deteriorating	10-☐

For the answer look up the number you checked in Figure 3.5.1. Note that all change must be *relative to last season*. Therefore some knowledge of the season length is essential *a priori* even if very approximate; try to estimate the entire lifetime of the growth process from beginning to end and then divide by five (there are two winters in a complete cycle).

3.6 – DOWNWARD-POINTING S-CURVES

A downward-pointing S-curve represents decline instead of growth. But here again the rate of well-established declining process undergoes rapid and slow periods. Negative growth and positive growth go through similar phases—seasons—and a few basic seasonal attributes remain unchanged between the two. For example, both positive and negative summers are characterized by centralization, leadership, top-down management with increased central control, and bureaucratic procedures. Other attributes—such as those concerning pricing, profits, and long-range planning—become reversed. For springs and falls, too, some attributes remain unchanged and others reverse. During a positive spring there is learning and a need for specialists to design and build, but during a negative spring specialists are also needed to restructure and reduce. At the same time, positive spring is characterized by investments, whereas negative spring is characterized by disinvestments.

For a well-established declining process the three graphs of Figure 3.5.1 must be reversed (mirror images with respect to the horizontal axis) and the above questionnaire must be modified as follows:

What are the prospects for the future in the case of a well-established declining process?
(compare to last season)

NEGATIVE	POSITIVE	
1-☐ Little negative and stable	Very high and rather stable	6-☐
2-☐ Little negative and deteriorating	High but deteriorating	7-☐
3-☐ Very negative and deteriorating	Low and deteriorating	8-☐
4-☐ Very negative and stable	Very low and stable	9-☐
5-☐ Improving	Improving	10-☐

For the answer you can look up the number you checked again in Figure 3.5.1.

3.7 – INTUITIVE USE OF S-CURVES

S-curves enhanced by the seasons metaphor can also be used simply qualitatively to obtain rare insights and intuitive understanding. The seasons metaphor dictates that in spring the focus is on *what* to do, whereas in fall the emphasis shifts to the *how*. The former appears early in the growth process, the latter late. The evolution of classical music can be visualized as a large-timeframe S-curve beginning its development sometime in the fifteenth century and reaching a ceiling in the twentieth century. In Bach's time composers were concerned with *what* to say. The value of their music is on its architecture and as a consequence it can sound good when reproduced by any instrument, even by simple whistling. But two hundred years later composers such as Debussy wrote music that depends crucially on the interpretation, the *how*. Classical music was still "young" in Bach's time but was getting "old" by Debussy's time (when you hear people say that they need to focus on the how, you can understand that they are referring to something that is getting old, see Figure 3.6.1.

One may wonder why Chopin is more popular than Bartók. Chopin composed during the "summer" of music's S-curve when public preoccupation with music went over a maximum. Around that time composers' efforts were rewarded more handsomely than today. The innovations they made in music were assimilated by the public within a short period of time because the curve rose steeply and would rapidly catch up with each innovation. But today the curve has flattened and gifted composers are given very limited space. If they make even only small innovations they find themselves above the curve and there won't be any time in the future when the public will appreciate their work. On the other hand, if they don't innovate, they will not be saying anything new. In either case today's composers will not be credited with an achievement.

THE EVOLUTION OF CLASSICAL MUSIC

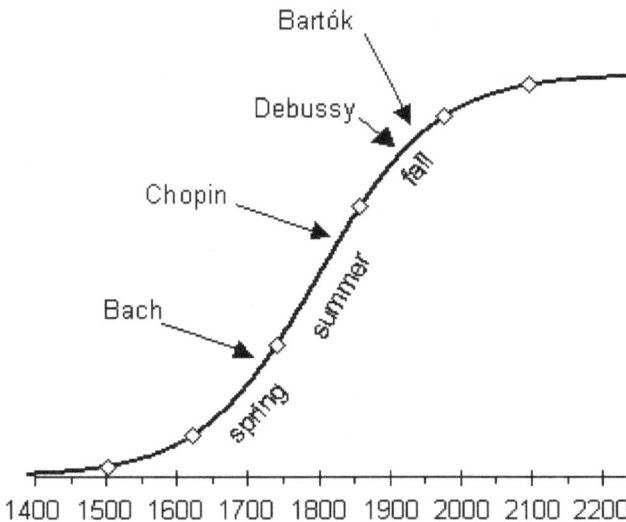

Figure 3.6.1 This S-curve has been constructed by only qualitative arguments and yet it seems accurate and informative. The vertical axis could be something like "importance", "sophistication", or "public appreciation", (always cumulative). The little circles delimit the seasons.

IN CLOSING

The S-shaped curve is a visualization of the natural law that governs growth in competition. This curve depicts the size—the population—attained by a certain time: *how far you have gone*. The second visualization of the same law is the bell-shaped curve representing the rate of growth, the life cycle. This curve is linked to how much momentum you have acquired: *how difficult it will be to stop you*. The third visualization is the up-and-down-and-up curve. It is linked to the force that drives the growth process: *the promise for the future*.

The ability to locate our position on the curve via the questionnaire on future prospects comes from the fact that deep down inside we know important things in an emotional way. Our knowledge may lack mathematical precision, but it unquestionably distinguishes optimism from pessimism, euphoria from anxiety, relaxation from stress. It also tells us whether the change is for the better or for the worse.

Once we have located our position on the curve, it becomes clearer what to do. Generally speaking we should be doing the opposite from what proved successful two seasons ago; examples:

- If you lose your job (that is, find yourself in a professional winter), you need to become entrepreneurial and opportunistic. Take risks, break rules, and explore all directions. These behaviors are opposite to those that helped you succeed when your job was at its Zenith. You were then conservative, conformist, obedient, and unidirectional. You worked long days then, asking no questions; you work less now but question more.

- During the early stages of a product's life cycle—winter—the sales force is opportunistic. Two seasons later—summer—the opposite behavior is appropriate; sales operations invariably become centralized and regulated, making use of automated procedures for price quotation and order intake.

- People in the fall season of their lives may wonder about what to do next. They should consider the opposite of what really helped them during their spring season. Youngsters typically benefit from learning activities such as reading, schooling, and apprenticeships. Older people then, even if they have the opportunity to go back to school, will benefit more from writing, teaching, and coaching. But it must all be tailored to the particular situation. For example, a young student who is poor should benefit from a scholarship; an older person who is rich will benefit (that is, will feel better) from contributing to a scholarship fund.

4 – SUBSTITUTIONS

In its simplest form natural growth in competition is a process in which one or more "species" strive to increase their numbers in a "niche" of finite resources. Depending on whether or not the "species" is successful over time, its population will trace an ascending or a descending S-curve. In a niche filled to capacity, one species population can increase only to the extent that another one decreases. Thus occurs a process of *substitution*, and to the extent that the conditions of competition are natural, the transition from occupancy by the old to occupancy by the new should follow the familiar S-shaped pattern of a natural growth process.

The first connection between competitive substitutions and S-curves was done by J. C. Fischer and R. H. Pry in a celebrated article published in 1971. It became a classic in studies of the diffusion of technological change. They wrote as follows:

> If one admits that man has few broad basic needs to be satisfied—food, clothing, shelter, transportation, communication, education, and the like—then it follows that technological evolution consists mainly of substituting a new form of satisfaction for the old one. Thus as technology advances, we may successively substitute coal for wood, hydrocarbons for coal, and nuclear fuel for fossil fuel in the production of energy. In war we may substitute guns for arrows, or tanks for horses. Even in a much more narrow and confined framework, substitutions are constantly encountered. For example, we substitute water-based paints for oil-based paints, detergents for soap, and plastic floors for wood floors in houses.[1]

They went on to explain that depending on the timeframe of the substitution the process may seem evolutionary or revolutionary. However, regardless of the pace of change, the end result is to perform an existing function or satisfy an ongoing need differently. The function or need rarely undergoes radical change.

A similar process occurs in nature, with competition embedded in the fact that the new way is vying with the old way to satisfy the same need. And the eventual winner will be, in the Darwinian formulation, the one better fit for survival. This unpalatable conclusion may seem unfair to the aging, wise, and experienced members of human society, but in practice it is not always easy for the young to take over from the old. Experience and wisdom do provide a competitive edge, and the substitution process proceeds only to the extent that youth fortifies itself progressively with knowledge and understanding. It is the combination of the required proportions of energy, fitness, experience, and wisdom that will determine the rate of competitive substitutions. If one's overall rating is low due to a lack in one area, someone else with a better score will gain ground, but only proportionally to his or her competitive advantage.

The opposite substitution, cases in which the old replace the young, is possible but rare. It is sometimes encountered in crisis situations where age and experience are more important to survival than youth and energy. But independently of who is substituting for whom, and in spite of the harshness ingrained in competitive substitutions, one can say that the process deserves to be called natural.

4.1 – ONE-TO-ONE SUBSTITUTIONS

A species population growing into an ecological niche that is already filled to capacity will progressively replace the incumbent species. A classical example was the replacement of horses by cars as means of personal transportation at the beginning of the twentieth century.

When automobiles were first introduced, they offered an attractive alternative to traveling on horseback. The speed and cost, however, remained about the same. In *Megamistakes: Forecasting and the Myth of Rapid Technological Change*, Steven Schnaars considers a cost-benefit analysis as one of the three ways to avoid wrong forecasts.[2] In this case such an analysis would have predicted a poor future for cars.

Ironically, one of the early advantages attributed to the automobile was its non-polluting operation. In large cities, removing horse excrement from the streets was becoming an increasingly heavy task, and projections for the transport needs of the future were ominous. For this and mainly for other more deeply-rooted reasons, cars began replacing horses rapidly and diffused in society as a popular means of transportation.

We can look at this substitution process in detail by focusing on the phasing-in period of the automobile 1900-1930. Let us look at only the relative amounts, that is, the percentage of cars and horses of the total number of transport "units" (horses plus cars.) Before 1900, horses filled 100% of the personal transport niche. As the percentage of cars grew, the share of horses declined, because the sum had to equal 100%. The data in Figure 4.1.1 show only non-farming horses and mules.

THE SUBSTITUTION OF CARS FOR HORSES IN PERSONAL TRANSPORTATION

As a percentage
of all "vehicles"

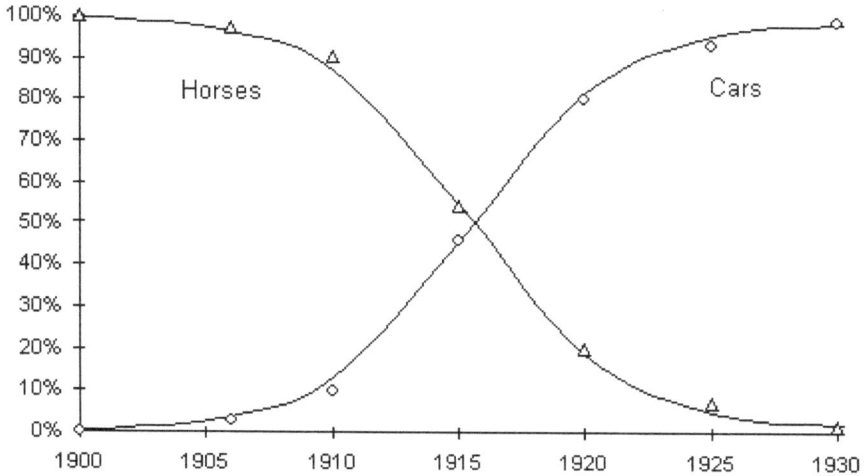

Figure 4.1.1 The data points represent percentages of the total number of transportation units, namely, cars plus non-farming horses and mules. The S-curves are fitted to the data points. The sum of respective ascending and descending percentages equals 100% at any given time.[3]

These trajectories are seen to follow complementary S-curves. Around 1916 there are an equal number of horses and cars on the streets, and by 1925 the substitution is more than 90% completed. It is interesting to notice that the fitted S-curve does not quite reach the ceiling of 100% for cars after 1930. This may be related to the fact that a certain number of horses were not replaced by cars. They are probably the horses found today in horseback riding and in horse racing.

The obsolescence of horse as a means of transportation illustrates the inevitable takeover by newcomers possessing competitive advantages. There are always two complementary trajectories in one-to-one substitutions, one for the loser and one for the winner. They indicate the shares, the relative positions, of the contenders. Because the ceiling is by definition 100%, the determination of these curves becomes easier and more reliable than usual S-curves (there is 1 in place of the parameter M in Equations 2.2.1 and 2.2.2). The niche size for shares is by definition 100% and it is not a function of time.

By looking at shares we focus on the competition and we evidence an advantage whose origin is deeply rooted, as if it were genetic in nature. This description thus becomes free of external influences: the state of the economy, politics, earthquakes, and seasonal effects such as vacations and holidays. In the case of the cars-for-horses substitution, World War I had no impact; the trajectories in Figure 4.1.1 continued their smooth evolution undisturbed.

Another advantage of focusing on relative positions in substitution processes is that in a fast-growing market the natural character of the process (the shape S) may be hidden under the absolute numbers that are increasing for both competitors. But the fact that one competitor is growing faster implies that the other competitor is phasing out. In Figure 4.1.2 we see the absolute numbers of horses and cars in the United States since 1850. During the first decade of the twentieth century the number of horses continued to increase as it had in the past. The number of cars increased even more rapidly, however. The substitution graph of Figure 4.1.1 reveals an indisputable decline for the horses' share during the decade in question.

THE OVERALL PERSONAL "VEHICLE" MARKET KEPT INCREASING EVEN AS THE USE OF HORSES DECLINED

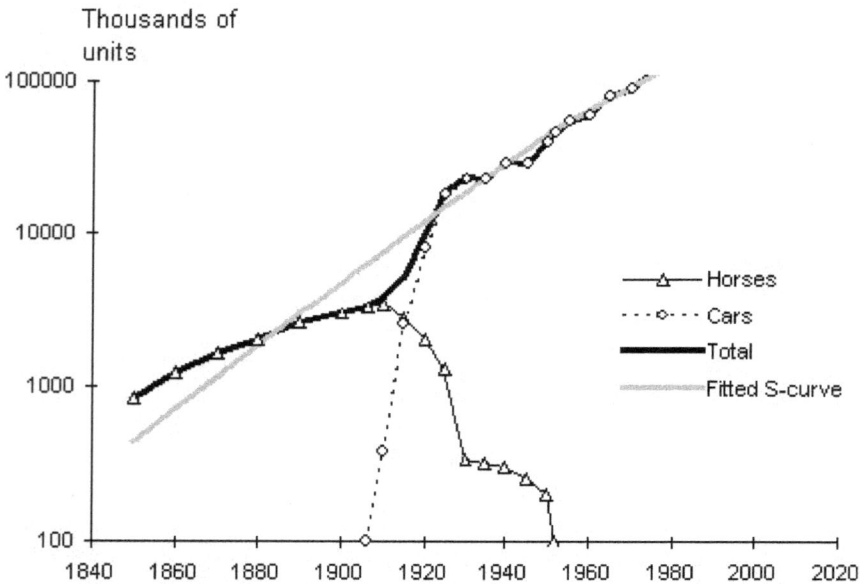

Figure 4.1.2 The numbers of non-farming horses (including mules) and cars in the United States. The vertical scale is logarithmic to accommodate the many-fold growth. The sum of horses plus cars grew practically unaffected across the substitution period and is amenable to an S-curve fit (thick gray line).[4]

Playing the devil's advocate, one may try to use this way of thinking to prove that given any two competitors, one of them must necessarily be phasing out. Since they are bound to grow at different rates, one will be always "losing" relative to the other. The fallacy of this approach is that two competitors chosen at random most probably do not constitute a niche. A natural one-to-one substitution is expected whenever there is direct transfer from one to the other with no third parties involved. The niche needs to be carefully defined. For example, do the two computer makers IBM and Hewlett-Packard together constitute one niche? Should we expect substitution of one by the other, or should they be looked at as only two out of many members of the bigger computer market? A necessary and sufficient condition for such a microniche to exist would be that the sum of the two shares is invariant over time, as was the case in Figure 4.1.1.

Other evidence that such a microniche exists would be to know independently that in a certain geographical or market segment these two are the only companies that offer products. In the latter case the geographical or market segment constitutes a niche, but whether or not a substitution process is taking place in a natural way will depend on how closely the evolution of the market shares resembles S-shaped patterns.

The S-curve pattern can be made to appear as a straight line when viewed through the appropriate "eyepiece." The logistic function used in the one-to-one natural substitutions—Equation 2.2.2 with $M = 1$— is such that if one divides the number of the "new" by the number of the "old" at any given time and plots this ratio with logarithmic vertical scale, one gets a straight line (alternatively one may plot the logarithm of this ratio on a linear scale). It is a mathematical transformation, described by Equation 4.1.1 and depicted in Figure 4.1.3.

$$\frac{"new"}{"old"} = \frac{X(t)}{1-X(t)} = e^{a(t-t_o)} \qquad\qquad 4.1.1$$

The interest in doing this transformation is to facilitate the detection of "naturalness" in a growth process from only a few data points. In theory even only three data points that fall on a straight line indicate the existence of an S-curve, albeit with poor confidence (the more points we have the higher our confidence). This eliminates the need for computers and sophisticated fitting procedures when searching for "naturalness" in substitution processes. All we need to do is look for a straight-line pattern in the data, the existence of which will be proof that indeed we are dealing with natural growth in competition.

Transforming an S-Curve into a Straight Line

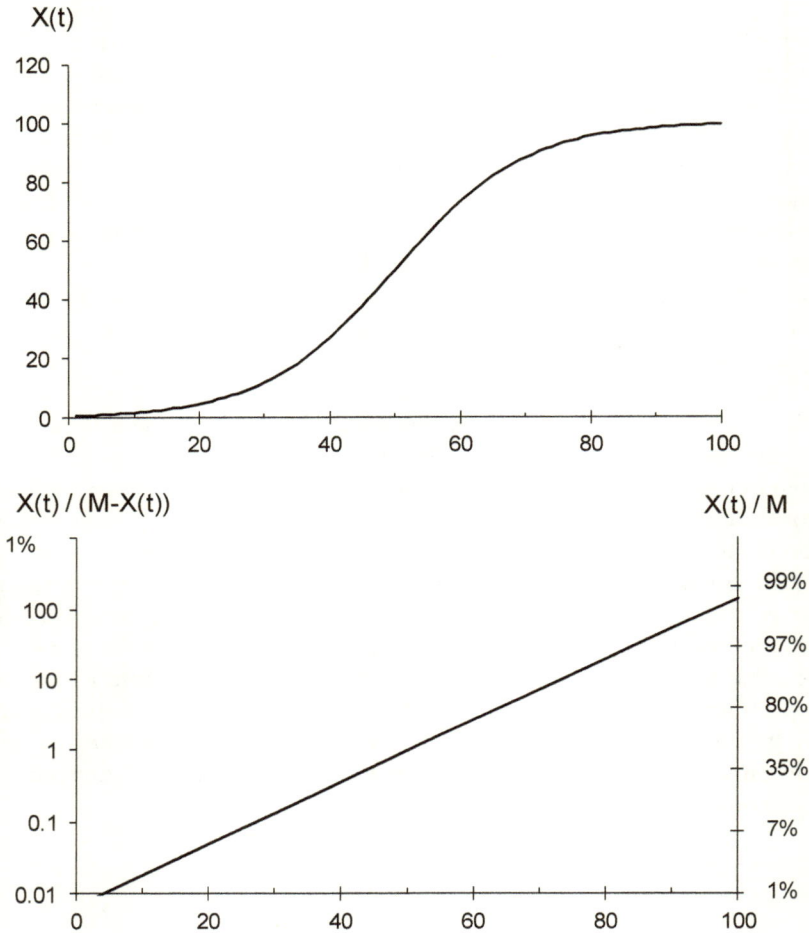

Figure 4.1.3 The S-curve at the top is transformed into a straight line at the bottom by plotting the ratio "new" to "old" on a logarithmic scale at the left while the share of "new" is designated by the nonlinear "logistic" scale at the right. This scale is nonlinear with 100% infinitely far upward and 0% infinitely far downward.

Let us illustrate this with a hypothetical scenario. Suppose you are concerned about the new hamburger stand that opened recently across the street from yours. You worry that its guarantee of home delivery in less than ten minutes may not only cut into your business but also put you out of it altogether. People may just decide to save the gas and order their sandwiches from wherever they happen to be. To make it easy, let us also suppose that the stand across the street has set up a public counting device, which advertises the number of hamburgers it has sold so far.

It is easy to find out if your competitor's way is going to be the way of the future. Here is a recipe. Start your own count of how many hamburgers you have sold since the competition appeared and track the ratio—your competitor's number divided by your number. Then make a graph on semi-logarithmic paper and plot this ratio every day (you can ask for logarithmic vertical scale on your computer's spreadsheet). By the third day you should be able to see how this ratio is lining up with the previous two days. A couple of weeks later you will have enough data points to reliably discern a trend. If the data points form a straight line (within the small daily fluctuations, of course), you may want to start looking around for another business. If, on the other hand, the trend is flattening or the pattern is such that no overall straight line is discernible, then chances are that the guys across the street are not here to stay, or if they are, they will not take all the business.

Looking at natural substitution processes in this way reveals straight lines. The straighter the lines, the more natural the processes. The longer the lines, the more confidence one can have in extrapolating them further. If the ratio of new to old has not yet reached 0.1, it may be too early to talk of a substitution; a natural substitution becomes "respectable" only after it has demonstrated that it has survived "infant mortality" as we saw in Chapter 3.

Another reason for which an *a priori* natural substitution may not display the expected trajectory is that the variable is not properly defined. For example the substitution of detergent for soap discussed in the article by Fisher and Pry would not have followed a straight line had they taken *all* soap. They carefully considered only laundry soap, leaving cosmetic soap aside. Complications can also arise in substitutions that look "unnatural" in cases of a niche-within-a-niche, or a niche-beyond-a-niche. In both cases two different S-curves must be considered for the appropriate time periods. In the straight-line representation such cases show a broken line made out of two straight sections.

When close scrutiny does not eliminate irregularities, it means that there is something unnatural after all. A substitution may show local deviations from a straight-line pattern, which can be due to exceptional temporary phenomena. But such anomalies are soon reabsorbed, and the process regains a more natural course.

Among the many examples of one-to-one substitutions quantitatively discussed in *Predictions* and in *Conquering Uncertainty* are: fossil-based for renewable energy sources, steamships for sail ships, information workers for manual laborers, women for men executives, telephone calls for letters, and consulting for accounting revenue within Arthur Andersen.

Below we will look into three examples taken from the Fischer-and-Pry article mentioned earlier because they illustrate a number of interesting points. Figure 4.1.4 shows the substitutions of synthetic for natural rubber, synthetic for natural fibers, and margarine for butter in the United States. All three depict the same slope (the three straight lines are parallel). This does not mean that *all* substitutions always follow this rate, but it does point to a business-as-usual aspect of society, and not only American society. The detergent-for-soap substitution mentioned earlier took place at the same rate in Japan as it had done in the United States ten years earlier.[5]

However, the replacement of natural by synthetic rubber shows a large "anomaly" during the war years. In the 1930s synthetic rubber was slowly making an appearance in the American market as a more expensive alternative of lesser quality than natural rubber, which was imported in large quantities from foreign sources. During the early stages of World War II, imports of natural rubber were largely cut off and, at the same time demand for rubber increased considerably. A large national effort during these years resulted in improving the quality and reducing the production costs of synthetic rubber.

Synthetic replaced natural rubber at an accelerated rate during the war years as can be evidenced in Figure 4.1.4. But as soon as the war ended, foreign sources of natural rubber became available again, and the substitution rate dropped despite the technological know-how already acquired. From then on the substitution process continued at a rate similar to other replacements, such as margarine for butter and synthetic for natural fibers to reach again war levels of production only twenty years later. The deviation, caused by the necessities of the war, disappeared leaving no trace when life got back to normal.

The solid-black points in Figure 4.1.4 show that none of the three substitution processes finally reached 100% completion. They all stopped at around 90%. Contrary to what may have been expected from the law of natural competition one-to-one substitutions do not always proceed to completion. A "locked" portion of the market share may resist substitution. In our three examples this locked portion was about 10% of the market; it could be larger. Competitive substitutions are natural growth processes and do follow S-curves, but the newcomer rarely replaces the incumbent completely.

WARS MAY INTERFERE WITH NATURAL SUBSTITUTIONS

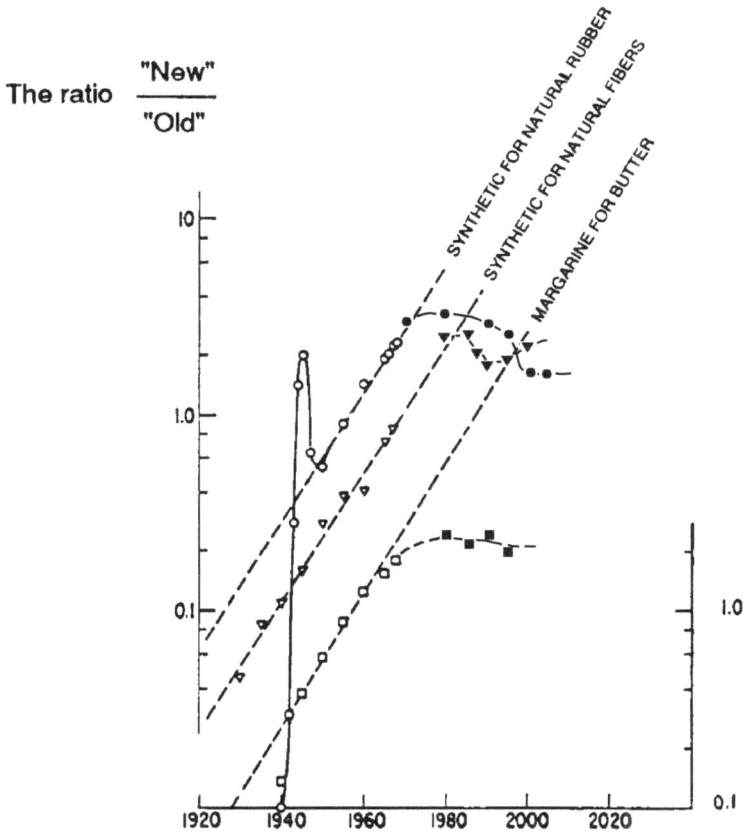

Figure 4.1.4 Three replacements in the United States published by J. C. Fisher and R. H. Pry in 1971. The data show ratios of amounts consumed. The logarithmic scale brings out the straight-line character of the substitutions. The only significant deviation from a natural path is observed for the production of synthetic rubber during World War II. The solid-back points show recent data.[6]

4.2 – CASE STUDY

DEC Microvax II Substituted for the Minicomputer Vax 11/750.

We saw in Section 2.3 that the DEC minicomputer Vax 11/750 phased out during 1986 and was replaced by the Microvax II, which was one-third the price for the same performance. Being much cheaper the new computer sold in much greater numbers (consequence of price elasticity). But before the sales of the Vax 11/750 dropped to statistically insignificant numbers I was able to establish that the substitution Microvax II for Vax 11/750 sales was following a natural course, that is, a logistic S-curve pattern. I plotted the logarithm of the ratio of the two products and obtained a straight line—this is the same as plotting the ratio on a logarithmic scale—see Figure 4.2.1. From the values of the ratio one can deduce shares of each product. Niche occupancy by Microvax II is indicated on the left-hand axis with a nonlinear scale (with a linear scale the pattern would be S-shaped). Obviously the trajectory of the Vax11/750 share followed a complementary course, that is, a straight line pointing downward with minus the slope of the gray line, not shown the figure.

THE MICROVAX II SUBSTITUTED FOR THE VAX 11/750

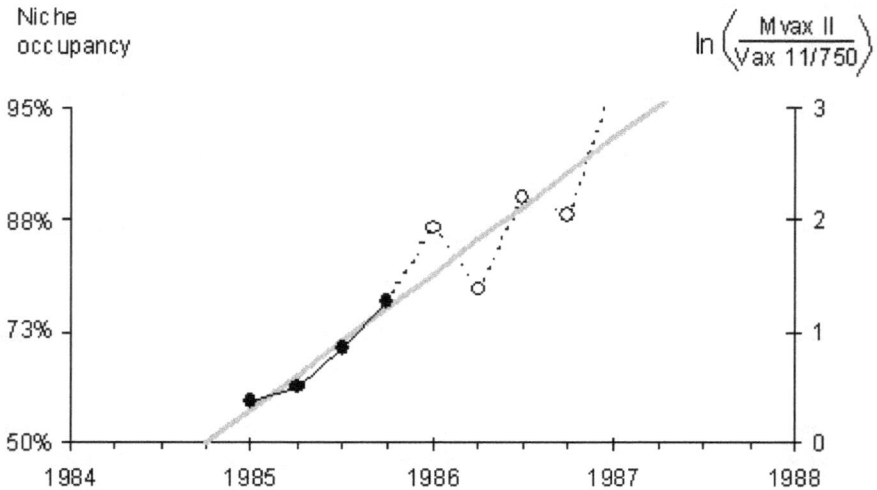

Figure 4.2.1 Vertically on the right-hand axis is plotted the logarithm of the sales ratio "new" to "old". On the left-hand axis the scale is nonlinear and marks the niche penetration by the "new" (Microvax II). The straight gray line is a fit based on the four black points. The white circles are later data.

Because Microvax II was selling in much greater numbers from the beginning, the substitution began at around 50% and traces only the second half of the S-curve. From the first four quarterly data points I was able to determine a straight line for the ratio "new" to "old", in this case Microvax II to Vax 11/750. The gray straight line forecasts this ratio and is in quite good agreement with later data (white circles). Notice that the data fluctuate more and more as we approach and go above the 90% level, as expected from our discussion on chaotic fluctuations in Chapter 3. But given the nonlinear scale of Figure 4.2.1, these apparently big fluctuations amount to only a few percent deviations from the projected trend.

The gray line of Figure 4.2.1 representing the ratio of "new" to "old" can be combined with the bell-shaped curve in Figure 2.3.1 representing forecasts for the "old" to yield future forecasts for Microvax II sales. This is shown in Figure 4.2.2 and turned out to be in rather good agreement with actual sales during the following three years.

The added value of my study, however, was not simply improved long-term forecasting accuracy. My forecasts were based on a new way of thinking and a science-based one for that. Marketers at DEC appreciated having such inputs in order to be able to make out-of-the box decisions on their long-range planning.

FORECASTED VS. ACTUAL SALES FOR MICROVAX II

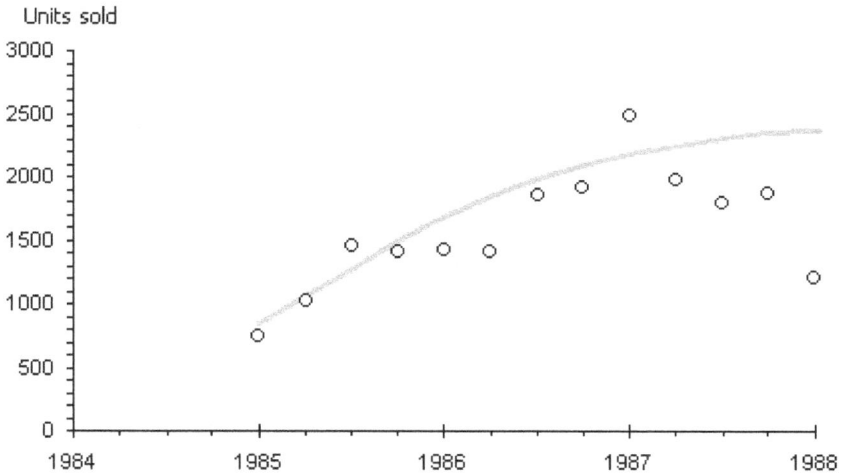

Figure 4.2.2 Forecast (gray line) and actual sales (white circles). The gray line has been calculated from the life-cycle line in Figure 2.3.1 and the straight line in Figure 4.2.1.

4.3 – SUCCESSIVE SUBSTITUTIONS

The introduction of a gifted new competitor in an already occupied niche results in a progressive displacement of the older tenant, and the dominant role eventually passes from the old to the new. As the new gets older, however, it cedes leadership in its turn to a more recent contender, and substitutions may thus cascade. For example, steamships replaced sailing ships, but later they themselves were replaced by ships with internal-combustion engines. While the total registered tonnage of the merchant fleet in the United States increased by a factor of almost one hundred during the last two hundred years, the percentages of the different types of ship show two successive substitutions.

In Figure 4.3.1, the vertical scale is again such that S-curves become straight lines. We can distinguish two one-to-one substitutions: steam for sail before 1900 and motor for steam after 1950. Between these dates all three types of boats coexist, with steam claiming the lion's share. It is worth noting that motor ships represented only 10% of the total tonnage as late as 1970. Steamships have been decreasing in favor of motor ships, but remained the dominant type of merchant vessel all the way to the end of the twentieth century; although they are often fueled by oil instead of coal, and in some cases use steam turbines instead of coal-burning external-combustion engines.

Internal-combustion engines, when first introduced in ships, started spreading "abnormally" rapidly, probably due to the momentum acquired in their swift propagation through transportation overland (replacement of horses by automobiles), which had just preceded.

Suddenly the realities of World War II, notably a shortage of gasoline, interrupted the accelerated introduction of motors in ships, and the substitution process was readjusted to a level and a rhythm that later proved to be the natural trend.

The little circle in Figure 4.3.1 reflects the situation in year 2000. This update is based on data from only tankers and indicates a fifty-fifty split between steam and motor propulsion engines. The 50-percent point comes earlier than expected. The discrepancy may be due to the fact that the update concerns only tankers. But it may also be due to a new phenomenon. There is a newcomer in our competitive picture, gas propulsion. The graph of Figure 4.3.1 was put together before ships with gas propulsion began diffusing into the market. The appearance of ships with gas propulsion may have accelerated the decline of steam ships. And the newcomer is most likely to eventually replace motor ships.

FROM SAIL TO STEAM TO MOTORS

Percentage of total tonnage

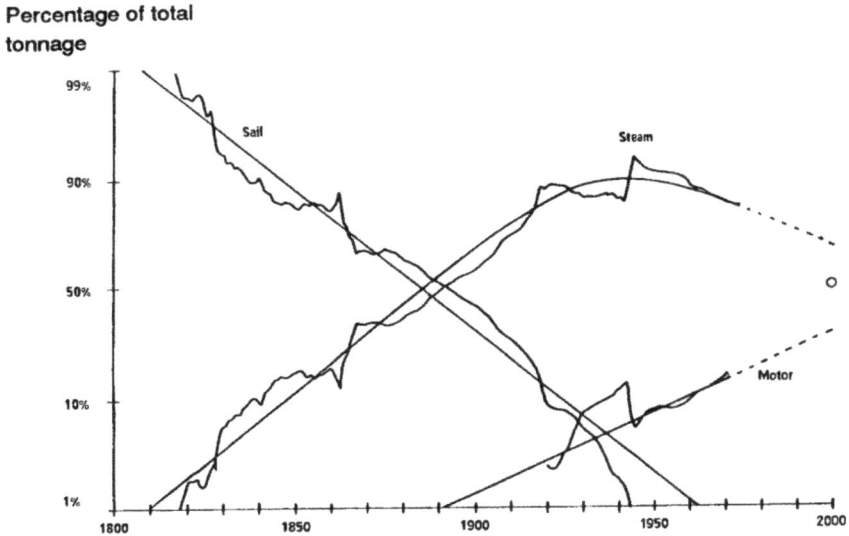

Figure 4.3.1 The percentage of US total tonnage of merchant vessels by type of ship. Again, the vertical axis shows the logistic scale that transforms S-curves to straight lines. The straight lines shown are fits to the data. The curved section is the transition period between the end of phasing-in and the beginning of phasing-out. Steamships substituted for sailboats between 1800 and 1920, at which time boats with internal-combustion engines started replacing steam ships. World War II seems to have brought this substitution process down to its natural course. The little circle at 50% is an update from Lloyd's Register database.[7]

The smooth lines in Figure 4.3.1 represent the description given by the substitution model as generalized by Nakicenovic to include more than two competitors.[8] It says that at any given time the shares of all competitors *but one* will follow straight-line trajectories. The singled out competitor, called the saturating one, will have its share determined as the remainder from 100% after all other shares have been subtracted. The saturating competitor is normally the oldest among the ones that were still growing. Usually it is also the one with the largest share, has practically reached maximum penetration, and is expected to start declining soon. The trajectory of a saturating share is curved. It traces the transition from the end of the growing phase, where the entity was substituting for its predecessor, to the beginning of the declining phase, where it will itself start being replaced by the one next in line. This happens precisely when the curvature of the resulting saturating trajectory drops to zero as described in detail by Nakicenovic. Every competitor goes through the saturating phase in chronological order.

The saturation phase can be seen as the culmination and, at the same time, as the beginning of the end. For a product it often corresponds to the maturity phase of the life cycle. It is the time when you face competition directly. You have done well, and everyone is trying to chip away at your gains. Your share is calculated as what remains after subtracting from 100% the trajectories of all the others. You are at the top, but you are alone; the model requires one and only one in the saturating phase at a time. This condition is necessary in order to produce a workable model, but it also matches well what happens in a multi-competitor arena—typically, the Olympic games where second and third places are usually not coveted by competitive individuals. Everyone competes for the first position. The nature of competition is such that there is always *one* front-runner, and everyone runs against him or her.

The reader will find many examples of successive substitutions in *Predictions* and in Marchetti's numerous publications.[9] The most celebrated example is the substitution of primary-energy sources, which has become a source of many far-reaching insights. It was first published by Marchetti in 1977.[10] I have been asked to update this picture on several occasions. Under *Case Studies* below I describe in detail my most recent update and its conclusions that became the object of a publication.[11]

4.4 – CASE STUDIES

Where Has the Energy Picture Gone Wrong?

The generalized Fisher-Pry diffusion/substitution model has been used in describing the primary-energy mix in world energy consumption over the last 150 years, see Figure 4.4.1 During the 150 years, wood, coal, natural gas, and nuclear energy have been the main protagonists in supplying the world with energy. More than one energy source was present at any time, but the leading role passed from one to the other. Wind power, waterpower, and other lesser sources have been ignored because they command too small a market share.

Figure 4.4.1 makes use of the logistic vertical scale that transforms S-curve into straight lines. It becomes evident from this picture that a century-long history of an energy source can be described—straight lines—quite well with only two constants, those required to define a straight line. (The curved sections are calculated by subtracting the straight lines from 100 %.) The destiny of an energy source is decided as soon as the two constants describing the straight line can be determined.

There are other messages in Figure 4.4.1 By looking more closely at the data we see that world-shaking events such as wars, skyrocketing energy prices, and recessions had little effect on the overall trends. Strikes may be more visible. In the coal industry, for example, such actions may result in short-lived deviations but the previous trend is quickly resumed.

Another observation is that there is no relationship between the utilization and the reserves of a primary energy source. It seems that the market moves away from a certain primary energy source long before the source becomes exhausted, at least at world level. This was true for wood and coal. It should also be true for oil. Despite the ominous predictions made in the 1950s that we would run out of oil in twenty years, we never did; more oil was found as the demand grew. Oil reserves will probably never be exhausted because other energy sources will be introduced in time. Well-established substitution processes with long time constants are fundamental in nature and will not be influenced by "lesser" reasons such as the depletion of reserves.

Environmentalists have opposed nuclear energy vehemently. This primary energy source reached 1% share in the world market in the mid 1970s. The rate of growth during the first decade, however, seems disproportionately rapid compared to the entry and exit slopes of wood, coal, oil and natural gas, all of which conform closely to a more gradual rate. At the same time, the opposition to nuclear energy also seemed out of proportion when compared to other environmental issues. Could it be that environmentalists did not react to nuclear energy per se but to its rate of growth instead?

As a consequence of the intense criticism, the growth of nuclear energy has slowed considerably, and has now approached the straight line proposed by the model. One may question what was the prime mover here—the environmental concerns that succeeded in slowing the rate of growth or the nuclear energy craze that forced environmentalists to react?

The coming to life of such a craze is understandable. Nuclear energy made a world-shaking appearance in the closing act of World War II by demonstrating the human ability to access superhuman powers. The word superhuman is appropriate because the bases of nuclear reactions are the mechanisms through which stars generate their energy. Humans for the first time possessed the sources of power that feed our sun, which was often considered as a god in the past. At the same time mankind acquired independence; nuclear is the only energy source that would remain indefinitely at our disposal if the sun went out.

Energy Consumption Worldwide

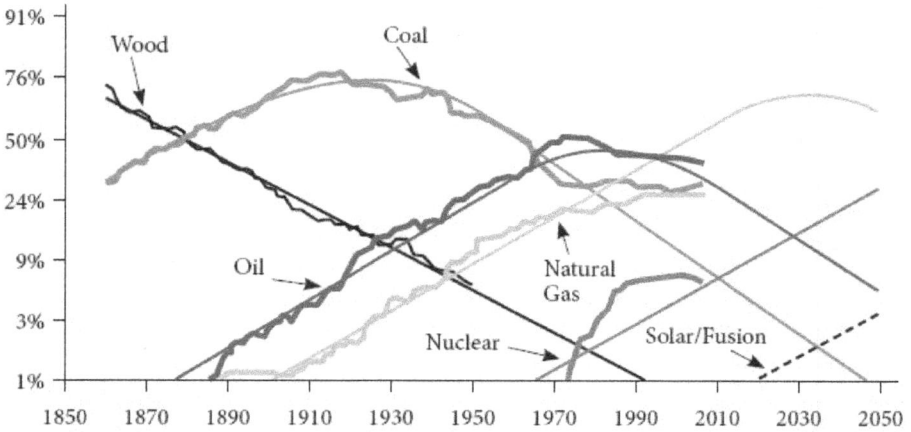

Figure 4.4.1   Data, fits, and projections for the shares of different energies consumed worldwide. For nuclear, the straight line is not a fit but a trajectory suggested by analogy. The futuristic source labeled "Solar/Fusion" may involve solar energy and thermonuclear fusion.[12]

    The figure also suggests that nuclear energy has a long future. Its share should grow at a slower more natural rate, with a trajectory parallel to those of oil, coal, and natural gas. A more mature less hastened diffusion of nuclear energy will meet less resistance from environmentalists if for no other reason the fact that a mature technology is less accident-prone. Indeed, in the last twenty years there has been less than one major accident in five years whereas in the early 1980s we witnessed five such accidents in three years.

    There is a hypothetical next primary energy source shown—fusion and/or solar and/or other—projected to enter the picture by supplying 1% of the world's needs in the 2020s. This projection is reasonable because such a technology, once demonstrated to be feasible, would require long time to be mastered industrially, as did nuclear energy. But even if we had such an energy source available today, it would have to diffuse at the natural rate, the rate at which other types of energy have entered and exited in the past; otherwise it could meet opposition comparable to that from environmentalists to early nuclear. One way or another the gas and nuclear cycles would still be traced out if somewhat earlier and smaller. Both these energy sources need to take their turn in playing a role comparable in importance to that of oil at its time.

But there is a significant "glitch" in the otherwise coherent energy picture of Figure 4.4.1. The share of coal stopped declining along the model's natural-growth trajectory in the early 1970s at the expense of natural gas. This may not be due to only the aggressively developing countries such as China who use coal ravenously. Developed countries such as the UK have been known to resist giving up coal. Whoever the culprit maybe the widening gap between the persistent level of coal use and coal's naturally declining trajectory becomes a source of pressure to the system, which may manifest itself in unexpected ways (possibly another case like the environmentalists vs. nuclear in the 1980s).

There is a secret concealed in this energy picture. As society moves from wood to coal to oil to gas and to nuclear society unwittingly pursues a strategy of fuel improvement not only because each new fuel is cleaner fuel but also—not unrelated—because each new fuel has higher energy content. Wood is rich in carbon but natural gas is rich in hydrogen. When hydrogen burns it gives water as exhaust; when carbon burns it gives CO_2 as exhaust. When wood burns very little hydrogen becomes oxidized to give water. Most of the energy comes from the carbon that oxidizes to give CO_2. On the contrary, when natural gas burns lots of hydrogen become water and very little carbon becomes CO_2. The molar ratio hydrogen/carbon for wood is about 0.1, for coal about 1, for oil about 2, and for natural gas (e.g., methane) about 4. For a fuel like hydrogen this ratio becomes infinite and the CO_2 emissions to the atmosphere null.[13]

Bio-fuels such as ethanol have a molar ratio of 3 and therefore on a quality basis they belong between oil and natural gas. To introduce bio-fuels on a big scale today would represent a move backward in the evolution of fuels in society.

The energy substitution described in Figure 4.4.1 took place in such a way that fuels rich in hydrogen progressively and consistently replaced fuels rich in carbon, and all that happened in a natural way (i.e., following an S-curve). The combination of energy sources according to the shares shown yields a hydrogen content that increases along an S-curve, see Figure 4.4.2). Society followed this S-curve on a global scale without the conscious intervention of governments or other influential decision makers. Bottom-up forces have safeguarded for one hundred years a smooth transition to energies that are more performing and less polluting.

The black dots in the top graph of Figure 4.4.2 have been obtained using the data points in Figure 4.4.1. Coincidental with the "glitch" mentioned earlier there is now a deviation from the S-curve pattern around 1972. It seems that hydrogen-enrichment process (decarbonization) stopped at that time. However, the persistent use of coal and its impact

Hydrogen Content of the Primary-Energy Mix (data)

Legend:
- The ratio H/(H+C)
- S-curve fit

Hydrogen Content of the Primary-Energy Mix (model)

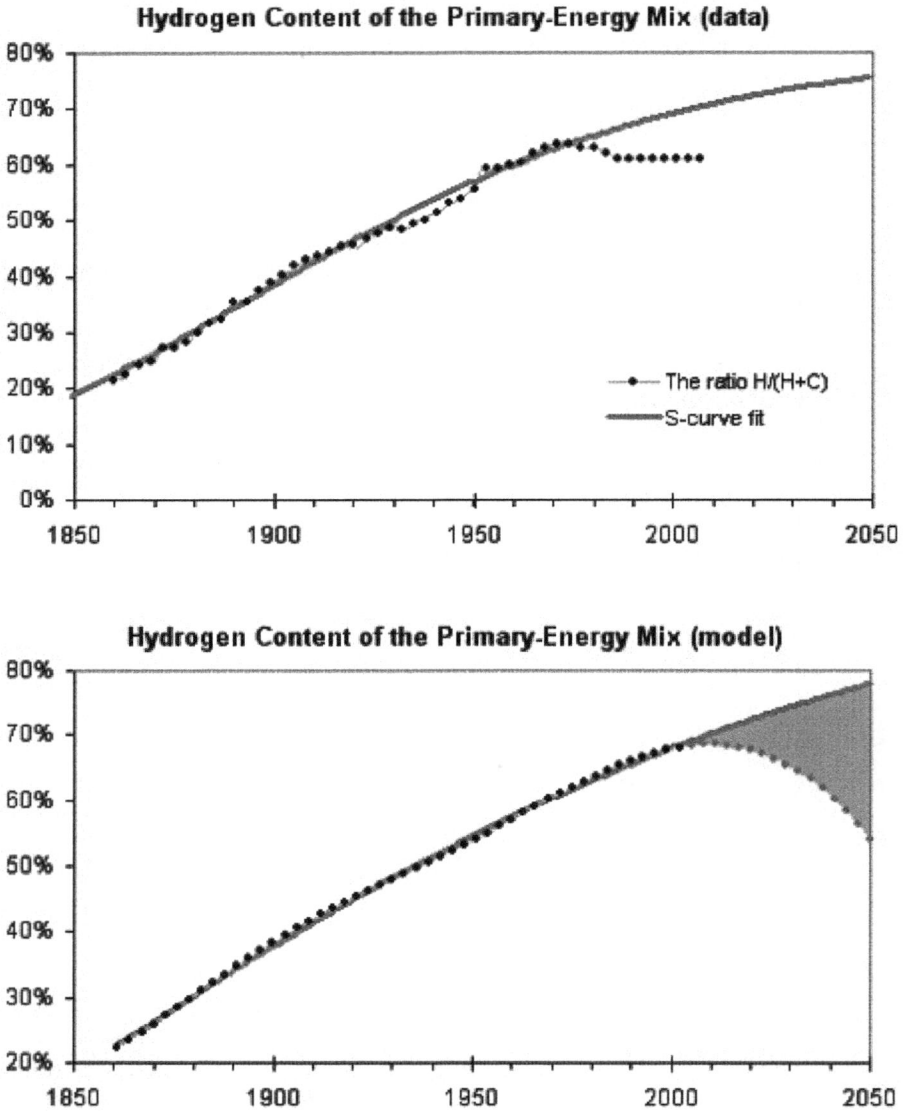

Figure 4.4.2   The black dots indicate the evolution of the hydrogen-content percentage according to the energy mix of Figure 4.4.1 from the data points (top graph) and from the model lines (bottom graph). The thick gray lines are S-curve fits to the black dots over the period 1860-1972 (top graph) and 1860-2008 (bottom graph). The gray area reflects the amount of hydrogen that needs to be provided from non-fossil types of energy.

on natural gas are not alone to blame for the missing hydrogen in our fuels today. Had coal continued declining and gas ascending along their natural paths, we would still be missing some hydrogen today. The black dots in lower graph of Figure 4.4.2 have been obtained using the smooth trend lines as defined by the substitution model in Figure 4.4.1. Here too there is a deviation from the S-pattern beginning around year 2000. This is because there is no hydrogen content in nuclear energy or in solar/fusion. As a consequence, the deviation from the S-curve becomes progressively more pronounced toward year 2050.

The gray area in the figure represents the "missing" hydrogen content. This amount of hydrogen should somehow be contributed by nuclear energy, if we want to continue the well-established natural course of de-carbonization. Nuclear energy can indeed do this in a number of different ways. For example, seawater can be split into hydrogen and oxygen via electrolysis or by direct use of nuclear heat. It must be noted that nuclear energy is not indispensable for the natural path to be maintained. Other energy sources such as solar, wind, hydroelectric, thermonuclear fusion or a combination thereof, could do the job but these technologies are still responsible for insignificant contribution to the energy picture worldwide and also present enormous technical and practical problems.

There is little doubt that society will eventually use hydrogen as its energy vector. It is the most potent fuel and progress cannot be stopped. The use of hydrogen as fuel has demonstrated survival of "infant mortality" with extensive applications in rockets. It is only a question of time before it diffuses to other social uses. After all, no niche in nature was ever left partially filled under natural circumstances and an S-curve that has been evolving for one hundred years (Figure 4.4.2) will most certainly proceed to completion. The catch phrase here is "natural circumstances". Can we trust circumstances to remain natural? Figure 4.4.1 indicates an anomaly; coal consumption began deviating from its naturally declining trajectory in the early 1970s.

Semiconductor Market Trends

In 1992 DEC and Siemens entered negotiations for a joint venture. Siemens had become interested in DEC's new microprocessor technology based on 64-bit microprocessors word length. But meetings between the two companies were hung up on differences of opinions when it came to evaluating the new technology's long-term impact. A vice president from DEC came to me and asked for "objective" projections of what should be expected in the microprocessor market.

DEC had been making minicomputers with microprocessors of progressively larger word width. The very first 4-bit machines were rapidly replaced by the widely accepted PDP 8 built with 8-bit microprocessors. There followed a decade during which 16-bit microprocessors progressively replaced 8-bit ones despite the latter's dominant role in the marketplace. Then came a hybrid 16/32-bit version for a short while, but poised for the dominant role in the market—comparable to that of the 8-bit paradigm—seemed to be the 32-bit technology. As for the expected market reaction to the up-coming 64-bit technology it was a big question mark.

In Figure 4.4.3 we see my analysis of market shipments data up to 1989 for the substitution of different microprocessor technologies. With a logistic vertical scale we evidence straight-line behaviors for all phasing-in and phasing-out technologies. The 64-bit technology was estimated to enter the market (that is, achieve 1% market share) sometime in mid-1995 and diffuse at a rate comparable to that of previous technologies and in particular the most recent entrant the 32-bit microprocessor.

Projections of S-curves are rather reliable, the more so when the ceiling does not need to be determined, as is the case with market shares. My projections in Figure 4.4.3 played a key role during subsequent negotia-

MARKET SHARES OF MICROPROCESSOR UNIT SHIPMENTS BY WORD WIDTH

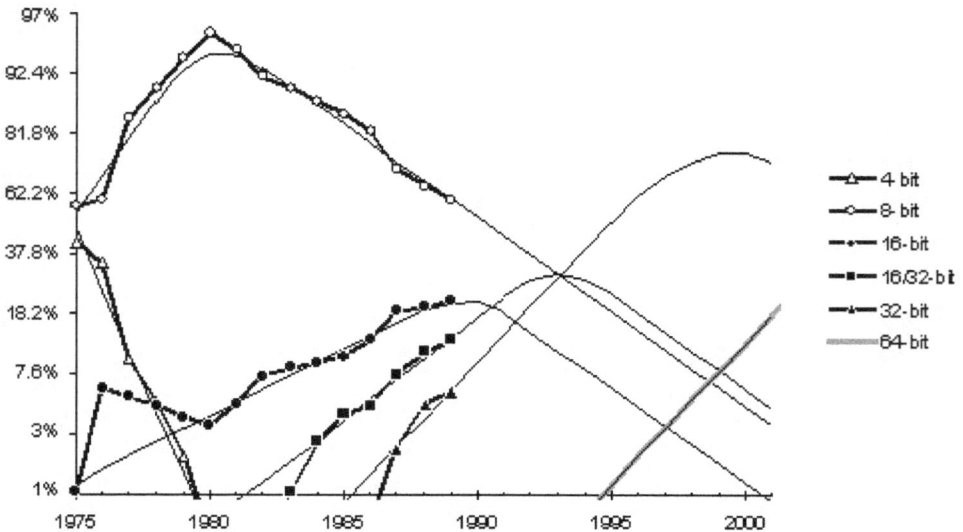

Figure 4.4.3 The smooth thin lines are model descriptions. The thick gray line is a scenario for the new 64-bit technology; its slope was chosen to be the same as for the 32-bit case.[14]

ions between DEC and Siemens. I even went as far as to supply forecast for unit shipments by folding the market-share projections from Figure 4.4.3 and the projection of an S-curve fitted on the sum total numbers of shipments in the data I used.

IN CLOSING

It is a hard fact of life that young will replace old. In all three processes, diffusion, substitution, and competitive growth, the entities under consideration obey the same law.

In their paper Fisher and Pry looked at the rate of substitution for a variety of applications and found that the speed at which a substitution takes place is not simply related to the improvements in technology or manufacturing or marketing or distribution or any other single factor. It is rather a measure of how much the new is better than the old in all these factors. When a substitution begins, the new product, process, or service struggles hard to improve and demonstrate its advantages over the old one. As the newcomer finds recognition by achieving a small percentage of the market, the threatened element redoubles its efforts to maintain or improve its position. Thus, the pace of innovation may increase significantly during the course of a substitution struggle. The curvature of the bends and the steepness of the S-curve traced out by the ratio of total-market shares, however—the slope of the straight line in the logarithmic graph—does not change throughout the substitution. The rate reflected in this slope seems to be determined by the combination of economic forces stemming from the superiority of the newcomer.

Fisher and Pry suggested that this model could prove useful to investigations in the many aspects of technological change and innovation in our society. In fact, its use has spread far beyond that application. I do not know if they realized back in 1970 the diversity of the areas of inquiry into which their model would diffuse during the decades that followed, but I agree with Marchetti when he says that they provided us with a tool for "Fishing and Prying" into the mechanisms of social living.

5 – CASCADES OF S-CURVES

Marketers have long used bell-shaped curves to describe the life cycles of their products. After all, product sales do grow in a competitive environment and the best-fit product normally wins. But marketers have a harder time accepting the fact that natural growth is capped and that their company will not continue growing exponentially, not even linearly. The only way growth can be sustained in a competitive environment is via a succession of S-shaped logistic steps as one market niche is filled after the other. Even then, the overall envelope will follow a logistic pattern on a larger scale.[1]

5.1 – JUST-IN-TIME REPLACEMENT

A well-known marketers' utopian pursuit is the strategy of product replacement timed so as to avoid any slowdown in the growth of their sales revenue. Evidently, launching products too closely together (the case may be argued for new Microsoft Windows operating systems) may frustrate customers and/or lead to "cannibalization" of their own market when the new product robs sales from the old one. On the other hand, delaying the launching of a replacement product may create a vacuum in a vendor's offerings and result in loss of customers to the competition. So the question becomes when is the optimum time to launch a replacement? The question can be generalized to: when is the right time to introduce change in an ongoing natural-growth process? No one wants to tamper with something that works well, but how old should become a product before its replacement is launched?

The criterion can be found in harmonic motion and not only because the concept of harmony implies goodness. Regularly spaced product life cycles produce a landscape pattern suggestive of a sine wave, and large-scale growth processes, such as the world energy consumption discussed in Section 3.3, have deviated from a natural trend so as to also produce a sinusoidal wave (Kondratieff's cycle).[2] The sinusoidal pattern is characteristic of the pendulum's harmonic motion.

The cascade of two identical logistics was studied as a function of the distance in time between them for different time constants. The logistics, representing cumulative sales, were cascaded in a mutually exclusive way, that is, the first logistic stopped when the second took over. This was essential in order to maintain an approximately constant market in terms of average sales per unit of time. Otherwise, we would not be addressing the replacement of products but the expansion of markets via rapid product launching, which is a different and rather debatable subject.[3]

In Figure 5.1.1, a straight line connects the centers of the two logistics and thus serves as a general trend. The difference between the envelope of the cumulative sales and the straight line was extracted and fitted by a sinusoidal wave. The fit involved four parameters: the time delay between the two logistics, and the amplitude, frequency and phase of the sine wave. The fitting process minimized the sum of differences squared, akin to a Chi Square. The fit was excellent and also stable against a factor-of-ten change in the time constant of the logistic used.

The overlap of the cascading logistics is rather small: 2.6%, 10.3%, and 32.7% of the replacement logistic coincide with 89.7%, 97.4, and 99.4 respectively of the incumbent logistic, see Figure 5.1.2.

A Harmonic Cascade of S-Curves

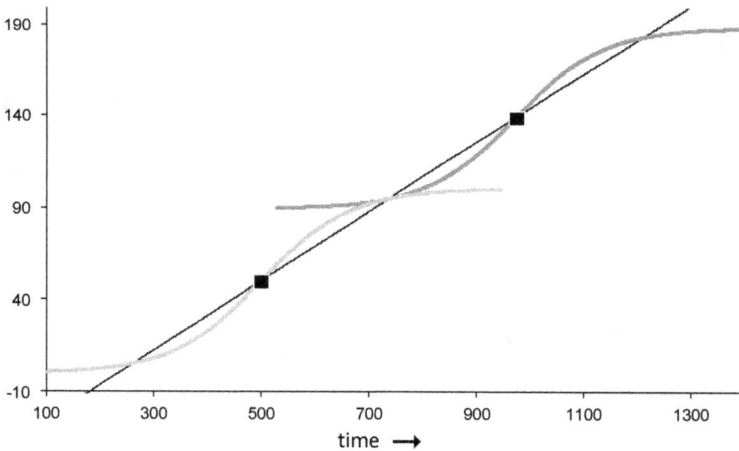

Figure 5.1.1 The same logistic pattern repeats (dark gray line) from where the previous one (light gray line) leaves off. The straight line connects the center points of the two logistics. The axes have arbitrary units.

THE OVERLAP BETWEEN THE TWO LOGISTICS OF FIGURE 5.1

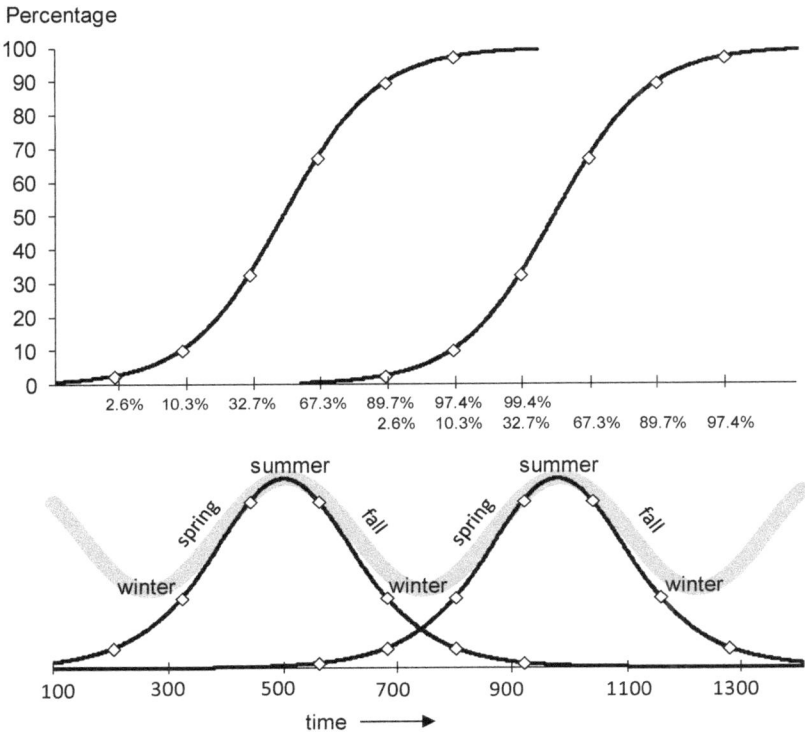

Figure 5.1.2 The two logistics of Figure 5.1.1 and their corresponding life cycles. The horizontal axis at the middle shows percentage penetration levels for each logistic. The horizontal axis at the bottom shows the same arbitrary time units as in Figure 5.1.1. The little diamonds delimit the business seasons.[4]

This recipe spells out in a quantitative way how to harmonically cascaded natural-growth processes. It can be used to time the launching of new products using only the sales information at hand. In order for the new product to achieve 2.6% penetration of its market when the old product reaches 89.7% penetration of its market, the launching of the new product—corresponding to the nominal beginning of the new logistic, namely its 1% level—must occur halfway down the phasing-out period of the incumbent product. This point in time falls between the two little diamonds on the declining side of the life cycle in Figure 5.1.2, the season of "fall" as defined in Chapter 3. Like farmers sowing in the fall the seeds for the next crop, product managers must sow the seed of their new product during the fall season of the incumbent product.

What we want to retain here is that if natural-growth processes are cascaded in a *harmonic* way, then there will be a periodic and regular swing between good and bad business seasons. This swing is not simply natural and inevitable. It is also desirable because it will play a significant role in triggering new growth, just as pruning the roses ensures healthier blossoms for the next season. The lesson for business executives facing a major transition between products, technologies, or other fundamental change is not to strive for minimizing its impact but to plan for and anticipate a low-growth period comparable in duration to the high-growth period they just enjoyed.

Proverbial wisdom has long claimed that there is goodness in every season. Some people may think that the most desirable climate is found on tropical islands like Mauritius and Seychelles. Not true! Our above argument based on harmony dictates a large and regular seasonal variation like that encountered in temperate climate, which has also been the cradle of most great civilizations. History is poor in significant cultures that emerged from the arctic or from the tropics, the former perhaps because of conditions hostile to life and the latter mostly because of lack of variation and motivation. Despite an idyllic setting, tropical islands are rather sterile. The expulsion of Adam and Eve from Paradise may have been, after all, an original blessing.

5.2 – FRACTALS OF S-CURVES

The big picture is not just the cascading from one S-shaped step to the next. It is a cascade of cascades, an endless stream of S-curves alternating with periods of chaos, as described earlier. Would the corresponding life cycles—the rate of growth—be a regular oscillation? Does the Kondratieff's cycle mentioned in Section 3.3 tick like a regular clock over the centuries, repeating its peaks and troughs at exact intervals? Are the random fluctuations of a few percent in magnitude observed during the last two hundred years the only deviations possible? If that is the case, how does one explain the shortening of life cycles (of products, technologies, etc.), and the paradigm shift, progressively crowding humanity's significant transitions in recent history?[5]

A group of people linked together with a common goal, interest, ability or affiliation—for example, a company or an organization—will have its own S-shaped evolution. The individuals now play the role of the cells in a multi-cellular organism, and their assembly becomes the organism. The population in its entirety—that is, the organization itself— can be seen as an individual. The same thing is true for products. A group of products, each with its own life cycle, can be described by a similar but larger curve representing the family or the technology life cycle. If we zoom back further, we may find that many technologies come and go, succeeding each other the way products do. Thus we find a fractal aspect in the S-shaped natural growth pattern.[6] That is, zooming in or out, we obtain the same S-shaped pattern, and the only difference is the timeframe (see Fig. 5.2.1).

S-curves are nested like Russian dolls. Consequently, there are many product seasons in one company season, many company seasons in one industry season, and many industry seasons in one global economy season. In all cases, the main characteristics of the social phenomena and human behavior associated with a given season are similar. But there are non-obvious connections across the different levels of S-curves. For the sake of the discussion, let us consider four levels of nested S-curves. Each level goes through natural growth steps with a life cycle of the same pattern but of different time duration. A typical situation might be as follows:

THE FRACTAL NATURE OF NATURAL GROWTH

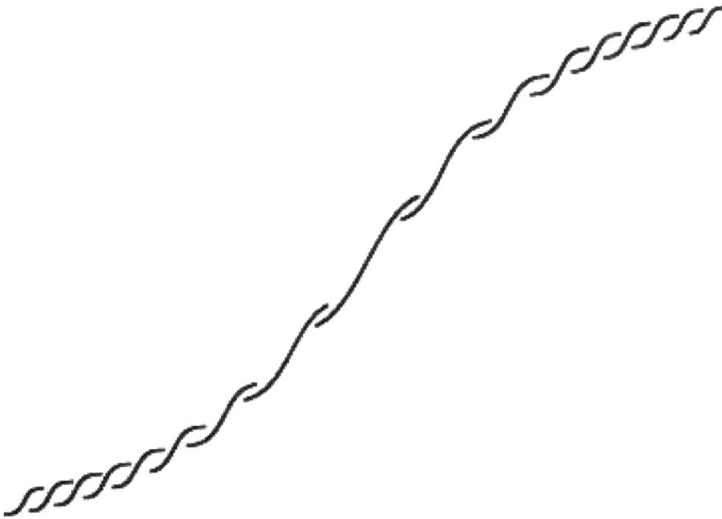

Figure 5.2.1 An overall S-shaped pattern decomposed into constituent S-shaped curves according to a rigorous procedure. The horizontal axis represents time.

Products, consist of units sold and may have a life cycle of 6 quarters.

Product families or *companies*, consist of a set of related products and may have a typical business cycle of 5 years— in the case of a product family, 5 years may be the duration of its life cycle.

Basic technologies or *industries*, consist of a set of related product families or companies and can have typical cycles of 15 years.

The economy, is the sum of all industries and has a cycle of 56 years (Kondratieff cycle).

S-curves at different levels are linked. For example, the high output of a summer season feeds the S-curves of one level below. That is why product replacement is least painful when the product family is in summer, just as the replacement of product families is least painful when the technology curve is in summer. Another link between S-curves of different levels occurs with innovation, which normally belongs in winter. Innovation in spring concerns the S-curves of one level below. For example, the spring of an industry brings product innovation. The spring of the economy brings industry innovation.

The graph in Fig. 5.2.1 has been constructed in a rigorous and quantitative way. The overall curve is given a certain thickness within which the constituent S-curves must be contained. Redundant solutions are eliminated by requiring all constituent curves to belong to the same class. That is, they must all have the same slope at their midpoint, so that the maximum rate of growth is the same for all sub-processes. Such a rule has a defensible interpretation in product sales, because it reflects the stability of consumer spending. People's average income (gross national product) does not change rapidly with time; therefore the buying power of individuals of a certain income class also remains roughly stable over a period of time. As products come and go, rapidly substituting each other, the maximum rate of product sales does not change appreciably on the average, and the larger the product niche, the longer its life cycle. As a consequence, life cycles become longer during the high-growth period and shorter during the low-growth period, as depicted in Fig. 5.2.2.

The large-scale S-curve that becomes visible when we zoom backward serves as an envelop for the succession of the smaller constituent curves. Its level defines the ceiling up to which constituents will grow and its steepness determines the length of their life cycle. The phenomenon of shrinking life cycles, an important concern of today's manufacturers, can be quantitatively linked to the saturation of the enveloping process (see Table 5.2.1). For a family of products, shrinking life cycles reflect how close to exhaustion a technology may be. On a larger scale, shrinking life cycles of families of products (for example, mainframe computers) reflect changing social patterns (such as a trend toward demand for more portable and personalized products). On an even larger scale, a large number of families of products—technologies, markets, and so on—with shrinking life cycles may reflect a global economic recession.

Because the decomposition of the envelope S-curve to the constituent product S-curves has been done quantitatively, we can relate the shortening of product life cycles to the overall level of saturation—how close it is to exhaustion—of the envelope. We can then monitor the drift of the width of life cycles over time in order to determine either how close we are to full saturation (life cycles getting shorter) or how far we are from a future maximal rate of growth (life cycles getting longer).

In practice, due to technical or other reasons, such as pent-up demand, we often find that the first few short-lived S-curves in a long chain are either understated or missing.

THE SHORTENING OF LIFE CYCLES

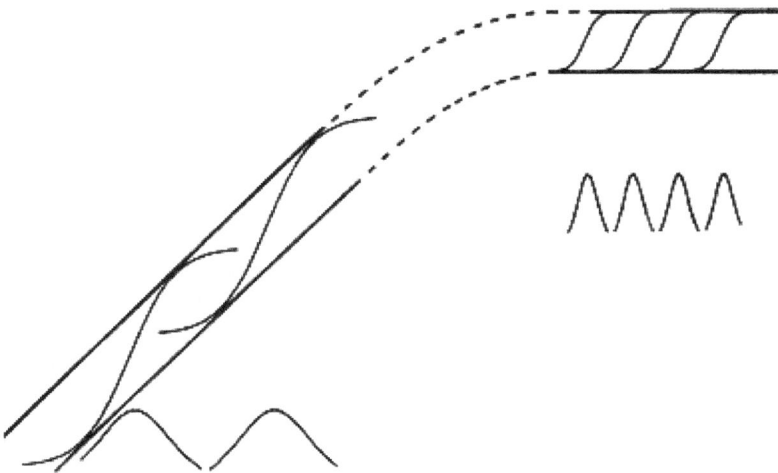

Figure 5.2.2 A geometric explanation of why the end of growth implies shorter life cycles.

Table 5.2.1 The relation between the shortening of life cycles and saturation

Life-cycle length (relative to longest)	Level of saturation (percent of ceiling)
0.17	3.1
0.19	4.0
0.20	5.2
0.22	6.9
0.24	9.1
0.30	12.8
0.41	20.0
0.70	31.4
1.00	50.0
0.70	68.6
0.41	80.0
0.30	87.2
0.24	90.9
0.22	93.1
0.20	94.8
0.19	96.0
0.17	96.9

Being able to estimate the level of overall saturation from observing life-cycle trends is a powerful approach. It implies that a non-specialist, such as a dock worker loading boxes onto trucks, may notice that the labels on the boxes change three times as frequently as they used to back in the good old days, and boast to his fellow workers that he knows that the technology behind these products is more than 87% exhausted. He may go further and argue that if things have been done right, the next-technology products should be showing up at the dock with the coming shipment.

This image may sound naive, but the approach offers valuable insights for tracking the overall life cycle of products, families of technologies, and social trends. Examining the evolution of the sub-processes can give us information about the remaining growth potential of the outer envelope. In other words, the shortening of product life cycles tells about the remaining growth potential of the product family. The shortening of product-family life cycles tells about the remaining growth potential of the company. The life cycles of companies tell about the remaining growth potential of the industry, and the life cycles of the industries about the whole economy.

An example of nested S-curves can be found in the aviation industry. Wide-body aircraft constitute a family with about a dozen members, each having its own life cycle. Early members, such as the DC10 and Lockheed Tristar, were shorter-lived than the Boeing 747. However, the later rapid appearance of the 767s, a number of Airbuses, MD11s, and 777s implied that these aircraft would have shorter life cycles than the 747s. As in the pattern of Fig. 5.2.1, the wide-body family of aircraft underwent successively the stages of: two short life cycles, one long, and again a number of short ones. We can thus conclude that the overall S-curve, describing the growth process of the wide-body family, is approaching a ceiling, with the 747 as the central long-lived product. In the future, we should expect little—if any—growth in the annual passenger-mile totals of wide-body aircraft. In fact, the average size of airliners on transatlantic flights has already shown signs of decline during the mid-1990s. In that light, the Airbus superjumbo (A380) will not have its own market. This aircraft must steal market share from the wide bodies in use. Even then their sales would probably never reach the volume of 1400 units that Airbus managers had originally anticipated.

We can zoom back and look at all of jet aviation as one family with two members. The first one—early jets—underwent a 15-year growth process. The second one—wide bodies—underwent a 30-year growth process. The picture suggests that there should be a new upcoming type of aircraft—possibly supersonic—with relatively high carrying capacity but narrower fuselage (single corridors) than today's wide bodies. The Concord could be this family's precursor. Because the life cycles of jet aircraft families have so far been increasing, we conclude that the overall diffusion in jet aviation has not yet passed the midpoint of its S-curve. An independent estimate positions the midpoint of this diffusion process in early 21st century.[7] One can thus safely surmise that this new family of supersonic aircraft will grow for longer than thirty years and will constitute the central long-lived family in jet aviation.

5.3 – CASE STUDIES

The MicroVAX Family of DEC Minicomputers

Digital Equipment Corporation (DEC) became successful thanks to the minicomputer, a market niche created and filled by DEC. The first technology of minicomputers, called PDP, was launched in 1959. In 1978

DEC launched a second architecture of minicomputers, called VAX, based on a 32-bit microprocessor. They replaced half the PDP sales by the mid 1980s. By 1990 DEC launched yet another architecture of computers, called Alpha, based on a 64-bit microprocessor. They replaced half the VAX sales by the mid 1990s. Each architecture had many product families, and each family many products.

As a strategy consultant at DEC, I was asked to study one family of products in detail, the MicroVAXes.[8] They occupied the $20,000 to $50,000 price range. I produced S-curve fits for each one of the computer models in this family and was able to deduce a life cycle for each. The family's first entrant was MicroVAX I. It had a short life cycle, and it was generally considered an unsuccessful product—unfairly so. It should have been seen as a precursor (see discussion in Section 3.1), an exploratory attempt that paved the way for the products that followed. MicroVAX II had the longest life cycle—three times as long as its predecessor. The life-cycle duration was already decreasing with the follow-up product, M2000, which lasted for a little more than half as long as MicroVAX II. Later models appeared in rapid succession and featured life cycles more than four times shorter than that of MicroVAX II, see Figure 5.3.1. According to Table 5.2.1, this product family should have been around 90% exhausted at the time of my study.

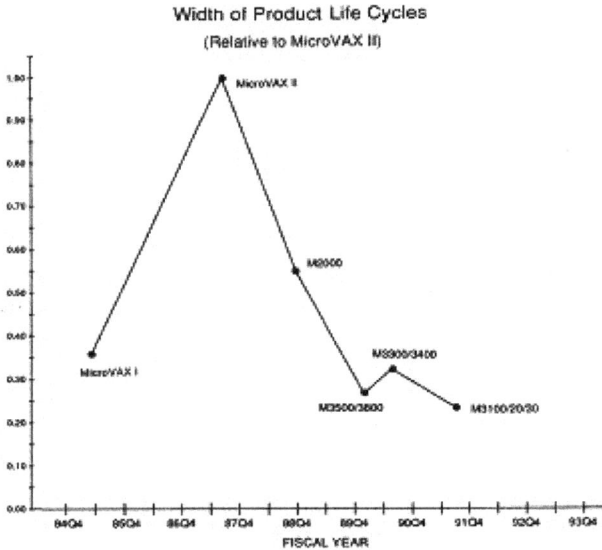

Figure 5.3.1 The rise and fall of product life cycles in the MicroVAX family of Digital Equipment computers.

I was able to obtain confirmation of this conclusion by analyzing the growth of MicroVAX as a single process. Despite a limited resolution (only a small number of models), the evolution of MicroVAX corroborated the fractal aspect of logistic growth.

Because of the trend toward smaller computers, the importance of MicroVAX over time was best represented by its market share in the micro-niche considered. The share rose and declined over the lifetime of this product line. Cumulated market share was fitted to a logistic curve in Figure 5.3.2.

In order to focus on the rate of penetration of the MicroVAX technology, the vertical scale was normalized to 100% when the process accumulating market share reached a ceiling. We can thus read saturation levels directly as a function of time. The starting point is 19% reflecting

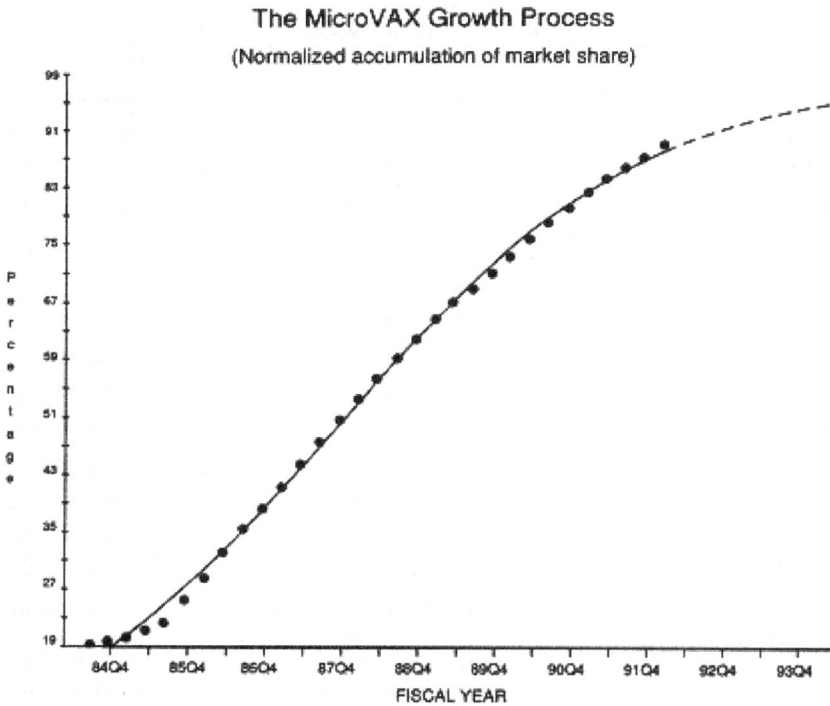

The MicroVAX Growth Process

(Normalized accumulation of market share)

Figure 5.3.2 The MicroVAX story as reflected by the technology's ability to fill its own market niche. The data points represent the accumulation of market share. The line is a logistic fit up to the second quarter of fiscal year 1992. The process is normalized to 100% at the ceiling of the fitted line. A jump from 0 to 19% at the beginning corroborates the notion of a sudden release of pent-up demand due to a delayed appearance.

the release of a certain pent-up demand (a 4th parameter —pedestal—was used in the S-curve fit as described in Chapter 2). At the time of my analysis the curve's penetration level was 87% in good agreement with our previous conclusion based on the shortening of the life cycles of this family's component products. It came as no surprise that soon afterward, this price range of computers was taken over by workstations and servers.

Following this study, I ventured further on my own knowing that the VAX architecture had many product families like MicroVAX. Zooming back, I was able to see the PDP, VAX, and Alpha technologies all behaving like single products inside DEC's overall company curve. In fact, the life cycles of these architectures were getting shorter. With the life cycle of PDPs taken as unity, the life cycle of VAXes turned out to be equal to 0.65, which, according to Table 5.2.1, corresponded to 70% completion of the company curve. It also implied that the Alpha architecture would have a life cycle equal to less than 0.4, and therefore should be 50% replaced, by something else, around the year 2002, by which time DEC as a company should be at around the 85-percent completion level of its overall curve.

In fact, DEC never got that far. In June 1998 it was acquired by Compaq, which subsequently merged with Hewlett-Packard in May 2002. Once again, the death of a species came not far from 90-percent completion of its curve.

Microsoft Windows Operating Systems

The state of maturity of the Windows operating systems as a family became the object of my study when I was asked to review claims for runway trends in the Information Technology industry.[9] Microsoft has been regularly releasing new operating systems. New software developments triggered by hardware improvements make it necessary to introduce major changes to the operating systems. This is a typical characteristic of "young" industries such as microchip production; they are mutational. But as the industry matures, "mutations" become rare and life cycles become longer. Figure 5.3.3 shows the evolution of the life cycle of Microsoft operating system as defined by the time between release announcements.

Windows XP was the operating system with the longest life cycle. Vista's life cycle was 57% of that of Windows XP and the life cycle of Windows 7 was 53% when Windows 8 came in 2012. With Windows XP at the center of the envelope S-curve for Windows operating systems and

TIME BETWEEN OPERATING SYSTEMS

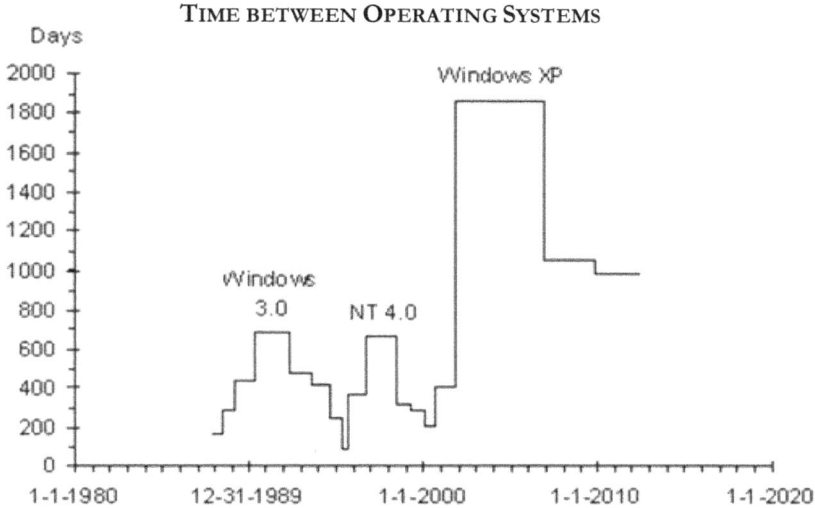

Figure 5.3.3 The duration of Microsoft Windows operating systems as defined by the time between new releases.

the life cycle being symmetric to a fist approximation, we can reasonably expect an end for this growth process by the late 2020s. Appropriately this coincides with an estimate for the end of Moore's law.[10]

Here we were able to make forecasts for the end of Microsoft's Windows operating systems from observations on the shortening of life cycles. Such forecasts would have been difficult to do—if not impossible—and certainly less defensible using other methods.

The Stages of Human Growth

There was an error in my first book *Predictions*. I had written that a newborn's size is around two feet six inches whereas in reality it is closer to twenty inches. The source of my error was that I had backcasted an S-curve fitted on my daughter's height measurements in elementary school and did not bother to go back and check with the original records. Needless to say that it became a source of embarrassment for me when a reader (working in a statistics office) wrote a tongue-in-cheek letter to the publisher wondering whether we were all bachelors!

On my part I ran to the medical library and obtained full sets of data on the evolution of the human size from conception to old age. It became immediately obvious that one S-curve could not describe the entire process. I tried to describe the complete dataset with as few S-curves as possible. I was able to discern three different processes, see Figure 5.3.4.

The first S-curve covers the period of gestation and extends to sometime beyond the age of one. The second S-curve covers from two to twelve years of age. The excess between ages thirteen and nineteen was amenable to a third logistic fit. The goodness of the fits deteriorated rapidly with changes in the definition of the datasets.

All three S-curves are partial, so in all three fits the fourth parameter (pedestal) was also determined. For the middle curve, corresponding to childhood, we see only half of an S-curve, but it contributes the largest-size chunk to one's height and covers more than 90% of one's total-growth period. Second in importance is the fetus/baby growth process with a comparable contribution to the final height but a much shorter time constant. Adolescence is a higher-order effect (less pronounced for girls) that begins at age thirteen and contributes less than 10% of the total

THE STAGES OF HUMAN GROWTH

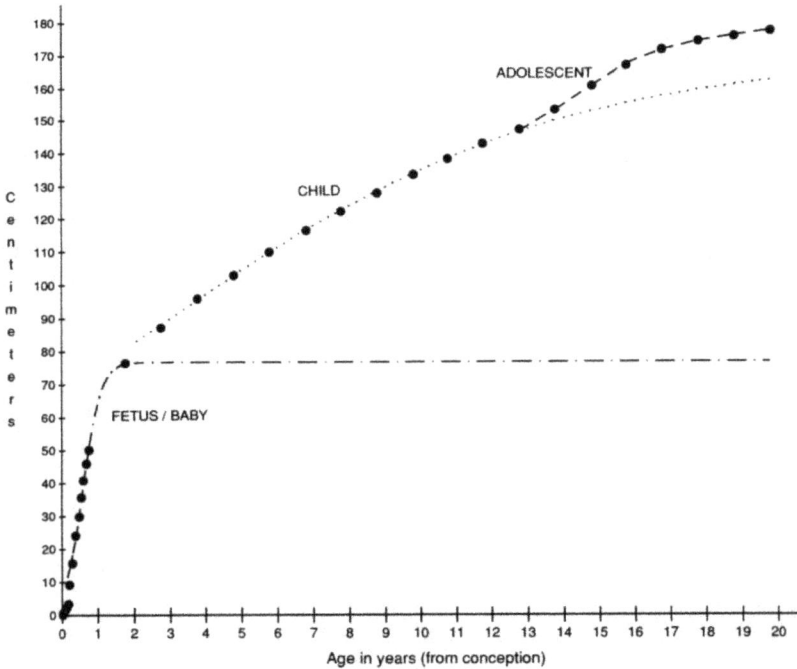

Figure 5.3.4 Data and three S-curve fits for phases of growth in size of a human male.[11]

height. A more in-depth study may discern finer logistic-growth processes around the egg and the embryo states. Finally, there is a relatively minor downward pointing S-curve describing the shrinking of one's height with old age, not shown in the figure.

My study of the human-size growth did not only serve to appease my publishers and reply to the vocal critic of my book. It also produced a number of insights. Evidently everyday terms such as fetus, baby, child, and adolescent have precise definitions reflecting growth processes that are distinct. Also the fact that fetus and baby belong to the same growth curve must be related to the fact that the distinction between these two states is largely "geographical", meaning inside or outside the womb. After all, the transition between them takes place abruptly, the ratio of gestation to babyhood from case to case could vary up to factors of 3, and the exact time of transition is most often arbitrary (induced labor/caesareans).

IN CLOSING

Sustained growth consists of successive S-shaped steps, each of which represents a well-defined amount of growth. A new S-curve begins where the previous one left off. Every step is associated with a niche that opened following some fundamental change (a mutation, a major innovation, a technological break-through, etc.). But all transitions display the characteristics of winter seasons.

When 10.3% of the replacement process overlaps with 97.4% of the incumbent we have a harmonic cascade of natural-growth processes. The everyday words **harmonic** and **natural** here have rigorous science-based definitions. The former concerns motion under a restoring force that is proportional to the displacement (harmonic motion) and the latter concerns a rate of growth that is proportional to the amount of growth already achieved but also to the amount of growth remaining to be achieved (logistic growth).

Between successive growth phases there is a lull in the overall rate of growth, a winter season that is both unavoidable and beneficial. Just-in-time replacement of products does not maintain constant or increasing sales. It ensures that a dip in overall sales will be of *natural* duration and size. Its duration should be comparable to the duration of the rapid-growth phase experienced while the last S-curve was steeply rising. The swing between high-growth and low-growth seasons stimulates the organism's vitality, and the timely anticipation of the winter season allows for the appropriate strategic planning that will contribute to the organism's longevity.

An old mathematical pastime has been describing any function as a sum of terms belonging to a class of functions, for example the Fourier analysis that decomposes functions into sines and cosines. In this tradition one may want to decompose any overall growth process into S-curve sections instead of sines and cosines and for a given process we may find that one S-curve component plays a major role, even if the overall pattern shows significant deviations from a large-scale S-curve. In an analogy with Fourier analysis we would say that this is the fundamental harmonic and that higher harmonics are expected to play less important roles. For the case of human-size growth discussed earlier the "fundamental harmonic" would be childhood.

6 – EVENT ENHANCEMENT

In Chapter 4 we argued that the winter business season ensuing from a substitution be it among products, technologies, or markets, cannot and should not be avoided. Marketer's only compensatory action is the classical product portfolio approach of the Boston Consulting Group, which advocates holding at all times a variety of products, not all of which would be in the precarious transitional phase simultaneously.

The Boston Consulting Group, founded in 1963 by Bruce Henderson, has become known for its growth-share matrix, a diagram of the normal relationship between cash use and cash generation. The concept behind the BCG matrix is something Henderson first came across with the US defense industry and later applied to electronics. Namely, that the more airplanes that were built, the less time each unit took, and therefore the cheaper they became to produce. This is a formulation of the economies of scale—the industry curve—discussed in detail in Section 2.7. The Boston Consulting Group derived a portfolio management picture positioning products in four quadrants according to two variables, market growth and market share.[1] They labeled the quadrants as follows:

- *Stars* occupied the high-growth high-share quadrant.
- *Cash cows* occupied the low-growth high-share quadrant.
- *Dogs* occupied the low-growth low-share quadrant.
- *Question marks* occupied the high-growth low-share quadrant.

Looking at the description of each quadrant and what usually happens to products, we realize that the BCG matrix supplies a well-defined direction for the evolution of things. Stars become cash cows, which become dogs, and when they become bigger dogs they effectively are question marks, some of which may become stars. This cyclical movement is driven by changes in growth and market share.

The labeling of each quadrant of the BCG matrix reflects the combination of market growth and product growth. For example, cash cows, despite their high rate of sales, are associated with a low-growth period of the market.

The celebrated BCG matrix of the Boston Consulting Group was among the first decision-making tools to divide the life cycle and product portfolio management into four phases. The BCG matrix has been generalized here to handle services, technologies, markets, and anything that grows in competition. Moreover, the approach has now become prescriptive, that is, once strengths and weaknesses have been identified, it estimates the growth potential of each one of them as well as the most appropriate strategy. This matrix is more general and self-contained. It handles the evolution over time of any business entity that grows in competition: products, services, technologies, markets, organizations, Strategic Business Units (SBUs), departments, functions, processes, and the like. The variables are somewhat different. Instead of market share, we look at the actual degree of satisfaction, and instead of market growth, we consider the amount of future interest expected. But the most important difference is that our definition of the four segments—the seasons— refers only to the entity's rate of growth across its life cycle.

In our matrix (see Figure 6.1), *opportunities*—spring—refer to entities in a phase of early growth; they correspond to *question marks*. *Strengths*— summer—refer to entities in a high-growth period; they correspond to *stars*. *Aging*—fall—refers to whatever undergoes declining growth and corresponds to *cash cows*. *In transition*—winter—refers to entities with very low growth; they correspond to *dogs*. The advantage of defining things this way is that now we can use the decision-support machinery of the seasons discussed earlier.

One interactive software tool developed at Growth Dynamics is a quick-feedback questionnaire that produces results online. The technique has been used with such firms as Baxter International (health and medical products), and HLB International (accounting firms) as well as in a number of business conferences. Figure 6.1 shows an example of results obtained during the Eighth Annual pricing conference in Chicago in April 1995.

One of our findings was that pricing managers treat pricing not only as an art but also as a science. This dual view indicates that there is no perceived clear-cut advantage of an instinctive versus an analytical approach to pricing, something we will examine in more depth in Chapter 9. Still, pricing as an art came out more important for the future but less under control at present.

Other highlights based on the perception of pricing managers at the April 1995 Chicago conference follow:

- Price wars were found in a winter season as if they were doubtful tactics (*dogs* in the classical BCG matrix).
- Similarly—but to a lesser extent—the use of software tools for setting prices was also found in a winter.
- Pricing according to value was found in a summer (a *strength*).

THE BCG MATRIX AS MODIFIED BY GROWTH DYNAMICS

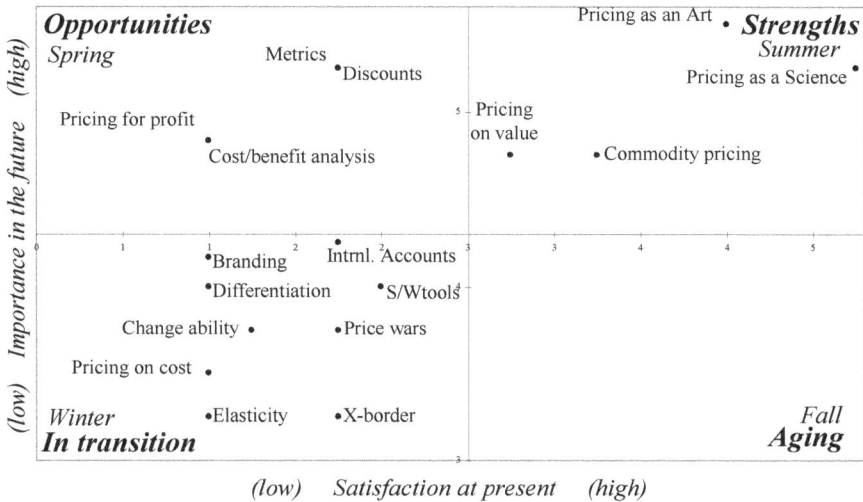

Figure 6.1   The data represent the answers given by the pricing managers participating at the Eighth Annual Pricing Conference in Chicago in April 1995.

One should expect such results to change with time, however. It is not excluded that price wars and software pricing tools become opportunities some time in the future.

We estimated the length of the business season for a few of the entries in our matrix. The audience's pricing practices were found to be in good agreement with the seasonal interpretation of correct business decisions. If we consider the US economy in early 1995 as being in a spring, pricing for value should be the predominant practice, whereas pricing for profit would be considered more appropriate for the next season. Accordingly, Figure 6.1 shows pricing for profit in the spring quadrant, since most managers considered it to be an opportunity for the future.

The original BCG matrix has been criticized as too simplistic. Its author, Bruce Henderson, explained that the BCG matrix was never meant to be prescriptive but was intended only as an innovative way to describe a business. In the modified version discussed above, the Growth Dynamics graphs can become prescriptive strategy-planning tools. By positioning many processes (or products) in their business season, one can develop guidelines about what to do according to the seasonal recommendations given earlier. Furthermore, the analysis can be enhanced in two ways. First, we can now determine more accurately—quantitatively—a product's position in the season and the season's length. Second, we can determine the remaining growth potential for each one of the entries in the matrix. These capabilities can be combined to enhance any event with a sizeable participation of people specializing or interested in a specific topic.

At Growth Dynamics we have put together and offering called *Event Enhancement* designed to enrich any conference, symposium, forum, or large meeting. It adds value and excitement by getting the participants involved and by tapping collective conscious and subconscious knowledge in an intelligent way.

A custom-made questionnaire based on the event's theme is distributed to all participants upon arrival. A half-an-hour introductory presentation is made to the full assembly the first day. The questionnaires are collected the same day and the data are entered into the computer and analyzed overnight. The results are presented the next day (15 min.) An interactive working session follows the results presentation. The session is tailored to the audience's interests (15 to 30 min.).

Besides a survey-type of analysis there is a modified-BCG type of analysis. When the results are presented use is made of the software package *Where Are You on the Curve and What to Do about It* to further explore the hottest issues in an on-line interactive work session where everyone contributes toward a comprehensive understanding of the most probable evolution of these issues over time.

The Event-Enhancement package adds spice and excitement to an event independently of the event's theme. At the same time valuable conclusions are extracted by tapping the collective knowledge of informed professionals in a sophisticated way. Finally, every participant becomes actively involved and feels ownership of a successful event even if he or she did not make a presentation (usually the majority of the attendees).

6.1 – CASE STUDIES

HLB International

HLB International is a worldwide organization of professional accounting firms and business advisers, each providing clients with a comprehensive and personal service relating to auditing, taxation, accounting and general financial and management advice. HLB members are well-established firms, capable of handling international assignments in all the main business centers and experienced in coordinating activities between countries. Formed in 1969, HLBI ranks in the top 12 international accounting networks, servicing clients through its member firms in over 100 countries.

In July 1994 HLB International celebrated its silver jubilee during a weeklong conference in Amsterdam attended by over 50 delegates. The event organizers wanted to enrich their program with visions of the future and invited me for a keynote speech on the theme: "The S-Shaped Adventure – A Piercing Look into the Future". I took the opportunity to suggest an event enhancement using the offering by the same name from Growth Dynamics.

The questionnaire shown in Figure 6.1.1 was put together following discussion with accountants to distill the one dozen or so of their most important issues (for example, the continuous recession and the use of Information technology). The one-page questionnaire was given to the participants upon their arrival and they were asked to return it by the next morning. I entered the data overnight on a prepared EXCEL workbook and the third day, after my keynote address, I presented them the results. My half-day session ended with a discussion and computer-aided brainstorming on the evolution of key concerns.

Figure 6.1.2 shows some survey-type results obtained from Part 7 of the questionnaire. They indicate that accountants were mostly worried about being informed, having qualified staff, and liabilities in that order. More interesting was the modified-BCG type of analysis some of which is shown in Figure 6.1.3. Here we see that their strength was in audits, tax/legal advice, and accounting consulting despite the fact that they many of them expressed interest in management consulting, perhaps because at that time the paradigm of Arthur Andersen emerging out of Andersen Accounting as one of the Big Six was still fresh in everyone's memory. Appropriately management consulting featured in the "Opportunities" quadrant of their matrix.

The discussion became animated when we tried to interactively estimate growth potentials for some of these activities. In order to find where on the curve they were we used the software package *Where Are You on the Curve and What to Do about It* described later in Chapter 9. But the first attempt was with the simple questionnaire that was presented earlier in Section 3.5.

Estimating growth potential was the added value of my intervention. The participants were experienced accountants each knowledgeable in specific areas. In fact, as it happens with most people, behind their judgment there was hidden knowledge even if they were not aware of it. Tapping this knowledge by probing their instinctive/emotional reaction contributed to improving the accuracy of growth-potential estimates.

PLEASE HAND THIS QUESTIONNAIRE COMPLETED TO REGISTRATION DESK NO LATER THAN WEDNESDAY MORNING !!!

Unless otherwise specified, please rate from 1 - 10; 10 = highest, 1 = lowest)

1. What % of your revenues comes from outside your country [%]

2. To what extent do you see alliances as a way to:

    2a. improve cross-border operations [ ]

    2b. complement your expertise [ ]

3. List the percentage of turn-over of your firm for each of these services?

4. How important are these services to you for the next 5 years?

5. Who do you think is the market leader in this field ? (independently of your own pursuits) use initials where obvious

6. How well do you satisfy your customers needs compared to the market leader in each service area ?

Columns (rated across questions 3–6):

	Audit	Tax, Financial & Legal Advice	Consulting on Accounting	IT Consulting	Management Consulting (no IT)	Recruiting Consulting	Knowledge Transfer (e.g. training, seminars, events, client publications)	Other: (please specify)
3.	%	%	%	%	%	%	%	%
4.								
5.								
6.								

7. Which of the following external pressures are of most concern to you ?

    [ ] continuing recession

    [ ] reputation of accounting profession

    [ ] separation of audit / non-audit

    [ ] being able to recruit suitably qualified staff

    [ ] audit liability and associated costs

    [ ] continued deregulation of "reserved areas" (e.g. audig, insolvency, investment advice, etc.)

    [ ] client defection to the Big 6

    [ ] capital shortages within partnership structure (external funding capability)

    [ ] use of IT to improve operations

    [ ] keeping abreast with latest information (e.g. changes to legislation)

    [ ] disclosure of full financial statement

8. What are your greatest strengths against the Big 6 ?

9. If you had to enter a forced marriage, which of the Big 6 would you choose as your partner ? _____ *optional*

10. Which, if any, of hte Big 6 is most likely to go under in the next five years and why ? (state most likely first) _____ *optional*

Company: _____ Name: _____ Title: _____ Country: _____

Figure 6.1.1   The questionnaire used with the HLB International event-enhancement application.

EXTERNAL PRESSURES

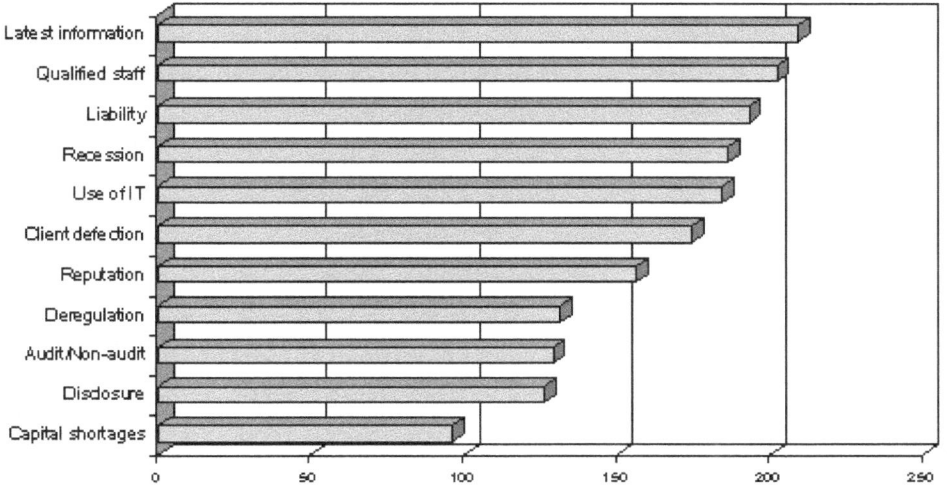

Figure 6.1.2 A typical survey-type result based on the questions (Item 7) in Figure 6.1.1.

EVOLUTION OF MAIN CONCERNS

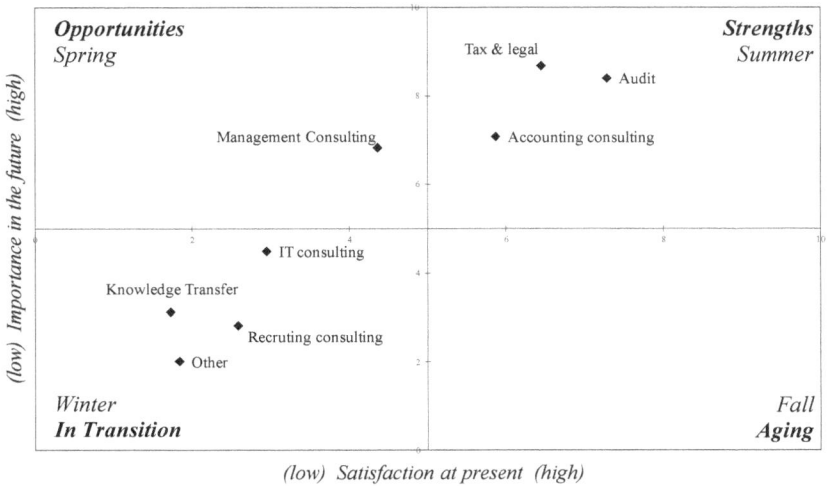

Figure 6.1.3 The modified-BCG type of analysis. Time normally runs in a clock-ward direction.

HRM FI Conference

In September 1994 DEC was one of the sponsors in the London conference of the Human Resource Managers and Training & Development Managers of leading financial institutions (HRM FI Conference). DEC's interest was with the financial institutions many of which were its customers. I was asked to add some excitement to the event in view of securing leads for DEC's new Learning-Services business line.

I studied the scope of the conference and together with colleagues we distilled fourteen questions of importance to human resource professionals in the Finance Industry, such issues as mergers & acquisitions, focus on core business, downsizing/redundancies, and the use of IT (see Part 3 in Figure 6.1.4). But in addition to these questions this time I introduced two ways to determine the company's position on the curve (see Parts 1 and 2 in Figure 6.1.4). The complete discussion of the six ways to find where you are on the curve is presented later in Chapter 9.

The two-page questionnaire was included in the folder each participant received upon arrival. Participants were asked to fill it out and hand it in by 16:00 the same day. That evening an assistant and I entered the data in our prepared EXCEL workbook and the next day the results were presented to the full assembly. Individuals were invited to come to the DEC stand in the afternoon and receive personalized feedback on how well their organization structures and human-resource management policies were suited to the overall business evolution of their company.

The general results included again survey-type results like those shown in Figure 6.1.2. For example, the 55 participants collectively rated focus on customers, the ability of the organization to change and adapt, and use of information technology as the three most important issues. The same three issues showed up as *strengths* (summer season) in the modified-BCG matrix, see Figure 6.1.5.

But now we had also determined each company's curve—via Part 1 of the questionnaire—and could pass judgment on the appropriateness of three of their major policies, namely improvements programs (BPR, TQM, benchmarking, etc.), employee profile solicited (specialists, entrepreneurs, generalists, etc.), and organizational style (centralized/decentralized). All this under the catchphrase: Is your company appropriately dressed for the season it is traversing?

The following two pages constitute the questionnaire that was printed on the two sides of a heavyweight sheet of paper.

SURVEY ON
BUSINESS EVOLUTION
&
THE ALIGNMENT OF
MANAGEMENT POLICIES

"He shall be succesful who acts according to the spirit of the times"
Niccolo Machiavelli, *The Prince*

Typical questions of HR professionals in the Finance Industry	• What are the growth areas in Finance today and tomorrow? • How are you guided in your strategy planning? • How do you choose organizational structures and management policies? • Is your company appropriately "dressed" for the business season it is traversing ? This survey is designed to tackle the above questions. Your experience will contribute to valuable insights!
A survey approach using Natural Growth Concepts	Theodore Modis, Ph.D., scientist, consultant and author and Susanne Seror, consultant, will present and interprete the survey results assessing the dynamic evolution of your business and management context. Business like the weather goes through seasons, and so do successful management policies. Our approach uses research and experience to diagnose the season and its evolution, and give advice accordingly. (See also the issue of *The Futurist* in the conference package) The results of the survey will be presented to you at the special breakfast briefing to be held in the Crystal Room of the May-Fair Intercontinental Hotel on Thursday, September 22 between 08:00 and 08:45.
Personalized feedback More information	For more complete and personalized feedback, visit the Digital stand on Thursday. You will be able to compare your position and business season, to those of the rest of the industry. You will get some evaluation of your company's growth potential.
Additional incentive: Win a Digital PC!	By handing in your survey by 16:00 on Wednesday, September 21, you will automatically participate at the lottery for a Digital Color Notebook PC.
Who is eligible for the PC lottery?	All delegates and participants at the HRM Finance '94 Conference who return the survey by the time indicated above. Digital and other conference organisation staff are NOT entitled to participate.

Please indicate:
Country: _____ Industry: _____

Optional information:
Name: _____ First Name: _____ Position: _____

Company: _____ Tel.: _____ Fax: _____

Or attach/hand in your business card

All information will be handled with strict
CONFIDENTIALITY

BUSINESS CARD

digital™

1. Please think of the evolution of your company. Choose either the whole company, the   Please indicate here (optional)
geography or the business segment you are responsible for:
(Use your best judgement and specify fractions of a year if necessary (decimals) in the grey boxes; follow the arrows)

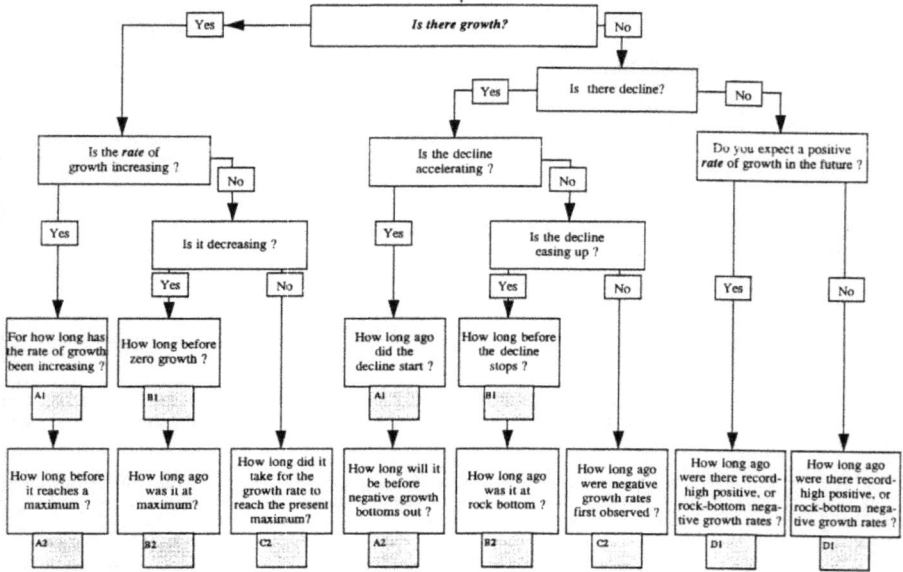

Yes   **Is there growth?**   No

Yes   Is there decline?   No

Is the *rate* of growth increasing ?	Is the decline accelerating ?	Do you expect a positive *rate* of growth in the future ?

Yes   No   Yes   No   Yes   No

Is it decreasing ?	Is the decline easing up ?

Yes   No   Yes   No

For how long has the rate of growth been increasing ?	How long before zero growth ?	How long ago did the decline start ?	How long before the decline stops ?
A1	B1	A1	B1

How long before it reaches a maximum ?	How long ago was it at maximum?	How long did it take for the growth rate to reach the present maximum?	How long will it be before negative growth bottoms out ?	How long ago was it at rock bottom ?	How long ago were negative growth rates first observed ?	How long ago were there record-high positive, or rock-bottom negative growth rates ?	How long ago were there record-high positive, or rock-bottom negative growth rates ?
A2	B2	C2	A2	B2	C2	D1	D1

2. For the company/geography/business segment you chose under question 1, please indicate:
(*if more than one, please rank them, 1=most important; please don't use same number twice*)

2a. where is most energy spent among the following strategic initiatives at present

☐ Business Process Redesign   ☐ Continuous Improvement   ☐ Total Quality Management (Excellence Programs)   ☐ Benchmarking

2b. what kind of employee profile you need most at present

☐ Entrepreneurs   ☐ Specialists   ☐ Process Agents (for management & execution)   ☐ Generalists

2c. which decision making style best characterizes the organization today

☐ Decentralized   ☐ evolving towards Centralization   ☐ Centralized   ☐ evolving towards Decentralization

3. Looking at the entire company from an HR perspective, please indicate performance & importance on a scale from 1 - 5 for each of the following: (*1=low, 5 = high, n/a = not applicable; please circle what is appropriate*)

	How SATISFACTORY is it TODAY	How IMPORTANT is it TODAY	How IMPORTANT will it be in 3 YEARS
3a. Mergers & acquisitions	1 2 3 4 5 n/a	1 2 3 4 5	1 2 3 4 5
3b. Downsizing/redundancies	1 2 3 4 5 n/a	1 2 3 4 5	1 2 3 4 5
3c. Hiring/retaining	1 2 3 4 5 n/a	1 2 3 4 5	1 2 3 4 5
3d. Flexible/peripheral workforce	1 2 3 4 5 n/a	1 2 3 4 5	1 2 3 4 5
3e. Horizontal career mobility	1 2 3 4 5 n/a	1 2 3 4 5	1 2 3 4 5
3f. Ability of organization to change & adapt	1 2 3 4 5 n/a	1 2 3 4 5	1 2 3 4 5
3g. Simplify business practice	1 2 3 4 5 n/a	1 2 3 4 5	1 2 3 4 5
3h. Focus on core business	1 2 3 4 5 n/a	1 2 3 4 5	1 2 3 4 5
3i. Manage & develop workforce competence	1 2 3 4 5 n/a	1 2 3 4 5	1 2 3 4 5
3j. Measure workforce performance	1 2 3 4 5 n/a	1 2 3 4 5	1 2 3 4 5
3k. Use of information technology	1 2 3 4 5 n/a	1 2 3 4 5	1 2 3 4 5
3l. Compete across borders & cultures	1 2 3 4 5 n/a	1 2 3 4 5	1 2 3 4 5
3m. Focus on customers	1 2 3 4 5 n/a	1 2 3 4 5	1 2 3 4 5
3n. Influence of HR in strategic business decisions	1 2 3 4 5 n/a	1 2 3 4 5	1 2 3 4 5

THANK YOU

Figure 6.1.4 This and the previous page constitute the questionnaire.

THE GROWTH POTENTIAL OF YOUR COMPETENCIES

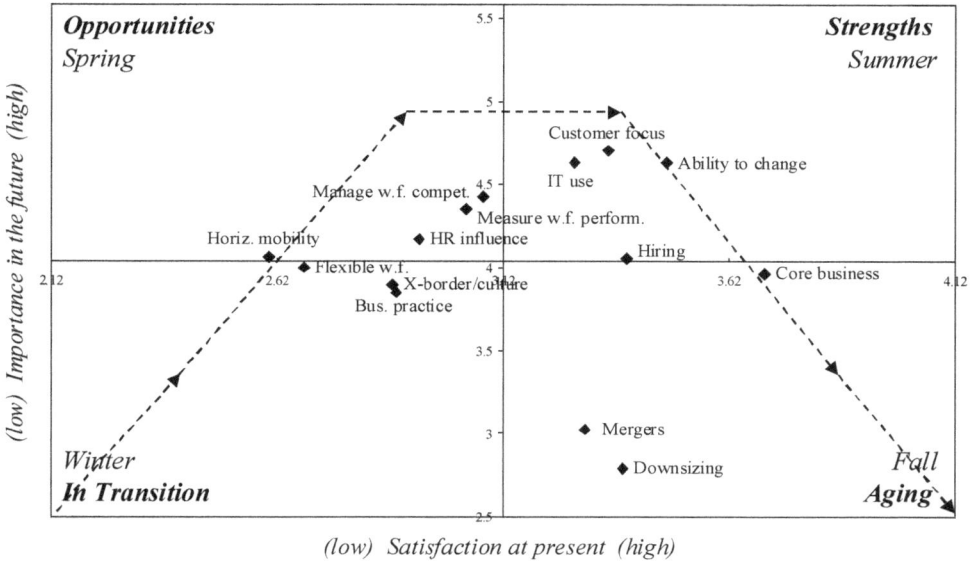

Figure 6.15 Concerns coming in and going out (aging); growing in importance over the next three years (opportunities); remaining important today as well as in three years time (strengths).

STRATEGIC INITIATIVES

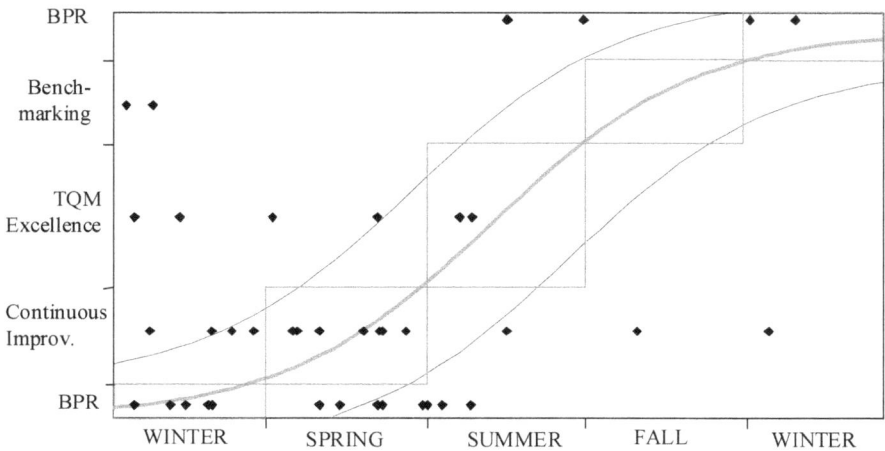

Figure 6.1.6 An S-curve template with seasons delimited. The thin gray lines define a band within which a company is doing the right thing for its season.

For each one of the three policies considered we produced graphs like the one shown in Figure 6.1.6 indicating where each participant's company stood. In the figure we see a pictorial S-curve and the associated seasons. All S-curves were normalized to a ceiling of 100% (half of the companies had a season length between 2 and 5 years). The thin gray lines delimit a width, determined by the season length, within which a strategic program is "in harmony" with the season being traversed. For example, TQM is appropriate in summer whereas benchmarking is not appropriate in "winter" that experiences a considerable amount of chaos.

Figure 6.1.6 indicates that less than 15% of the answers were completely out of line with the season. However, the other two variables performed less well and at the end only 20% of the answers had all three strategic initiatives in line with the season.

Finding oneself inside the band delimited by the thin gray lines is goodness because it implies that a path of least resistance is being followed. Each black dot in Figure 6.1.6 represents a participant's inputs and in fact, our program had the capability of showing the participant's name when hovering over the dot with the cursor. We exploited this feature late in the afternoon when people came by our stand to find out how they had done. Revealing someone's position being way off the natural path often raised wisecracks from teasing colleagues. Of course, they had been warned when they received the questionnaires that they could use a pseudonym.

IN CLOSING

Events involving large gatherings usually feature a few "star" speakers on the stage and many passive listeners in the audience. Excitement and enjoyment are unevenly split between these two groups. The Event-Enhancement methodology presented here permits everyone to become involved contributing inputs that will shape the event's final conclusions. Besides adding some excitement the methodology endows participants with a feeling of ownership of the results achieved.

But events involving large gatherings also feature an audience usually consisting of experts. These people have experience and knowledge some of which they may not even be aware of. Tapping this knowledge efficiently with a sophisticated tool can produce valuable results. At the end participants will take away insights beyond those prepared ahead of time and handed out by the speakers.

7 – The Life Cycle of Services

In 1989 Alain Debecker and I presented a paper in the international conference on "Diffusion of Technologies and Social Behavior" at IIASA, in Laxemburg, Austria. The topic of our paper was a quantitative determination of the service life cycle of computers. I was proud of that work because in order to formulate the technique we had put into practice an "exotic" mathematical procedure called convolution of functions, which up to that time had been a purely academic exercise for me.

Most people in business are familiar with the application of logistic growth to the sale of products even if they ignore its mathematical formulation. They all use a bell-shaped curve to refer to a product's life cycle. The corresponding S-curve, for a product's cumulative sales, is also something with which they feel comfortable.

Business people, however, are less in tune with the mortality of their products. Hardware maintenance contracts for machines sold closely follow unit sales. At the beginning the number of contracts increases at the same rate as sales, but instead of the familiar S-curve, contracts reach a peak and then slowly start declining as machines become old and obsolete. In Figure 7.1 we see the familiar forms: the sales life cycle, the corresponding S-curve of cumulative sales, and the less familiar service life cycle. Notice that the last graph peaks only after the product has completed its sales life cycle. Qualitatively the business world is aware of the service life cycle. They refer to it as the product's end-of-life curve. Quantitatively, however, they fall short of being able to predict when the product will peak and at what rate revenue will decline afterwards. As product life cycles become shorter, how will service life cycles be affected?

An article in the *Harvard Business Review* addressed this question.[1] Graphs and figures livened up the discussion, but the treatment remained qualitative and rather pictorial. It corroborated the intuition but did not help with quantitative forecasts. Determining the service life cycle is interesting for other reasons besides the ever-increasing importance of service revenue. It provides knowledge of the installed base, its actual and future size, which is crucial in marketing strategies for add-ons (follow-up sales in terms of accessories, upgrades, etc.), and a variety of services. This is why together with Alain Debecker we undertook the study of a quantitative approach for determining a product's *life span* as opposed to only its *sales life cycle*.[2]

SALES AND SERVICES PICTORIALLY

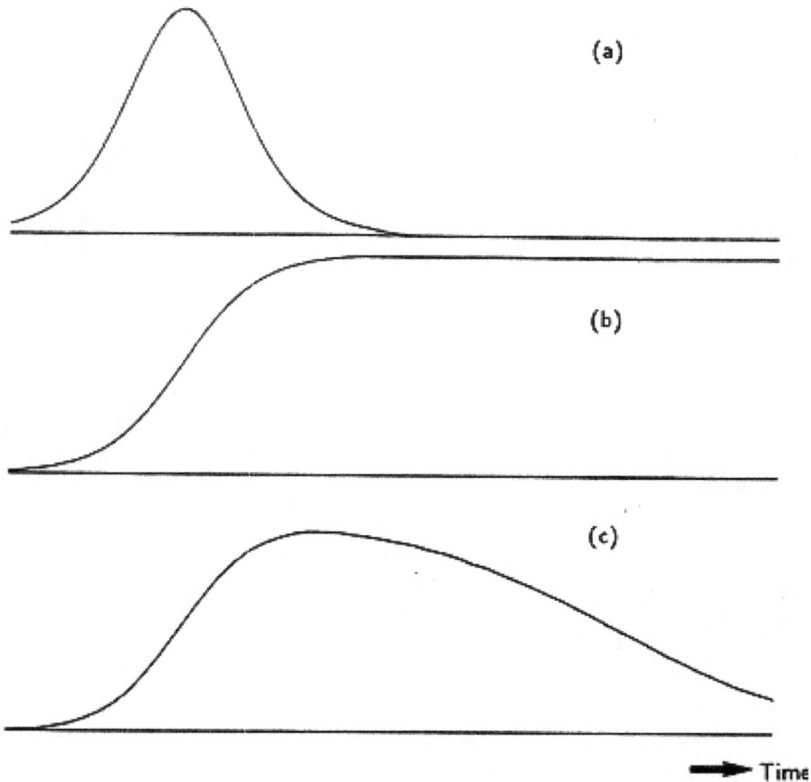

Figure 7.1. (a) Life cycle of sales, (b) Cumulative number of sales, (c) Number of service contracts active at a given time.

Logistic growth as formulated in the Equation 2.2.1 accurately describes situations where a niche is being filled under natural competition, be it an ecological or a market niche. The situation becomes more complicated when one is interested in tracking down the survivors of a generation over time. The total number of units sold of a particular product increases with time reaching its ceiling at the end of the products life cycle. The number of products *in use*, however, never reaches the same ceiling, as there is certain mortality among the products sold. Out of one hundred units sold in a month, 98 may be still alive a year later and only 50 in five years time. This erosion comes from aging and obsolescence, and sets in right from the beginning. While populations grow happily along their S-shaped birth curve, they are at every point in time subject to certain mortality.

Mathematically the case calls for a convolution function, the folding of logistic growth with a mortality function. What shape should the latter have? Sales follow a bell-shaped curve over time. To introduce mortality we began with the simplest possible assumption of a constant percentage decay rate, in other words, an exponential decay (the mathematical formula is given in Appendix A.3.

When we first applied this formulation to real data we obtained good results, particularly for old products for which the sales life cycle had finished years ago and service contracts were already beyond their peak and declining, see Figure 7.2.

SERVICE LIFE CYCLE WITH EXPONENTIAL MORTALITY

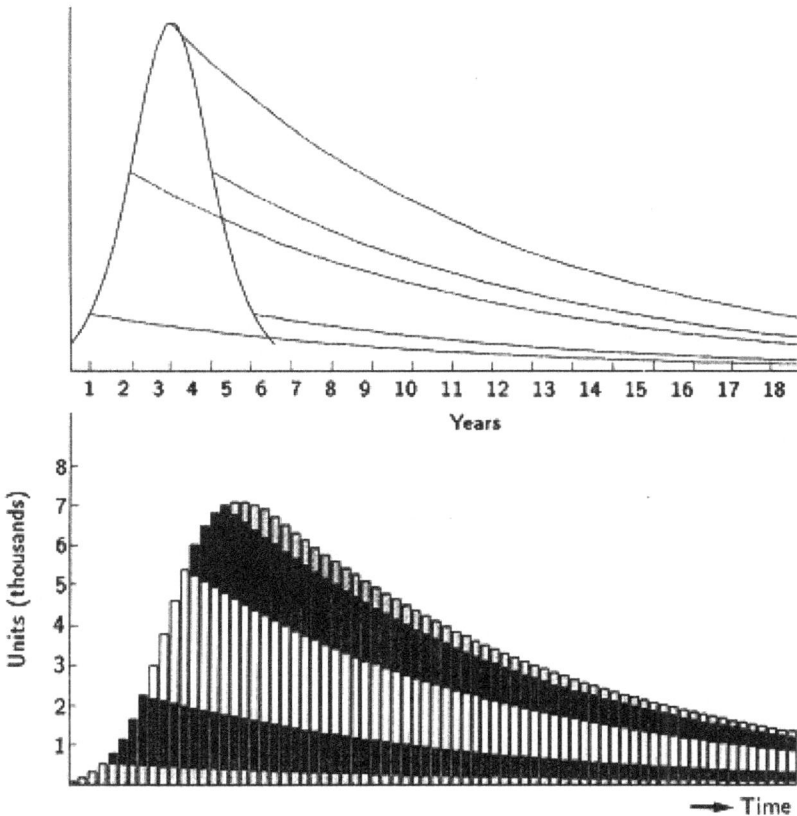

Figure 7.2. Above: life cycle outlining sales of service contracts and exponential mortality rates. Below: the integrated number of contracts with finer time bins (trimesters). The overall envelope represents total survivors at a given time.

However, there was a difficulty with relatively young products where the rate of decay was so low that it implied they would be around for a very long time. This fact contradicts the increasingly rapid cycling of products witnessed in the computer industry. The second difficulty was more revealing. When tracking decay rates in a number of areas we found that they were not constant over time. These observations prompted us to raise the level of sophistication for mortality, namely to try a second-degree function for the decay rate, which yielded a logistic pattern for the mortality, see Appendix A.3.

SERVICE LIFE CYCLE WITH LOGISTIC MORTALITY

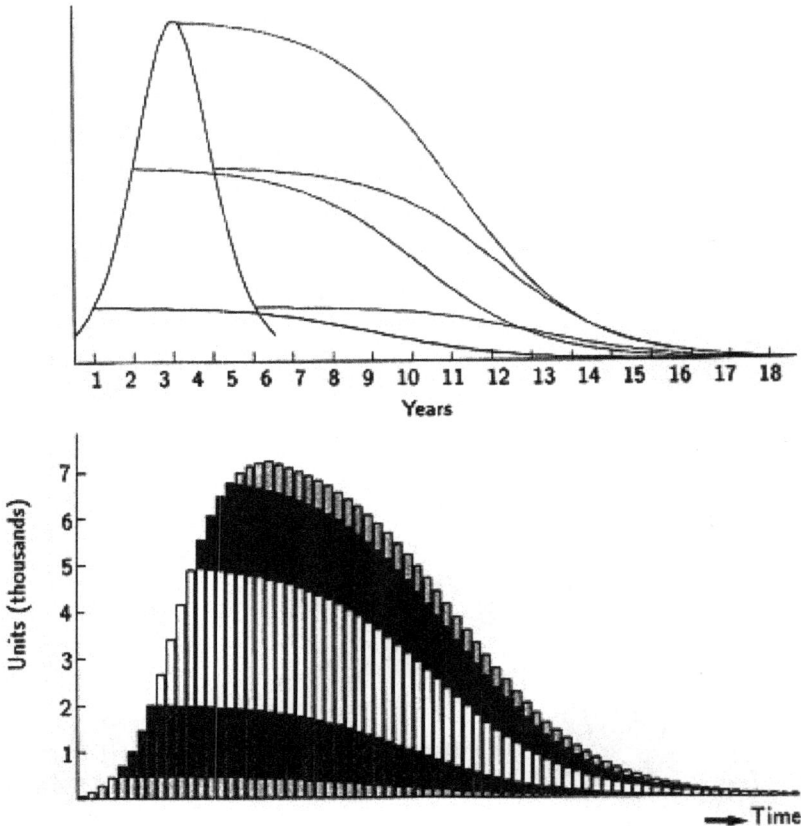

Figure 7.3. Above: life cycle outlining sales of service contracts and logistic mortality rates. Below: the integrated number of contracts with finer time bins (trimesters). The overall envelope represents total survivors at a given time.

So we ended up with an S-curve describing the machine sales but also another S-curve describing the mortality of these machines once they are installed in the field. Arriving at a logistic (S-curve) mortality was not entirely circumstantial. An older study on the appearance and survival of supertankers had revealed to us an exemplary S-shaped mortality for that "species". In addition, Marchetti has investigated human mortality and has also established logistic laws for the process.[3] However, what is important is that the logistic mortality better fits the data on the computer service contracts we were trying to describe. The new convolution function involves five parameters that must be determined by a fit, three from the logistic growth of contract births (Equation 2.2.2), and two from a logistic mortality normalized to 100%. This is graphically depicted in Figure 7.3.

To make forecasts one needs to determine the five parameters and for that it is necessary to have at least five measurements, namely monthly or quarterly data points on active contracts. But in practice, and in order to limit the uncertainties involved in logistic fits, one needs many more than five data points. The parameter determination is again a fitting procedure involving the minimization of a Chi Square formed as follows:

$$X^2 = \sum_i w_i (D_i - Q_i)^2$$

where D_i are the data points, Q_i the theoretical calculation form the convolution function and w_i are the weights (related to the uncertainties of the data).

There is a longer discussion on the weights in the Appendix but here we only say that the weights were generally taken to be uniform, except for some cases where they were adjusted through knowledge of the particular business situation. An example is shown in Figure 7.4. For this old computer model, even though we are missing the early data, we have enough points (monthly data for six years) to make a reliable determination. In fact, ignoring the most recent year (the last twelve points) in the fitting procedure has a negligible effect on the parameter values and the forecasted trajectory. Repeating the operation, that is dropping the last twenty-four points, still replicates closely the parameter values originally found. In conclusion, we can say that as long as the historical data go far enough to hint at the decline beyond the peak, the parameters determination shows a remarkable stability.

There was a problem, however, involving young products, that is, products for which the historical service data had not yet reached the peak. In these cases a 4- or 5-parameter fit, involving exponential- and

Service Life Cycle of an Old Product

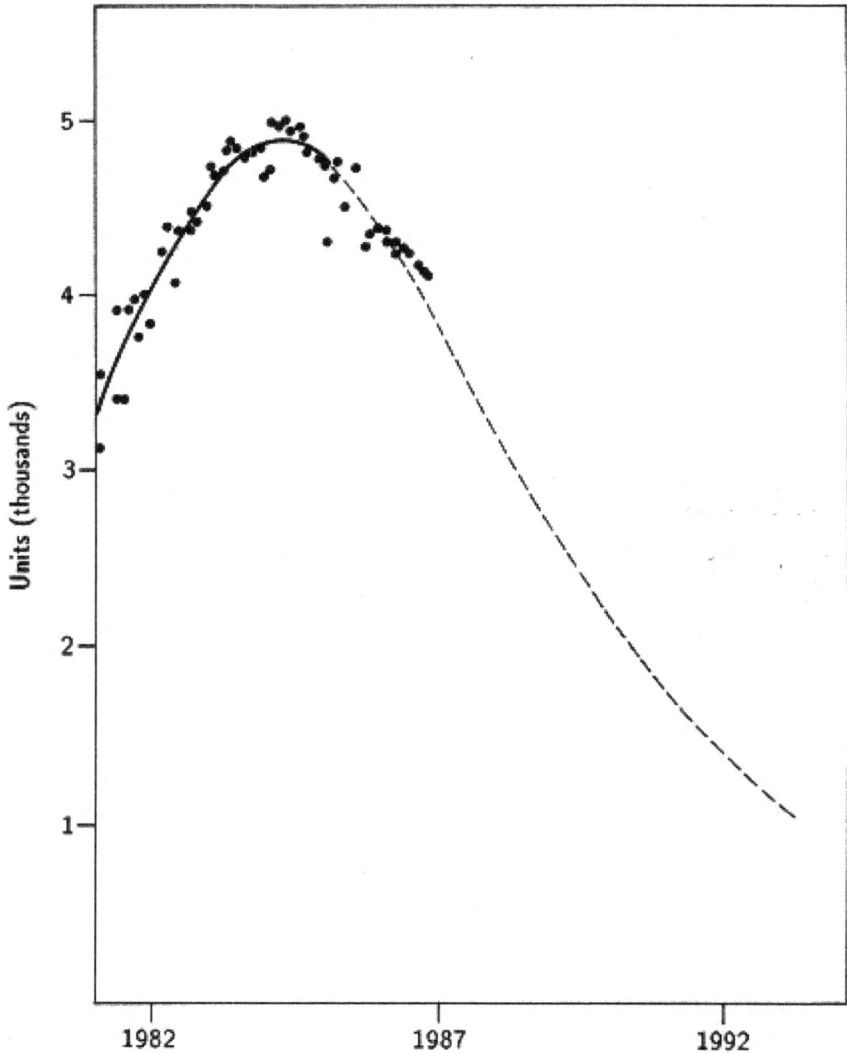

Figure 7.4. Monthly data and fit for the hardware service contracts of an old computer model. Each point represents the number of active contracts at the time. The fit (solid line) is based on the data up to the end of 1985, two years before the end of the historical window. The dotted line is the extrapolation of the convolution function determined from the fit and constitutes the main ingredient in the forecast of the service revenue.

logistic-mortality convolution functions respectively, produced a *null* mortality most of the time. The best fit found by the program would be a simple S-curve growth with zero mortality. This was seen in terms of the fact that the difference between contracts sold and contracts active was very small in the early days of a new product. The program could not determine mortality parameters if a simple 3-parameter growth logistic could describe the data just as well, see Figure 7.5.

Although this was a comforting feedback on the robustness and stability of the parameter determination method, it precluded the determination of contract mortality for young products. At the same time it inspired a resolution to the problem through factorization, namely adopting a two-step procedure. First fit the contract sales data, that is, the appearance of new contracts to a simple 3-parameter logistic. Once the ceiling was determined this way, we could fit the active-contract data to the convolution function, but this time with the ceiling *M* fixed at the value already determined from the sales fit. Clearly the procedure demands knowledge of two sets of data, sales of contracts as well as the contracts still active as a function of time.

SERVICE LIFE CYCLE OF A YOUNG PRODUCT

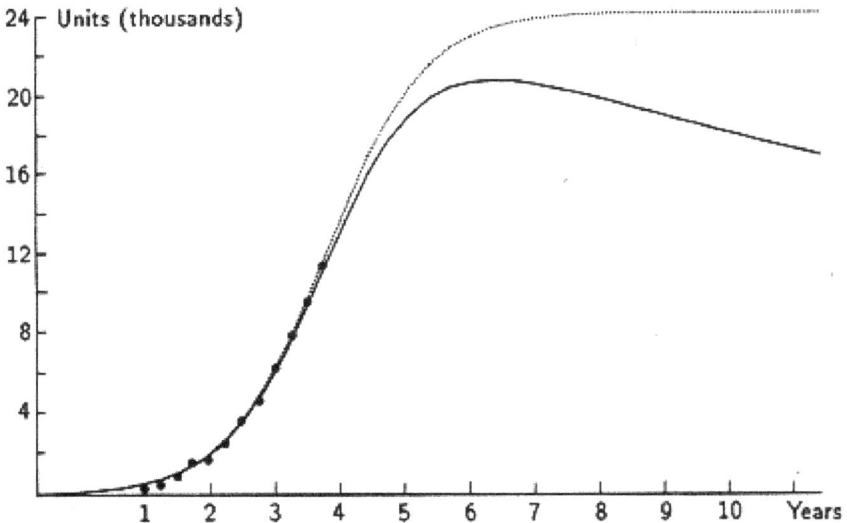

Figure 7.5. Quarterly data and fit for the active contracts of a young computer model. The fitting program yielded a null mortality (dotted line). The solid line suggests the realistic evolution taking mortality into account.

The approach described above sheds some new light on the concept of technological obsolescence. The usefulness of a generation of computer models decreases with time not because of aging, in other words material fatigue that would result in frequent breakdowns, but mainly because of obsolescence. Computer models do not drop out of use individually like used cars. They phase out together as their technological generation becomes outdated. In Figure 7.3 we see that the number of models in operation declines along an S-curve from the day of sales. The end-of-life point (taken here as the 1% of sales that remain at a certain date) is reached at approximately the same date for all models. People who bought the very first models will keep them for up to 16 years. Those who bought the last few models, sold say six years later, will only keep them ten years. This generation of computers had a sales life cycle of six years and a service lifecycle of 16. Perhaps unfairly, the models fabricated last, even though perfected and more reliable are endowed with shorter lifetimes.

7.1 – CASE STUDY

The Minicomputer VAX 11/780

DEC's first groundbreaking minicomputer was the VAX 11/780. It turned out to be a very successful product and helped establish DEC as a major player among the computer manufacturers presenting serious competition to IBM. The VAX 11/780 was introduced on October 25, 1977. It was the first member of the VAX computer family, the first commercially available 32-bit computer and the first one MIPS (one million instructions per second) machine.

The computer and its operating system (VMS) had been designed both from scratch. The result was a really reliable, powerful and user-friendly system. The affordable price level allowed many institutions and universities to acquire it.

For many years, VAX 11/780 remained the base system every computer speed benchmark referred to. Several programming languages could be used, such as Fortran-77, Cobol, Bliss-32, PL/I, BASIC, PASCAL, CORAL 66, and a netware software called DecNet. A dual processor version was launched in 1981 (the 11/782) and various other systems followed, from the small VAXstation 1 up to the VAX 9000 mainframe. But a few of the original model 11/780 were still in use in the year 2000.

Nevertheless in the late 1980s, several years after the original model's sales had dropped to zero, pressure was mounting in the company's manufacturing division to stop the fabrication of spare parts for this model. At that time I was working in a Management Science group of the company's Filed Service division where we undertook a study to forecast the service revenue still expected from this model.

The company kept rich historical statistics in its databases including active service contracts. Because this product was quite old, the two parameterizations of mortality (exponential and S-curve) gave comparable results. From a graph similar to that of Figure 7.4 we obtained our answer that the expected service revenue from machines installed in clients' premises over the next several years would be around 25% of what the model had already brought in. This unexpected conclusion was sufficient to convince the manufacturing division to continue the fabrication of key hardware components.

In retrospect, DEC earned millions of dollars in service revenue by using the service life-cycle technique. I doubt that such saving would have been achieved had we simply circulated the *Harvard Business Review* article with its qualitative treatment of the subject among the managers of the manufacturing division.

IN CLOSING

Unlike cumulative product sales, service contracts display a mortality over time. The evolution of service contracts is best described and forecasted through the use of a convolution function of two logistics: one representing the growth of contract sales (three parameters) and the other representing contract mortality (two parameters).

For young products it is recommended to factorize the process into two fits, births of contracts first and active contracts afterwards. Computer models in operation phase out independently of the date they were sold. As their technological generation becomes obsolete, early sales and late sales all drop out of use at around the same time. Beyond hardware service revenue forecasts, the approach offered here helps determine the strategically important installed base, which is the market for add-ons, software, follow-up products, and a multitude of other services.

8 – VOLTERRA-LOTKA

Industrial applications of biological models have a long history. One of the pioneers of this work was Alfred Lotka with his classic book *Elements of Physical Biology*.[1] At the heart of all biological models lies the logistic growth, Equation 2.2.1, which can also be written as follows:[2]

$$\frac{dX}{dt} = a_x X \frac{(M - X)}{M} = a_x X - b_x X^2 \qquad\qquad 8.1$$

where a_x and M constants, and

$$b_x = \frac{a_x}{M}$$

The solution of this equation is the ubiquitous S-shaped curve that enters extensively into everyday life. But Verhulst's equation deserves more credit than that. In its discrete form it is responsible for the whole science of chaos. Furthermore, as generalized in the Volterra-Lotka formulation, this equation can account for all types of interference between competing species. Finally, one might justifiably expect that in its full generality, the growth equation, in a discrete form, with cross terms to account for all inter-relations between competing species, would give a *complete* picture, in which growth, chaos, self-organization, complex adaptive systems, and other trendy academic pastime ensue as special cases. But let us concentrate in the simple and practical case of the two-competitor niche, something for which there is extensive literature.[3,4,5]

The S-curve describes the growth in competition of a species population. The origin of competition is due to the fact that members of the same species elbow each other in a crowded niche. In the presence of more than one species, the S-curve law does not generally apply, because one species may interfere with the growth rate of another. More terms must be added to the mathematical formulation to take this interaction into account, and the S-curve becomes distorted. Exceptions are one-to-one substitutions. They involve two competitors and yet their "market" shares follow S-shaped patterns, see the case of cars and horses discussed in Section 4.1.

There are two bends in the graceful shape of the celebrated S-curve. The first one (exponential rise) is due to the capability of the species to multiply. The second one (niche-saturation slowdown) is due to the competitive squeeze caused by the limited space.

The First Bend

If you put a pair of rabbits on a fenced-off range, you can watch their population increase by going through the successive stages of 2, 4, 8, 16, 32,..., 2^n in an exponential growth. If the average rabbit litter is greater than 2, you will see a steeper exponential growth. The same is true with products because they too have a capability to multiply. Depending upon its *attractiveness* every product sold will bring new customers. *Attractiveness* is the equivalent of the average rabbit litter. It is defined as:

$$Attractiveness = e^a$$

where a is the constant a_x in Equation 8.1. The more products sold and the more attractive they are, the higher the rate of sales will be. Sales will grow at a constant percent rate—that is, exponentially—for a while, with a time constant which depends on the attractiveness. (If a product's attractiveness is smaller than unity, we are dealing with an unsuccessful product and its sales will quickly dwindle down to zero.) The first bend of the S-curve comes from the first term in the right-hand side of Equation 8.1.

The Second Bend

The rabbit-population explosion ceases when a sizable part of the niche becomes occupied; the same is true with products. If the growth equation is to be valid for late *as well as* for early times it must contain a term that represents the fact that the niche capacity is finite. This is the negative term in Equation 8.1. The coefficient b_x expresses the strength of internal competition between members of the same species. In other words, it says that the percent rate of growth is also proportional to the still-empty space in the market niche. The second bend of the S-curve comes from the second term in the right-hand side of Equation 8.1.

8.1 – MORE THAN ONE SPECIES IN THE SAME NICHE

Two parameters, the attractiveness and the niche capacity (related to a_x and b_x) fully determine the S-shaped pattern evidenced in the evolution of a species population diffusing in its ecological niche. But what happens if besides rabbits we also have sheep on the range? After all, sheep also eat grass and in greater amounts than rabbits. Their presence will certainly suppress the rabbit population explosion. Worse yet, what happens if there are foxes? Competition between rabbits and sheep is not the same as between rabbits and foxes. Just think of the fact that faced with a finite amount of grass, sheep would probably lament at the rapid multiplication of rabbits, while foxes would undoubtedly rejoice.

It all has to do with how one competitor influences the growth rate of the other. Sheep and rabbits have a negative effect on each other's population by reducing each other's food supply, but while foxes damage rabbit populations, the latter have a positive influence on fox populations. Whenever there is more than one competitor in the same niche, we must consider the interaction between them, namely, how one's rate of growth depends on the existence of the other. We then need to introduce a third term in the growth equation to take this coupling into account. For two competitors X and Y the equations become:

$$\frac{\mathrm{d}X}{\mathrm{d}t} = a_x X - b_x X^2 + c_{xy} XY$$

$$\frac{\mathrm{d}Y}{\mathrm{d}t} = a_y Y - b_y Y^2 + c_{yx} XY$$

8.1.1

The values of c_{xy} and c_{yx} are related to the overlap, how much one steps on the feet of the other, or in other words, how many sales you will lose (or win), because your competitor won one. With the system of equations 8.1.1 we can formulate a measurement for one's ability to attack, counterattack, or retreat, as the case may be.

8.2 – ATTACKER'S ADVANTAGE, DEFENDER'S COUNTER-ATTACK

The attack of a new species against the defenses of an incumbent lies at the heart of corporate marketing strategies. This kind of struggle has been rigorously formulated by biologists and ecologists. Farrel tells of how in the 1930s George Gause, at Moscow's Zoological Museum, studied the competition between a traditional brewer's yeast and one used in Ukraine to make the refreshing milk drink called kefir, popular in Asian and Middle-Eastern countries.[6] He first grew the two yeasts in isolation and observed the S-shaped natural-growth pattern for each. He then put them together in the same test tube and let them compete for the same food. He found that each influenced the other's growth. But the brewer's yeast is tolerant to the alcohol that is produced as it grows; the kefir yeast is less so. In a mixture, this gave the brewer's yeast an increasing advantage as fermentation proceeded, and it outgrew its competitor. Simple S-curves did not describe the growth processes well, but the Volterra-Lotka mathematical formulation involving coupling constants did.

The parameters c_{xy} and c_{yx} are related to the attacker's advantage and the defender's counterattack.[3] The former quantifies the extent to which the attacker inhibits the ability of the defender to keep market share. The latter quantifies the extent to which the defender can prevent the attacker from stealing market share. The business strategy and tactics of attack and counterattack have been qualitatively described by Peter Drucker[7] and especially by Richard Foster.[8] The nature of the attacker's advantage has been clearly established by Cooper and Kleinschmidt[9]—professors respectively in industrial marketing and technology management, and in marketing and international business—who studied over 200 new products and determined that the most significant parameter in gaining market share is a "superior product that delivered unique benefits to the user." This and price considerations impact the magnitude of the attacker's advantage.

Under attack, the defender redoubles its own efforts to maintain or improve its position. A high value for the defender's counterattack implies a face-on counterattack within the context "we do better what they do". An effective counterattack, however, with long-lasting survival-sustaining consequences implies eventual adoption of the new technology, some sort of death for the old company, which is painful to assimilate culturally. Companies hesitate to embark on such undertakings. Because of this hesitation, Foster refers to defender's counterattack as the defender's *dilemma* and cites tens of examples in which a defender refused to acknowledge, or reacted too late, to an attacker's onslaught. A classical case was NCR's belated and traumatic transition to computerized cash registers.

Figure 8.2.1 shows a more recent example, the competition in the early Greek mobile-telephone market, a two-competitor struggle. The two firms launched their products simultaneously. One firm, Telestet, became an early market leader thus assuming the role of the defender. But the coupling parameters, determined from the data, were both negative, $c_{xy} = -0.8$ and the $c_{yx} = -0.6$ indicating much overlap and fierce competition of the sheep-rabbit nature. Every time Panafon would close a sale, Telestet would lose 0.8 potential sales, and every time Telestet would close a sale, Panafon would lose 0.6 sales. The difference was crucial. The model showed curves that eventually deviated from S-curves. With data up to the end of 1995, the model's prediction was that Panafon would become leader within a few months. By mid 1996 Panafon's market share had indeed been established higher than Telestet's.

MOBILE-TELEPHONE SALES IN GREECE

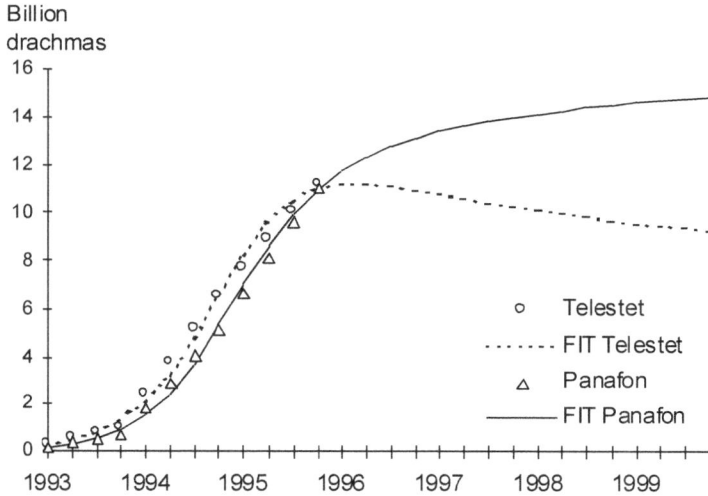

Figure 8.2.1   Quarterly sales for the two competitors of the Greek mobile-telephone market. Despite early dominance by Telestet, the model successfully predicted the shift in Panafon's favor by mid-1996.

Kristina Smitalova and Stefan Sujan, professors of mathematics at Comenius University and the Slovac Academy of Science respectively, in Bratislava, Slovakia, studied and classified the various coupling schemes in a rigorous way.[10] They distinguished and labeled six ways in which two competitors can influence each other's growth rate, according to the sign of the two coupling parameters involved. They are tabulated in the boxed text below where the entries can be taken as definitions for the corresponding form of competition.

Pure competition is what we have between rabbits and sheep. Each one influences negatively the growth of the other, but not with the same importance (sheep are fewer but eat more). Market examples are the mobile-telephone case mentioned above, or the competition between different-size computer models.

Predator-prey is the case of cinema and television. The more movies made for cinema, the more television will benefit, but the more television grows in importance, the more cinema suffers. Telefilms are not shown in movie theaters. Had been no legal protection, (restricting permission to broadcast new movies), television would have probably "eaten up" the cinema audience.

ALL POSSIBLE INTERACTIONS BETWEEN TWO SPECIES

− − *Pure competition* occurs when both species suffer from each other's existence.

+ − *Predator-prey* occurs when one of them serves as direct food to the other.

+ + *Mutualism* occurs in case of symbiosis, or a win-win situation.

+ 0 *Commensalism* occurs in a parasitic type of relationship in which one benefits from the existence of the other, which nevertheless remains unaffected.

− 0 *Amensalism* occurs when one suffers from the existence of the other, which is impervious to what is happening.

0 0 *Neutralism* occurs if there is no interaction whatsoever.

A typical case of mutualism is software and hardware. Sales of each one trigger more sales for the other.

Add-ons and accessories, such as car extras, constitute an example of commensalism. The more cars sold, the more car accessories will be sold. The inverse is not true, however; sales of accessories do not trigger car sales.

Amensalism can be found in the case of ballpoint pens and fountain pens described in detail below. The onslaught of ballpoint sales seriously damaged fountain-pen sales, and yet the ballpoint-pen population grew as if there was no competition.

Examples of neutralism are encountered in all situations in which there is no market overlap. For example, a sports store that sells both swimming-wear and skiwear. Depending on the geography there might be a negative correlation of seasonal origin, but the sales of one do not in general affect the sales of the other.

8.3 − COMPETITION MANAGEMENT

The intriguing fascination of the marketplace is that *the nature* of competition can be changed over time. For some business people achieving a change in the competitive roles is perhaps more handsomely rewarding than making profits. It is something that species in nature cannot do. Rabbits will never eat meat, and whenever humans tamper in such areas, either academically (genetic engineering) or industrially (mad-cow disease), they are invariably criticized, justly or unjustly.

But things are different in industry. In contrast to the jungle, a technology, a company, or a product does not need to remain prey to another forever. The competitive roles can be radically altered with the right decisions at the right time. External light meters, used for accurate diaphragm and speed setting on photographic cameras, enjoyed a stable *commensal* relationship with cameras for decades. As camera sales grew, so did the sales of light meters. But there came a time when technological developments enabled cameras to incorporate light meters into their own box. Soon the whole light-meter industry became prey to the camera industry. Sales of external light meters diminished while sales of cameras enjoyed a boost, and the relationship passed from *commensalism* to a *predator-prey* one.

The struggle between fountain pens and ballpoint pens, mentioned earlier, had a happier ending. Another case of genetic re-engineering in the marketplace, the substitution of ballpoint pens for fountain pens as writing instruments went through three distinct stages.

Before the appearance of ballpoint pens, fountain-pen sales were growing undisturbed to fill the writing-instrument market. They were following an S-shaped "rabbit curve" when the ballpoint technology made its appearance in 1951. As ballpoint sales picked up, those of fountain pens declined for the period 1951-1973. Ballpoint pens did not belong to the same species, neither did they constitute a one-to-one substitution, and yet they cut deep into the fountain-pen sales. A simple S-shaped pattern could not have described this transition but the Volterra-Lotka equations did, with attacker's advantage = -0.5 and defender's counterattack = 0, see Figure 8.3.1. These numbers imply a competitive advantage for ballpoint pens, which by winning one customer inflict losses of half a customer to fountain pens. Fountain pens staged a counterattack by radically dropping prices for many years. Their average price dropped as low as seventy-two cents. But the counterattack was ineffective—the corresponding coupling constant remained equal to zero. While counterattacking fountain pens lost market share and embarked on a well-established extinction course.

But eventually the prices of fountain pens began rising. The average pen price in the US reached $3.50 in 1980 and continued rising. In 1988 a Mont Blanc Masterpiece Diplomat retailed at $280, while a Waterman Le Mans 100 Briarwood cost $400. The fountain pen underwent what Darwin would have described as a "character displacement" to the luxury niche of the executive pen. The strategy of fountain pens since the early 1970s has been a retreat into non-competition. Indeed, the two coupling constants must both equal to zero for the Volterra-Lotka equations to do justice to the sales data of writing instruments in this period. In other words, we have two species that do not interact—*neutralism*—but each

THE STRUGGLE BETWEEN BALLPOINT AND FOUNTAIN PENS

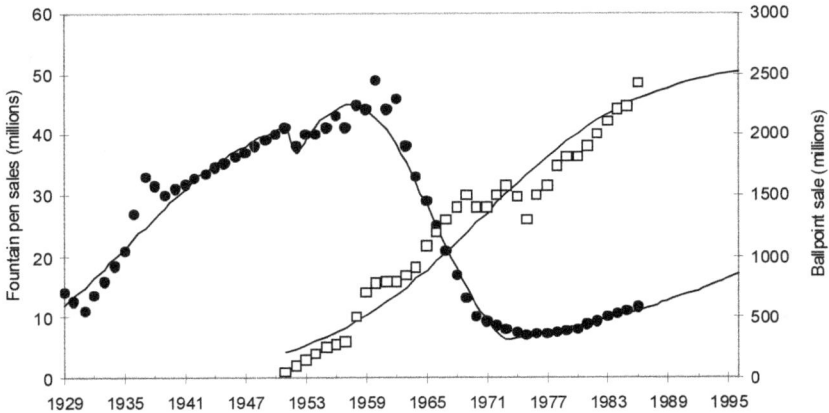

Figure 8.3.1 Sales (millions of units) of fountain pens and ballpoint pens in the US. The lines are the biological-model descriptions. Before 1951 and after 1973 we see S-curve patterns for each competitor. Between 1951 and 1974 we see a typical *amensal* type of competition where the attacker has an advantage (- 0.5), while the defender's counterattack is null. This case study has been discussed by Farrell.[3] The data for this graph have been digitized from a graph therein. Missing-year data have been interpolated.

follows a simple S-curve growth pattern. As a consequence fountain pens have secured for themselves a healthy and profitable market niche. Had they persisted in their competition with ballpoint pens, they would have perished.

Having quantified the competitive mechanisms during the period 1951-1973, it is amusing to play the following scenario. What would have happened had fountain pens undergone their character displacement five years earlier? The model's answer is a significantly higher number of sales for fountain pens today. Is it believable?

One could argue so. Fountain pens would have embarked on an upward trajectory earlier, starting from a stronger position. Enhanced fountain-pen content in everyday life could have cultural repercussions over time, and produce societal preferences and habits. At the end, a more favorable average-citizen disposition could have conceivably led to a more important role for the fountain pen today. Consequently on the average, their price would have to rise less, and their image a little more popular and a little less exclusive.

Character displacement is a classical way to diminish the impact of competition. Another name for this is *Darwinian divergence*, encountered among siblings. In his book *Born to Rebel*, Frank Sulloway—a historian-of-science turned sociologist at MIT's program in science, technology, and society—demonstrated that throughout history first-born children have become conservative and later-borns revolutionary. First-born children end up conservative because they do not want to lose any of the only-child privileges they enjoy. But this forces later-borns into becoming rebellious, to differentiate themselves and thus minimize competition and optimize survival in the same family.[11]

8.4 – ADVERTISING AND IMAGE BUILDING

The Volterra-Lotka equations require three parameters per competitor to describe growth in a two-competitor niche. One parameter represents the ability to multiply, another the size of the niche, and the third one interference from the other competitor. Consequently, we have three choices for action; or six, if we want to take into consideration the parameters of the competitor. To increase the prospects for growth then we could try to change one or more of the following:

- The product attractiveness (increase ours or decrease theirs)
- The size of the market-niche (increase ours or decrease theirs)
- The nature of the interaction (increase our attack or decrease their counterattack)

Each direction of action in principle affects only one parameter.[*] But it is not obvious which change will produce the greater effect; it depends on the particular situation. The concrete actions may include performance improvements, price changes, image transformation, and advertising campaigns. Performance and price concern one's own products only, but advertising via the appropriate message can in principle produce an effect on all six of the parameters. The question is how much of an effect will a certain effort produce. Some advertising messages have proven significantly more effective than others. Success is not necessarily due to whim, chance, or other after-the-fact explanations based on psychological arguments. The roles and the positions of the competitors at a given point in time determine which advertising message will be the effective one. We can illustrate the effectiveness of advertising messages with an example typical of competitive technological substitutions: woven carpets and tufted carpets.

---

[*] The truly independent variables are attractiveness, time constant, and occupancy, as defined below. They are related, but not one-to-one, to the parameters accessible to change. Consequently, some parameters will change together. A. The time constant of the multiplication process is defined as: *time constant* $= 1/\log(attractiveness)$. B. The occupancy is defined as: *occupancy* $= 1/[(time\ constant) \times (niche\ size)]$.

The Six Dimensions of Advertising Action

	Attractiveness	Niche size	Competition
WE:	↗ Our products are good	↗ You need our products	↘ We are different
THEY:	↘ Their products are not good	↘ You do not need their products	↗ We do better what they do

Figure 8.4.1 The six possible independent advertising messages according to our model.

Woven carpets were made on a loom in a manner similar to plain cloth, except that extra wrap yarns were introduced and raised by wires to form loops. Most of today's carpets are made with needles that punch loops through a backing and retreat to leave tufts. Examining the backing of a typical modern carpet reveals the use of glue to hold the tufts in place. This revolution in carpet making began in the 1950s. Tufting changed the requirements for the yarn. Long, continuous filaments were preferred, as they didn't pill or fuzz. Wool yarns have fibers as short as the annual growth of a sheep's hair. This put a fiber such as nylon in a very good position, especially when DuPont invented a bulked form of continuous fiber. The combination of this and tufting created a new "species" that satisfied a growing demand for carpeting and caused the displacement of woolen-woven carpets by nylon-tufted ones.[12]

The model description of the data indicates that the attacker's advantage = -2.2 and the defender's counterattack = -2.6. This is a typical situation of *pure competition* between two similar-species contenders even though the attacker sells in greater numbers. The fate of the defender is eventual extinction.

Could the makers of woolen-woven carpets have secured for themselves a market niche as did fountain pens? And if it were possible, what line of action should have they followed? Let us explore alternative lines of action—via advertising campaigns—and their effectiveness in shaping a different future for woolen carpets back in 1979. Let us rate the different scenarios stemming from changing the six parameters one at a time *by the same amount*, which to a first approximation can be taken as equivalent to comparable effort investment. It is a sensitivity study on the effectiveness of the corresponding advertising message.

SUBSTITUTING NYLON-TUFTED CARPETS FOR WOOLEN-WOVEN ONES

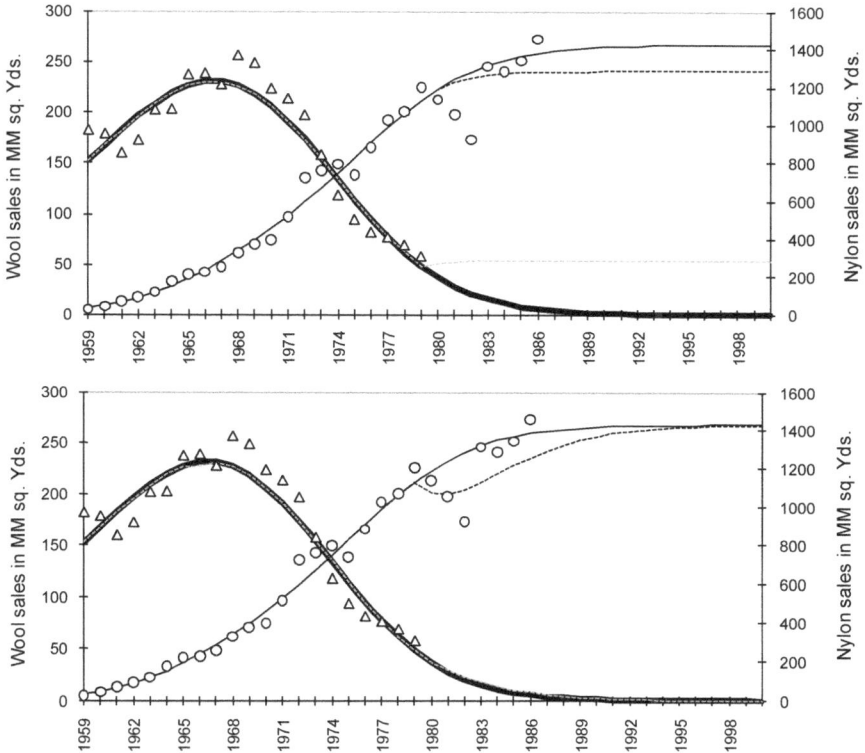

Figure 8.4.2 Triangles represent wool (left-hand axis); circles represent nylon (right-hand axis). The dotted lines indicate two scenarios of comparable change in the respective parameters: on the top following an advertising campaign under the slogan "Wool is different from nylon"; on the bottom under the slogan "Wool is better than nylon"

Figure 8.4.2 shows two of the six possible results. Effective campaigns would be those that emphasized attractiveness and differentiation with messages like "wool is good" and "wool is different from nylon." On the other hand, a counterattack along the lines: "wool is better than nylon", would have been very ineffective.

Table 8.4.1 below shows the complete list of possible advertising messages and their effect on the evolution of wool and nylon sales in 1979. Each message represents an *independent* direction in which the full traditional advertising machinery would have to be launched. There should be no cross talk between directions. For example, to obtain maximum benefit from the "wool is good" campaign one *should not* mix connotations such as "wool is better than nylon" or "nylon is bad". Each message would have to be developed and exploited separately.

Although the detailed execution of the advertising campaign (media, wording, style, etc.) remains crucial, the effectiveness ratings of the above directions come in a non-obvious if not surprising order, and could not have been arrived at by intuitive or other methods used by advertising agencies. Furthermore, the order may be completely different at another time or another market.

Table 8.4.1 shows the results of the complete sensitivity analysis following six scenarios played for the wool-nylon case study. Playing the scenarios from wool's point of view, we measure effectiveness according to how much wool benefits.

Finally there is a way to assess the size of the advertising investment called for. An advertising campaign along the lines of "our product is good" impacts the product's attractiveness just as price dropping does. (Price can be quantitatively related to volume change via the price elasticity, see Appendix A.3). The costs that would have incurred from price dropping alone can thus be compared to those of an advertising campaign that would achieve the same result. Naturally, this assessment may result in an overestimate or an underestimate depending on how the advertising campaign in question rated to the "our-product-is-good" alternative in the sensitivity analysis. I would like to point out, however, that if we relied on price dropping alone for the survival of woolen carpets, their price would have to be dropped by more than 100% !

TABLE 8.4.1 SENSITIVITY ANALYSIS

MESSAGE	EFFECTIVENESS	WOOL	NYLON
Wool is good.	Highest	Slowly rising from '79 level	Little compromised
Wool is different from nylon.	High	Stabilizes at '79 level	Little compromised
You do not need nylon.	Medium	Stabilizes at 0.5 of '79 level	Huge loss of market
Nylon is bad.	Poor	Stabilizes at 0.3 of '79 level	Serious loss of market
Wool is better than nylon.	Negligible	Null	Temporary losses only
You need wool.	Null	No effect	No effect

The case of the Greek mobile-telephone market mentioned earlier—Figure 8.2.1—is more malleable. As we indicated, it was possible for Telestet to have anticipated its eventual loss of the leading position. Had its managers taken action in the beginning of 1996 toward increasing the attractiveness of their products by 10%—for example, by dropping prices by 8%—they would have safeguarded their lead. Of course, Panafon may have rapidly responded in kind, but this is what the business game is all about, and to a large extent, it can be successfully, and painlessly, simulated on your personal computer!

8.5 – CASE STUDIES

A Major European Beer Producer

In 2002 an independent consultant who had a project with a major European beer-producing firm asked me for help to understand the competitive dynamics in the beer market. His client, despite a dominant position in the market, had been progressively losing market share for ten years. It was again a case where the market leader had more than 50% market share, which rendered a Volterra-Lotka analysis of a duopoly—this manufacturer versus all others—appropriate.

Application of the classical approach based on Equations 8.1.1 yielded the picture shown at the top of Figure 8.5.2 with the determined parameters shown in Table 8.5.2.

The two negative competition coupling constants indicated pure competition of the type between two species vying for the same resource. The magnitude of the constants showed evidence for some competitive advantage by this producer who generally suffered almost half as much as all others from in this struggle. And that seemed to be the saving grace for this producer because its attractiveness (in part reflected by the price) was considerably smaller than that of all others. Even the virtual niche size, in the hypothetical case where each competitor would have been alone, was smaller for this producer. It was not surprising then that market share had been slowly moving from this producer to the others, a situation to become worse in the future according to the graph at the top of Figure 8.5.2. The crucial question for this producer at that time was how to best

TABLE 8.5.2 – THE SIX PARAMETERS OF THE VOLTERRA-LOTKA EQUATIONS

	Attractiveness	Niche size	Competition
This manufacturer	1.046	187	-1.33
All others	1.899	516	-2.50

manage the competition, in other words what marketing effort (in advertising and image building) would prove most effective.

A TWO-COMPETITOR MARKET

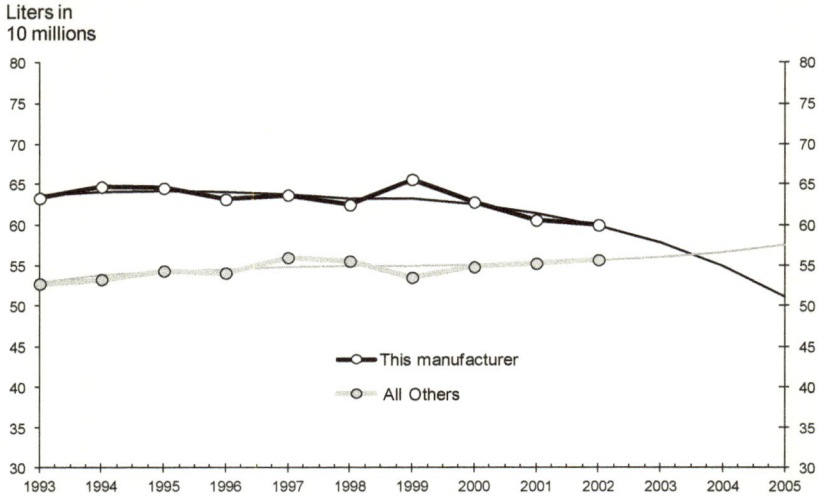

FOLLOWING 10% CHANGE TOWARD DIFFERENTIATION

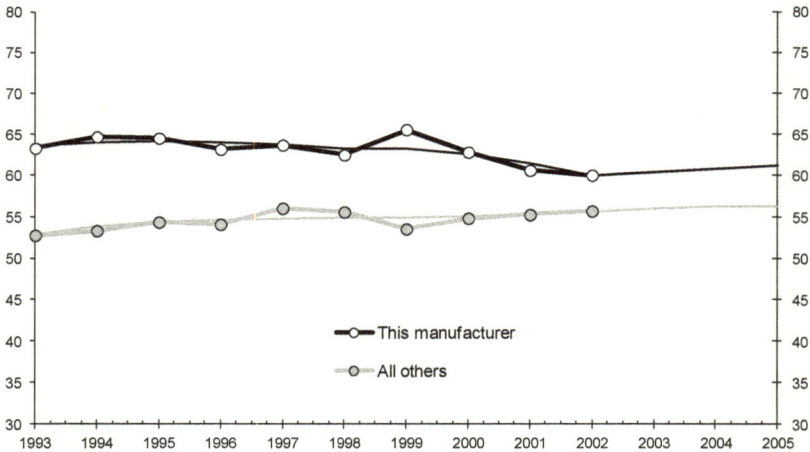

Figure 8.5.2   The Volterra-Lotka picture in 2002 (top) and a scenario for the future (bottom).

I played six scenarios each time changing one and only one of the six parameters in Table 8.5.2 by 10%. The biggest benefit was obtained for a 10% decrease in the absolute value of the coupling parameter representing the attacker's advantage (-1.33 in Table 8.5.2). Such action reflects a move toward differentiation via an advertising campaign along the lines "We are different", see Figure 8.4.1. As we see at the bottom of Figure 8.5.2 a campaign of this kind and magnitude would change this producer's trajectory from a declining trend to a gently rising one. The complete scenario-playing analysis is summarized in Table 8.5.3.

TABLE 8.5.3 SENSITIVITY ANALYSIS FOR THIS BEER PRODUCER

MESSAGE	EFFECTIVENESS	THIS PRODUCER	ALL OTHERS
Ours is different	Highest	Slowly rising from '02 level	Slowly rising from '02 level
You need ours	High	Slowly declining from '02 level	Slowly rising from '02 level
Theirs is bad	Poor	Declining from '02 level	Serious decline from '02 level
Ours is better than theirs	Negligible	Serious decline from '02 level	Little decline from '02 level
You do not need theirs	Negligible	Serious decline from '02 level	Remains flat at '02 level
Ours is good	Negligible	Serious decline from '02 level	Rising from '02 level

Nobel Laureates

In Section 2.6 we looked at the competition for Nobel Prizes only among Americans. The assumption was that there is a limited resource, the total number of Nobel laureates that the US will ever claim. The implication was that this number is capped. In other words, there will be a time when all Nobel Prizes will be awarded to nationals from other countries. Up to that time, Americans will be elbowing each other to win prizes and the fewer left in their "niche" the harder it will be to win one. This reasoning gave rise to an S-curve for US Nobel awards.

But there is also competition between Americans and other nationalities and the Volterra-Lotka equations can take this into account. The niche in this case would be all Nobel Prizes awarded annually, not only the ones destined for Americans. To the extent that US Nobel laureates represent about half or more of all Nobel Prizes every year, it is a good approximation to consider a duopoly, that is, a niche with only two species: Americans and all others grouped together. The species "all others" is rather inhomogeneous but with US Nobel laureates and all Nobel laureates both being well defined as species candidates, "all others" also becomes a well-defined species candidate.

Because there were large fluctuations on the yearly data the numbers were grouped together inside time bins of decades before the analysis. Once again the six constants in Equations 8.1.1 were determined via a global fit minimizing a Chi Square as described in Section 10.1 (the detailed technicalities of how the fit was done are described in Section 10.4).

The fit was of acceptable quality (70% confidence level) and the results are graphed in Figure 8.5.3 and tabulated in Table 8.5.4. The American trajectory is S-shaped (but not logistic) and the long-term forecast is roughly a 50-50 split of all Nobel Prizes between Americans and all other nationalities.[13]

NOBEL LAUREATES PER DECADE

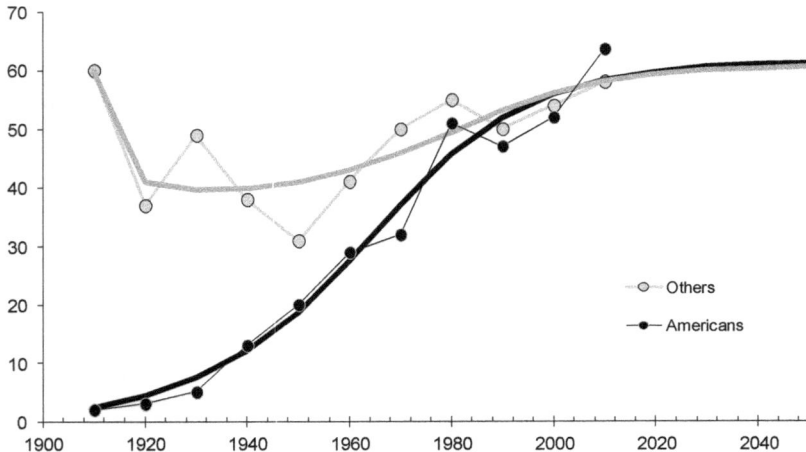

Figure 8.5.3 Decennial data points and solutions to the Volterra-Lotka equations (the last data points—awards for year 2010 not yet known—had been scaled up by 10/9). Despite its S-shaped form the black line is only *approximately* logistic.

TABLE 8.5.4 THE SIX PARAMETERS OF THE VOLTERRA-LOTKA EQUATIONS

	Attractiveness	Niche size	Competition
Americans	1.5	26	0.6
Others	1.7	37	0.4

Of particular interest are the values of the coupling constants. They are both positive indicating a win-win nature for this competition. In a symbiotic relationship each competitor benefits from the existence of the other, which is in line with the dynamics of scholarly research (each publication triggers more publications). But Americans benefit more when non-Americans win Nobel Prizes than vice versa. The ratio c_{xy} / c_{yx} is about 1.5 implying that one Nobel Prize won by a non-American will trigger 1.5 times more Nobel Prizes for Americans than the other way around. This is counteracted to some extent by the smaller attractiveness constant for Americans, which reflects the species' ability to multiply. If it is greater than 1, the species population grows; if it is less than 1, it declines. The values in Table 8.5.4 translate to attractiveness for Americans and all others of 1.5 and 1.7 respectively. This indicates that each American Nobel laureate generally "broods" 1.5 new American Nobel winners whereas for all others this number is 1.7.

All in all, the number of American Nobel Laureates in the long run should stabilize around an average of 61.4 per decade barely higher than 60.6 for all others.

Interestingly the US trajectory turned out S-shaped, which suggests that a logistic fit could have been a reasonable approximation but not for the cumulative numbers. The fit should have been on the numbers per unit of time. The limiting resource in this case would have been the annual number of American laureates. This number was zero at the turn of the 20th century and progressively grew to 8 by 2009 (6.4 on the average during the last 9 years). The meaning of competition in this picture would be that Americans elbow each other every year for one of their "quota" prizes that grew along an S-curve and in the 21st century reached a ceiling of 6.1.

The forecasts for American Nobel laureates from the Volterra-Lotka approach are comparable to the number of Nobel laureates won by all other nationalities together. But the fitted parameters gave rise to some interesting insights. The competition between Americans and all others for Nobel Prizes is of the win-win type. Locked in a symbiotic relationship both sides are winning but Americans are profiting more by 50%. At the same time, the ability of Nobel laureates to "multiply", i.e. the extent to which a Nobel laureate incubates more laureates, is lower for Americans than it is for other nationalities. One may ponder whether the roots of this last observation have something to do with the fact that chauvinistic traits tend to be more endemic in cultures with longer traditions.

All conclusions need to be interpreted within the uncertainties involved. Confidence levels of 70% indicate that there is 7 out of 10 chances that the Volterra-Lotka description is the right way to analyze this competition, not very different from the S-curve fits in Section 2.6. For the intermediate future—ten to twenty years—the logistic normalized to reasonable population projections would result in forecasts compatible with those of the Volterra-Lotka approach. Still, I would favor Volterra-Lotka because it addresses a more general type of competition. In any case, very long-term forecasts cannot be reliable and the whole exercise must be repeated with updated data sets in a couple of decades, by which time it may be appropriate to consider more than just two players.

IN CLOSING

The S-curve model enhanced with two-species interactions, as presented above, accounts for the three most fundamental factors that shape growth: the attractiveness of one's offering, the size of its market niche, and the interaction with the other competitor, (in cases where there is more than one competitor, one can often reduce the situation to a two-player picture by considering the major competitor only, or by grouping all others together). Naturally, there are other factors that influence growth, such as channels, distribution, market fragmentation, total market growth, market share, frequency of innovations, productivity in the ranks, and organizational and human-resource issues. Many of them can be expressed as combinations of the three fundamental ones. Alternatively, one could envisage elaborations of the model—adding more parameters—to take more phenomena into account.

As it stands, the model provides the base line, the trend on top of which other higher-order effects will be superimposed. It guides you through effective "genetic" manipulations of the competitive roles in the marketplace. It should be used as a front end to what is usually done. The model works equally well for products, for corporations, for technologies, or for whole industries. Only the time scales differ. The pleasure is all the strategist's, who now has a quantitative, science-based way to understand the crux of the competitive dynamics and to anticipate the consequences of possible actions.

Logistic S-curves are special cases of solutions to the Volterra-Lotka system of equations. The Volterra-Lotka Equations 8.1.1 reduce to the logistic Equation 2.2.1 whenever the coupling constants c_{ij} become zero.

Whereas logistic growth describes competition only among the members of one species, the Volterra-Lotka system of equations handles competition also with other species. It is advisable then to consult the Volterra-Lotka approach—whenever possible—even if one is interested only in logistic growth because it can shed light on how to apply the logistic-growth equation. In the US Nobel-laureates study the Volterra-Lotka solution dictated that a logistic S-curve should have been fitted on the annual numbers and not on cumulative numbers. Had we done so in Section 2.6 we would have obtained an answer very close to the black S-shaped curve of Figure 8.5.3.

Deciding whether to fit S-curves on cumulative or on per-unit-of-time data is a crucial first step for all logistic-growth applications and constitutes treacherous terrain for inexperienced S-curve enthusiasts. I myself mastered it only later in my career.[14]

PART TWO:
METHODS AND TOOLS

9 – COMPLETING THE PANOPLY

Oedipus became king of Thebes, according to the ancient Greek tragedy, by resolving the long-standing riddle "Which unique being walks at times on two, at times on three, at times on four legs, and is weaker the more legs he walks on?" see Figure 9.1. To set a winning strategy we need to answer a somewhat-related question: "Where are we on the curve?" The time frame can vary. If it is decades, we are probably addressing a whole life, or a company's existence from beginning to end. If it is years or months, we may be concerned with a product's life cycle, or a business season, and there will be many of them before the company or the technology ceases to exist. Knowledge of the position on the curve is of primordial importance. It is also a prerequisite for all strategy setting because strategies depend crucially on this position. For these reasons we have developed a software package at Growth Dynamics *Where Are You on the Curve and What to Do about It* that determines this position in six different ways ranging from the simplest to the most sophisticated one. Knowing this position, strategies can then be set according to the seasons metaphor discussed in Chapter 3.

WHERE ARE YOU ON THE CURVE?

Figure 9.1 A visual representation of the riddle the sphinx put to Oedipus.

9.1 – WHERE ARE YOU ON THE CURVE

Wishful thinking is a strategist's worst enemy because belief projection becomes the main determinant of most strategies. Long-range planning sessions often turn into battles of opinion where the need arises for objective science-based tools like *Where Are You on the Curve and What to Do about It*.

The simplest way to establish one's position on the curve is to ask his or her opinion on the matter. Naïve as this proposition may sound it should not be hastily discarded because these people are knowledgeable, if biased. I generally begin a positioning session with strategists by drawing a large S-curve on the flipchart and asking each one to indicate with a dot where he/she thinks we presently are. (If I notice uneasiness or excessive difficulty in the participants' decision-making process, I offer them a downward-pointing S-curve as an alternative). This pin-the-tail-on-the-donkey exercise is carried out openly with everyone watching. Arguments have been made in favor of a blind procedure where each participant places the dot in private. But I found that allowing them to influence each other triggers fruitful discussions, averages out some of the biases, and broadens the scope of the collective vision.

There is a valuable byproduct in the above exercise. The participants are also asked to estimate the timeframe of the overall growth process. Even if imprecise, such an estimate is an indispensable ingredient for the next way to establish one's position on the curve, namely the questionnaire based on the S-curve's second derivative described in Section 3.5. In answering the question "What are the prospects for the future?" the participants are expected to make comparisons with last season the length of which can vary considerably. The length of a product's season—five or ten years—is much shorter than the length of a company's season—ten or fifty years. For the growth process under discussion in my strategy session the season length is approximated with $1/5$ the time span between the 1% (nominal beginning) and the 99% (nominal end) penetration levels of the S-curve drawn on the flipchart (i.e. four seasons but two winters).

The above two determinations of the position on the curve permit a first check for consistency, the greater the agreement the higher our confidence. If the agreement is not good, we retain the second more reliable result whose precision is by construction half a season. But there is increased uncertainty, the more so the greater the discrepancy of the two methods. This positioning and the estimate of the overall time span will serve as inputs to the next more sophisticated way to determine the position on the curve described below.

Using Data from Company Records and Annual Reports

By the time we enter STRATEST1.xls, the EXCEL-based part of the software, we need to have consensus as to our positioning on the curve so far. If the participants disagree significantly with the position already determined and cannot all agree on a new different position (half-season alternative choices are offered by the program at this time), we must invoke the third method, a quantitative record-based determination of the position. In so doing elements from the second method above—based on the S-curve's second derivative—will now be applied in a quantitative and more objective way using data from company records and/or annual reports as well as educated guesses by the participant. This step furnishes precise determinations—if not necessarily accurate—of the position and the season length, which take precedence over previous values. For the sake of simplicity the program suggests to skip this step the first time around, but it should be done at some later time as it provides another answer and thus offers one more consistency check. This step becomes indispensable if our S-curve on our flipchart early on was an upside-down one.

The approach has been coded into a flow chart questionnaire asking about the company's (or the product's) growth as a function of time and is particularly suitable for growth processes that span many years, such as companies, technologies, and careers; if you chose it, you will be asked to quantify recent growth. The red section of the flow chart relates to the rare negative growth process depicted by a downward-pointing S-curve. Give your answers in years (use decimals). If the overall timeframe of the growth process is much smaller than a few years, you should understand "time units" in the place of "years", where the length of a "time unit" corresponds to that of a "season". If the process is of a large timeframe (say more than 20 years from 1% to 99%), then it is recommended that decades be used.

Following three numerical inputs the program returns the graph of an S-curve and the corresponding life cycle indicating where present resides on each. The flow chart, shown in Figure 9.1.1, begins by asking whether there has been growth or decline following which the paths shown in Figure 9.1.1a or in Figure 9.1.1b are chosen.

The two examples shown in Figures 9.1.1a and 9.1.1b give rise to the S-curves and the life cycles shown in Figures 9.1.2a and 9.1.2b respectively. The participant had to estimate the near-future evolution of the growth pattern, e.g. in how long for the midpoint of the growth process to be reached, and that is usually where the major part of the uncertainty comes from.

The seasons are delimited (but not labeled) in Figures 9.1.2. The present position is Early Summer in the example of Figure 9.1.1a and

Early *Negative* Summer in the example of Figure 9.1.1b, both indicated by black square dots. The season length is calculated as 1.4 years in both examples and is shown on top of Figures 9.1.2.

The participants may want to look at the graph and consult the strategy advice before proceeding with the questionnaire. This would be the case whenever a quick answer is needed. The questionnaire requires at least half an hour to fill out, but for several participants and taking into account the discussion that will be invariably triggered by the results, one can reasonably expect this exercise to last the better part of half a day.

Still, there is merit, particularly if the graphs in Figure 9.1.2 look reasonable, to have the participants go into the questionnaire without first looking at the graphs and thus become overly influenced by the precise determination of the position in the season. This would be the case whenever there is interest in evaluating the participants' intellectual versus emotional judgment (see next section).

The flow chart in Figure 9.1.1b also allows for the rare possibilty where neither growth nor decline has been recently witnessed. In all cases the participant is asked to provide estimates on how things will evolve in the future. At this point we must remember that the top questions in the flow chart (is there growth, decline, or no change) refer to last season the length of which was determined in the earlier stages of the exercise. However, the flow chart entries will yield a new more precise position in the season (the one indicated in Figure 9.1.2 with a square dot) the length of which is displayed at the top of the worksheet.

So far the position on the curve has been estimated via a combination of three different methods: pin the tail on the donkey, optimism/pessimism based on the 2nd derivative, and using company data and personal judgment. It is time to pause and digest the result. The participants should reach consensus or otherwise they should reiterate. In case of irreconcilable disagreements, they can always vote on which half season they believe they are in. One way or another it is essential to enter the questionnaire with a definite position on the curve. The more questionable the accuracy of this position, the higher the questionnaire's added value. After all the questionnaire brings two more ways of establishing where we are on the curve.

Alternatively, the questionnaire can serve as a tool for measuring and monitoring strategic performance. If the first three methods have established a rather coherent picture and there is little doubt where we are on the curve, the questionnaire will provide an excellent quantitative metric for the accuracy of the participants' rational judgment as well as the soundness of their instinct. This is done via judiciously chosen questions that exploit the seasonal attributes discussed in Chapter 3.

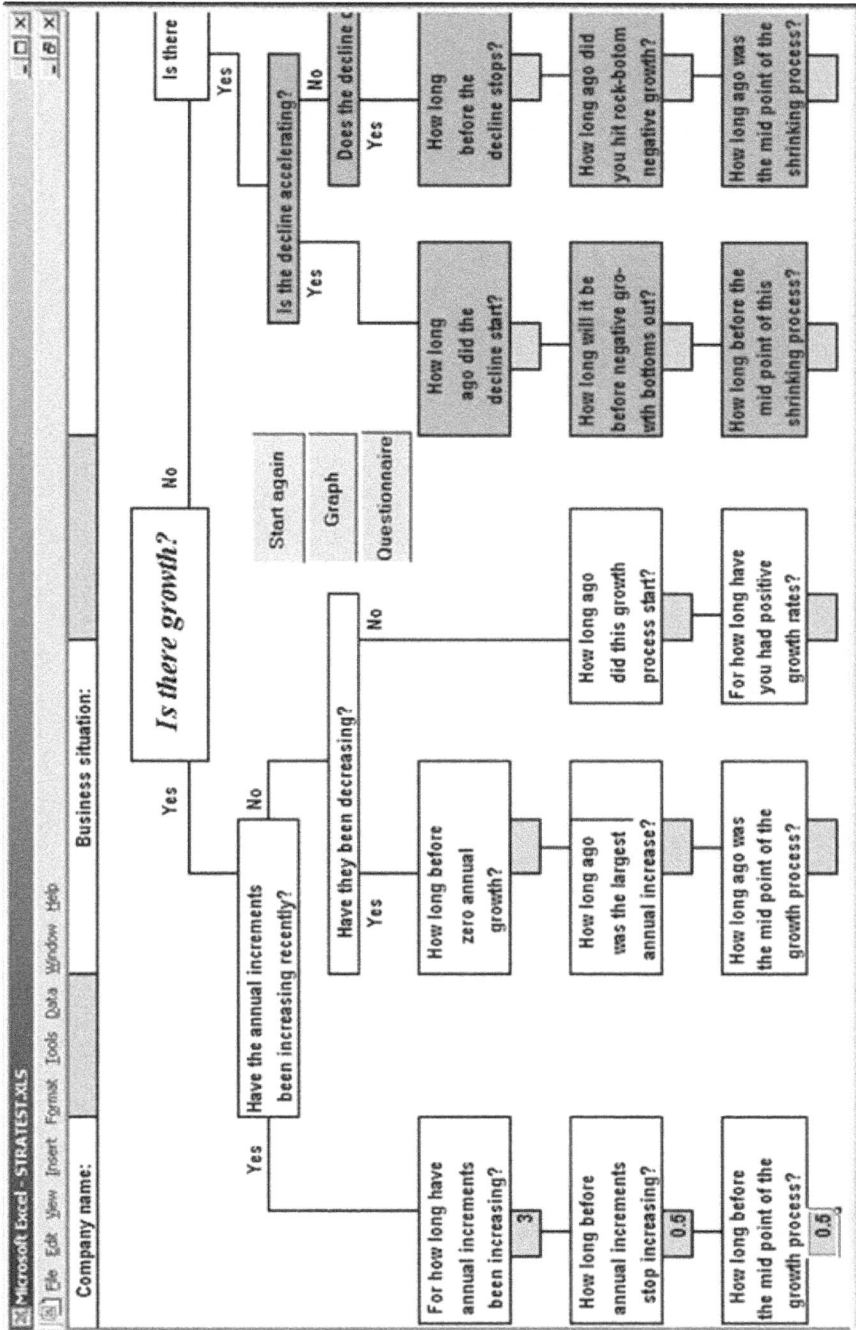

Figure 9.1.1a A flowchart example showing growth.

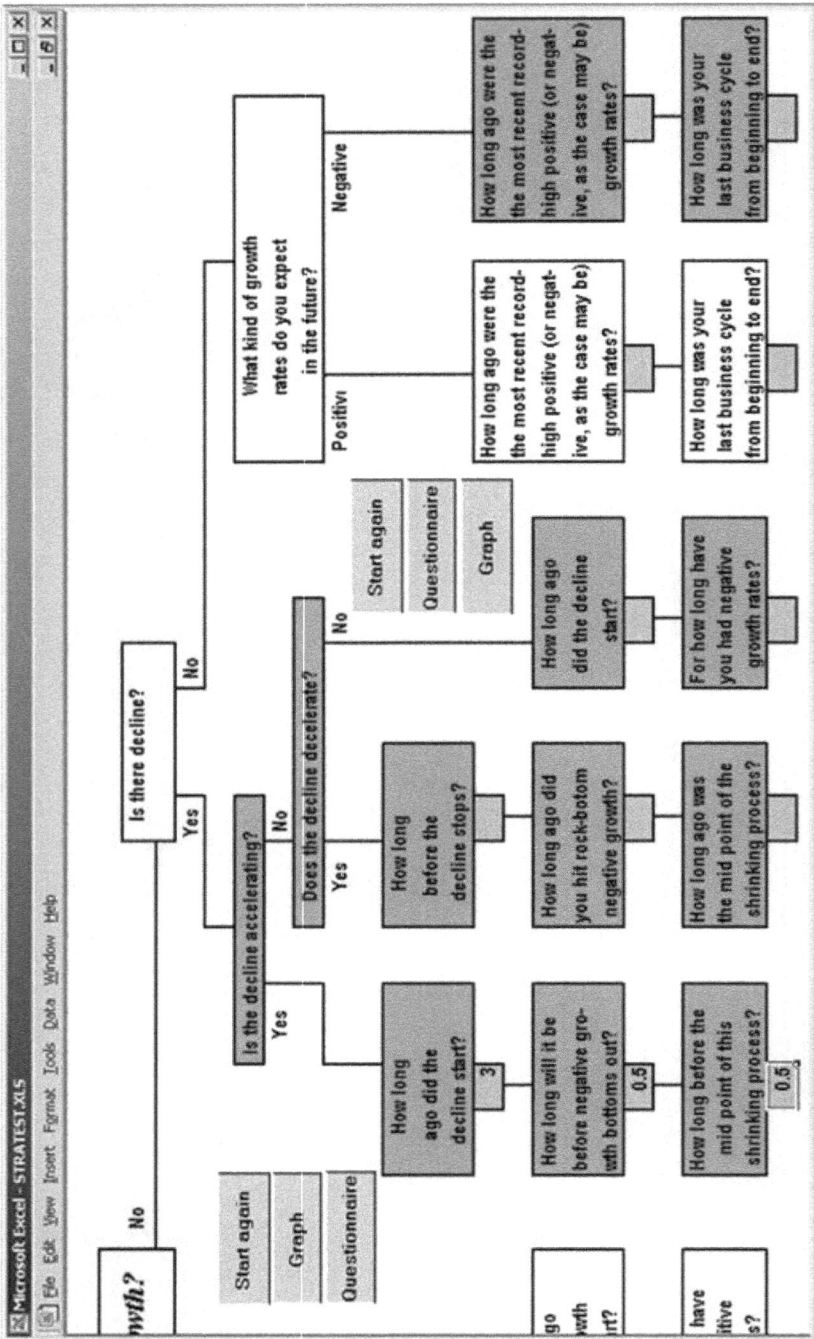

Figure 9.1.1b A flowchart example showing decline and the part of the flow chart for the rare neither-growth-nor-decline case.

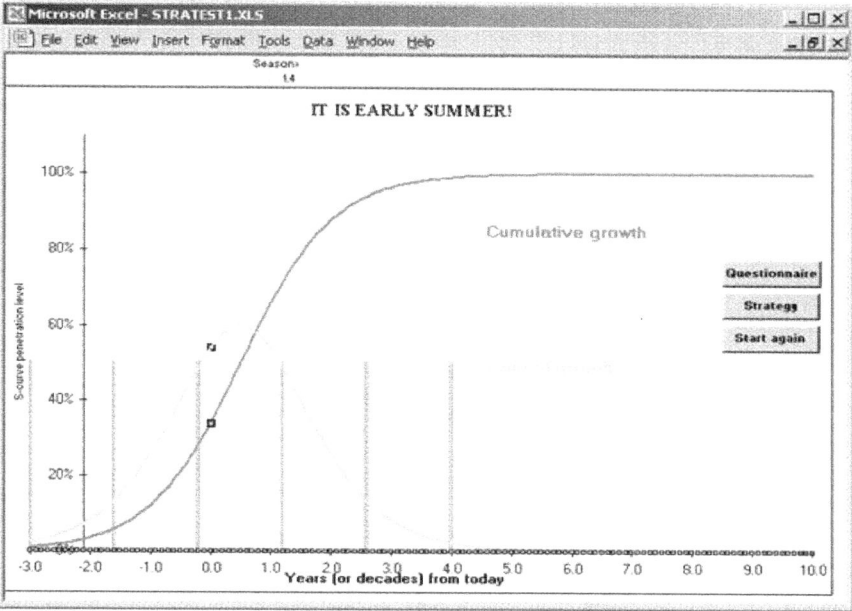

Figure 9.1.2a The S-curve and life cycle corresponding to Figure 9.1.1a.

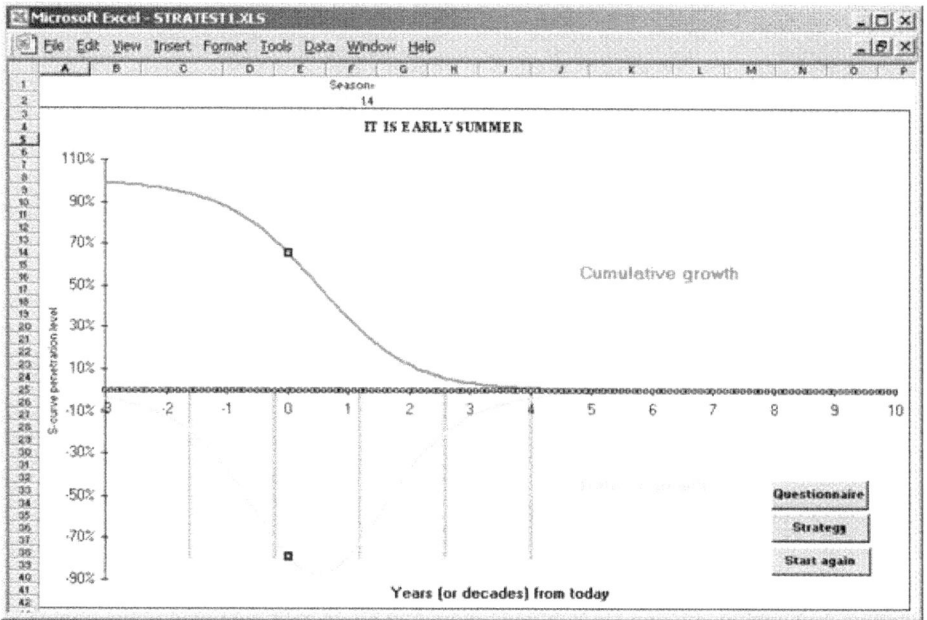

Figure 9.1.2b The S-curve and life cycle corresponding to Figure 9.1.1b (a negative season).

9.2 – INSTINCT VERSUS RATIONALE

Companies that find themselves in a business winter are frustrated, not knowing if and when they will come out of it, while other companies that may look good on paper (profitable, on budget, and with great balance sheets) may suddenly be seen to stumble upon a strategic catastrophe and collapse spectacularly and unexpectedly. In such cases strategic management is becoming overshadowed by a cloud of uncertainty and confusion. Strategic performance enjoys success that is seasonal. There are times when effective optimization demands that leaders step back, relinquish power, and delegate decision making.

Strategic performance measurement has not been the object of rigorous study. The profit impact of market strategy (PIMS) data base has produced many good observations on strategies that had good results, in general operational terms.[1] But although many tools have been devised and put in place for measuring and monitoring the performance and productivity of the middle and lower ranks, CEOs and Managing Directors are still being measured in a nonsystematic way. Erratic board reviews and stockholder judgment often come too late and, like tidal waves, sweep dynasties away overnight.

We saw in Chapter 3 that each season requires particular behavioral patterns for success. These patterns combined with understanding time frames and life-cycle positions offer mechanisms for measuring strategic performance. The approach consists of checking quantitatively whether the leadership is in harmony with the "spirit of the times". Furthermore, since many seasonal attributes refer to qualitative or emotional (that is, instinctive) appreciation of the situation, the approach allows us to evaluate a leader's performance in terms of his or her intuitive understanding of the situation.

Here is an example of the type of questions that can be asked:

BUSINESS	INTUITION
Your pricing policy is: a) Cost-based b) Value-based c) Arbitrary (decadent profits) d) Customer-driven (potentially unprofitable)	If your division were likened to a play, it would be: a) A romance b) A comedy c) A tragedy d) A satire

Let us say that we want to check the strategic performance of a man who is chief executive of a company's manufacturing division. We ask him to answer two multiple-choice questionnaires, one concerning his intuitive understanding, and another one concerning his business practices. He can mark more than one choice by specifying different weights according to his priorities. If his pricing is value-based and the CEO likens his division to a tragedy, he is doing something wrong. Either his instinct or his pricing is inappropriate. Tragedy corresponds to the fall season, when the correct pricing policy is cost-based. Value-based pricing schemes are appropriate in spring, which is likened to a romance.

The CEO's answers will then be gauged against the quantitative estimate of the position in the life cycle, obtained via the three methods described earlier. If the position turns out to be halfway between summer and fall, our manager gets 75 percent for intuition and only 25 percent for rationale on the basis of his answers to these two sample questions. The perennial argument of whether instinct or rationale is best for business can thus be answered for a particular individual in a particular situation.

The software package *Where Are You on the Curve and what to Do about It* uses dozens of questions to probe rationale and instinct. Most of these questions are shown in Figure 9.2.1 (those concerning rationale in Figure 9.2.1a and those concerning instinct in Figure 9.2.1b). In the example of the figures, the participant gets a grade of 96.1% for intuition and 91.8% for rationale. It is obvious why the estimate of the life-cycle position plays a key role in this approach.

I have used this approach with high-level executives on several occasions. My experience has produced one unexpected result. Although it is not possible to establish unquestionably superior performance of instinct over rationale or vice versa, the variance seems to be systematically biased. It appears that emotions more than reason are prone to erratic fluctuations. Specifically, I found that for the number of executives tested, rational and intuitive performance varied, with sometimes one and sometimes the other performing better. But in all cases, the spread among the intuitive questions was larger than the spread among the rational questions. If this result is significant, it means that instinct, even if it is at times more reliable (better average grade), is fundamentally a cruder instrument of judgment. This observation makes sense. Knowledgeable executives are likely to be coherent in their judgment, which may be subject to common wishful-thinking bias. Their gut feeling can be less biased, but will spread more from question to question.

An evaluation of instinctive versus rational strategic performance is not necessarily a determination of a genetic or life-long characteristic. Rationale, like instinct, can have good or bad days.

Of course, there are individuals who have more of an instinctive gift than others, and there are situations that call for more intuition than thinking. Thus it is useful to monitor the performance of one's instinct and rationale from case to case and from time to time through the questionnaires of Figure 9.2.1a and 9.2.1b. The multiple-choice answers permit more than one entries with different weights; 4 is the highest priority, 1 the lowest, and the same priority cannot be assigned twice.

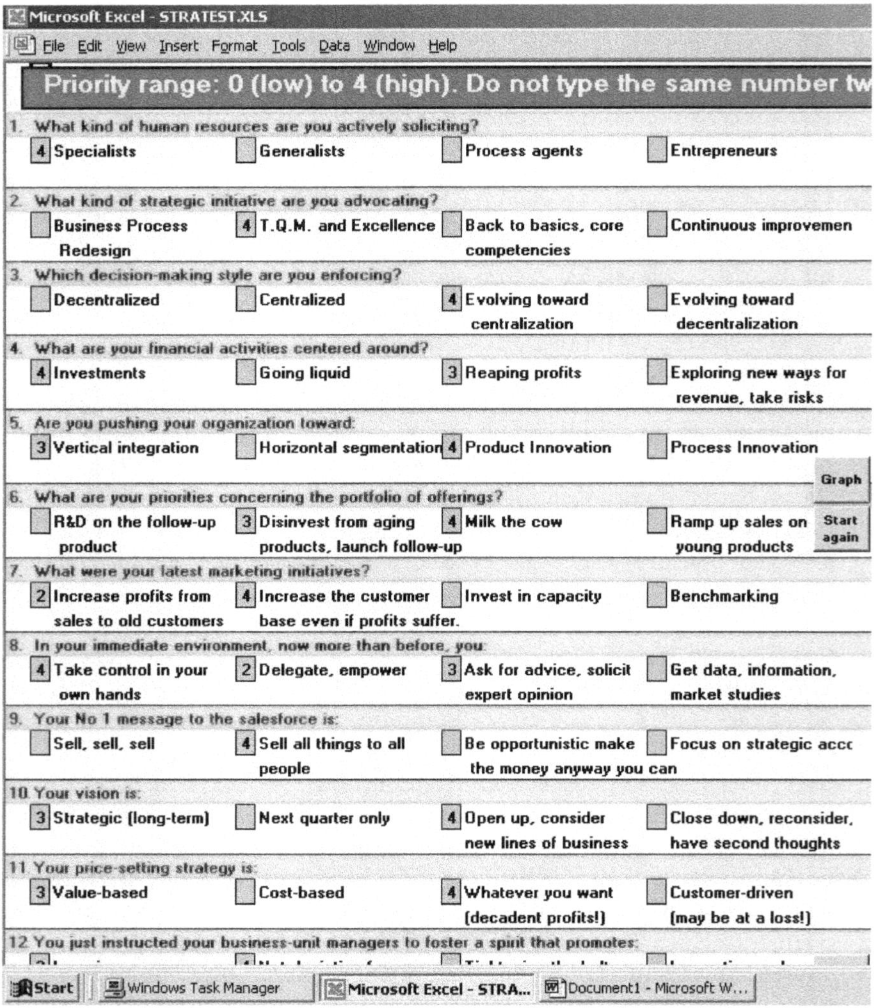

Figure 9.2.1a Sample answers to questions addressing one's rationale.

Microsoft Excel - STRATEST.XLS

File   Edit   View   Insert   Format   Tools   Data   Window   Help

1. What is your main concern these days?   Start again

| | Survival | 4 | Fun & games | | Sobering up | 3 | Keep up the pace of good progress |

2. What characterizes best your environment right now?

| | Chaos | 3 | Order, clockwork operations | 4 | Hard work | | Loss of market share |

3. What kind of knowledge do you feel is needed the most?

| 3 | In-depth (specialized) | 4 | In-breadth, applicable horizontally | | From text books, libraries, academia | | Innovative cross-discipline solutions |

4. Is your business at present going through

| 4 | A boom | | A recession | | A depression | 2 | Growth opportunities |

5. You believe that at this time, the key to success is

| | Efficiency | | Wise wastefulness | 3 | Innovation, change | 4 | Excellence |

6. Where are you looking at   Graph

| 3 | Ahead of you | 4 | Far ahead | | Right and left | | At others |

Start again

7. If you were in a play, would it be a

| 4 | Comedy | 3 | Romance | | Satire | | Tragedy |

8. Are you preoccupied with

| | WHAT to do | 3 | HOW to do it | | WHY are you doing what you are doing | 4 | Try to keep things from changing |

9. Your work makes you empathize (best identify) with the role of

| | A composer (music) | 4 | A performing artist | 3 | An administrator | | A philosopher |

10. What best describes your situation

| 4 | You have what you want | | You do not have what you want | | You have what you do not want | | You do not have what you do not want |

11. What are the feelings which prevail with you these days?

| 3 | Hope, excitement, elation | | Frustration, anxiety, confusion | | Blame, denial, panic | 4 | Comfort, boredom, decadence |

Graph

12. Do you think the time is right for   Start again

| | Learning | | Teaching | 4 | Enjoying | 3 | Experimenting |

13. Picture your business situation as being in a couple. What would best describe your at present situation?

Start | Windows Task Manager | Microsoft Excel - STRA...   Document1 - Microsoft W...

Figure 9.2.1b Sample answers to questions addressing one's instinct.

The typed answers produce two clouds of points in the graph with the S-curve (turquoise for intellect, purple for instinct). These clouds may spread across more than one season. An average for each cloud is calculated and indicated by a point with black outline. The position of the two averages relative to the previously established position on the S-curve translates to performance ratings, which are higher the greater the agreement. In the examples of Figures 9.1.1 - 9.2.2 the respective ratings are 96.1% for instinct and 91.8% for rationale. As is often the case, intuition gives a more accurate answer. What is not typical in this example is that the spread of the rationale points is larger than that the spread of the intuitive points. As a rule, it is the other way around, namely the spread of the rational points is smaller. Businesspersons display a general knowhow when making business decisions, even if their opinions are biased by the very targets they set for themselves. Their intuition, however, is less biased on the average.

Decision-support tools like *Where Are You on the Curve and What to Do about It* are particularly helpful during stressful times, when the instinct may be affected more than the intellect and the need for objectivity becomes more crucial.

RATING INTUITION AND RATIONALE

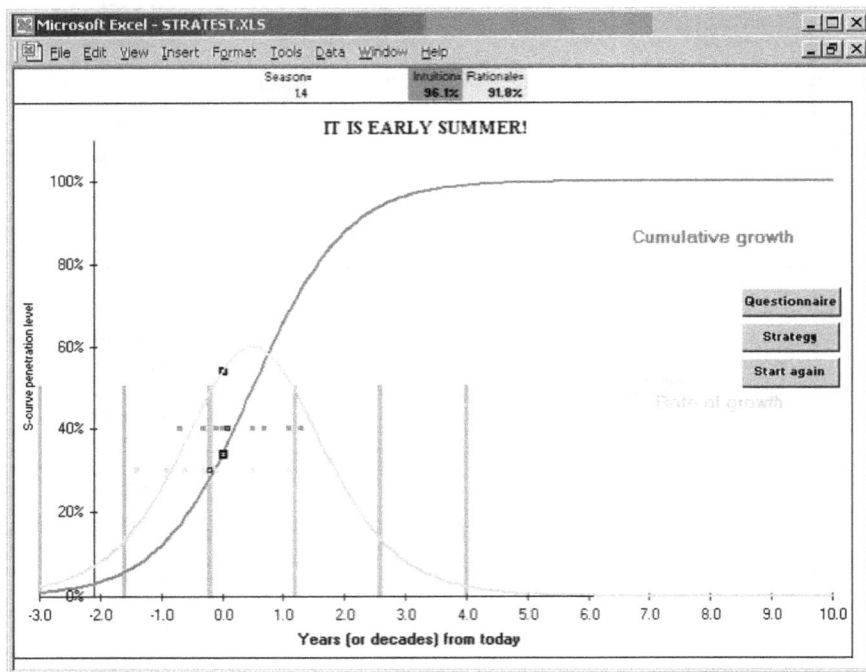

Figure 9.2.2 The curves of Figure 9.1.1a with the answers of Figure 9.2.1. The turquoise points (lower cloud) reflect the answers of Figure 9.2.1a; the purple points (upper cloud) reflect the answers of Figure 9.2.1b. The points outlined with black indicate the respective averages. The distance of these averages from the position on the curve (big black square points) determine the performance measures highlighted in purple and blue at the top of the worksheet.

9.3 – COULD YOU TAKE AIM AT AN APPLE ON YOUR SON'S HEAD?

Successful businesspersons, especially those making head-lines, take pride in claiming that "it is all in the guts". They rarely admit the value in the know-how transmitted through an MBA. Successful entrepreneurs have rarely been heard to give credit to their university professors as many renowned professionals in the arts and the sciences do. Most often credit for business success goes to some popular, folkloric, street-wise education gained outside schools, or to some genetic heritage.

Instinctive performance can carry one a long way, particularly during prosperous times when conditions permit one to "dance" one's way through good business decisions. The difficulties show up during economic recessions, when markets start saturating, competition becomes cutthroat, and the game changes from prosperity to survival. As in the performances of musicians and acrobats, heavy psychological stress results in insecurity, panic, and mistakes. William Tell may have been the rare exception, daring to take aim at the apple on his son's head. Most good archers would tremble too much under the stress of what was at stake.

Stress is quite evident among the executives who claim, "We had no difficulty positioning our products back when business was booming, but now the issue has acquired crucial importance. How can we be sure we are not making a mistake?" They are simply expressing their need for systematic guidelines in order to continue doing what they had been doing, apparently by instinct. Are there such guidelines? How does one obtain them?

Averaging the opinion of experts is one frequently used technique. This exercise can be greatly improved with interactive software tools, such as the modified BCG graph described in Chapter 6. But it remains subject to collective biases, inasmuch as the experts all belong to the same company or industry (unavoidable if they are supposed to be experts.)

The seasons metaphor, presented in Chapter 3 and discussed in more length in *Conquering Uncertainty*, can provide strategy guidelines following an accurate positioning on the curve.[2] Essential strategy elements have been hard-coded into the software package *Where are you on the Curve and What to Do about It* and will be obtained when the user hits the Strategy button in the worksheet depicted in Figures 9.1.2 and 9.2.2. They are reproduced below.

9.4 - STRATEGY ADVICE DEPENDING ON THE POSITION IN THE SEASON

As given in the software package from Growth Dynamics *Where are you on the Curve and What to Do about It*. For a more extensive discussion see *Conquering Uncertainty*.[3]

Season of Summer:
Advantage: High profits   **Disadvantage:** Low creativity

Summer is a season of order and profitability. The system becomes centralized and conservative. Good leaders are in demand and enjoy stability. Strategies become long-term. Process agents are also in demand. Conveniently, many of the specialists have naturally evolved into bureaucrats.

Early Summer:
Expand market share. This is the time for vertical integration: Sell all things to all people! But the good days will not last forever. Think of the approaching turning point.

Late Summer:
You are at the turning point! Cash cows are getting old. Competition is progressively becoming felt more seriously. You must plan for diminishing growth.

Season of Fall:
Advantage: Bearing fruit   **Disadvantage:** Aging

The hallmarks of this season are: denial, blame, and panic, in that order. Operations should become cost-driven. It is also the moment to launch the replacement product. It is a season of aging but also fruit bearing; a season to teach what you have learned. Cross-disciplinary generalists must be recruited to devise ideas for profitable new business. Buzz words include: Benchmarking, productivity, core competencies, back to basics.

Early Fall:
Sober up and tighten the belt. Do productivity and benchmarking studies to find out what you are not doing quite right.

Late Fall:
Cost-cutting and face-lifting operations are no longer effective. Consider redesigning your processes. Begin searching for entrepreneurs.

Season of Winter:

Advantage: New ideas   **Disadvantage:** Low profits

It is the hardest but also the most fertile season. It is time of chaos, innovation, and fundamental change. A turbulent bottom-up period when leaders fall and new directions are set. The company becomes segmented, decentralized, and horizontal. Fashionable buzz words are: empowerment, culture, change management, business process redesign (BPR), strategic business units (SBUs), niche markets. Strategies become short-term. Concerning human resources, bureaucrats are being exterminated and the rest of the workforce trained and re-skilled toward entrepreneurship and opportunism. Prices are market-dictated; survival is at stake. Death comes naturally in winter but it doesn't have to be this winter!

Early Winter:

This is time for entrepreneurship, and risk-taking. Encourage new ways of thinking and new lines of business. The more new initiatives, the better.

Late Winter:

This is the time of selection. Most of the "mutational" new ideas will die; only a few—the fittest—will survive.

Season of Spring:

Advantage: Excitement   **Disadvantage:** High investments

Spring is a season of hard work and continuous improvement. It is also a time of learning and investments. The recommended human resources are specialists, engineers, designers, men and women who resemble well-hardened and sharpened tools. The organization progressively abandons the decentralized, horizontal, entrepreneurial model, and moves toward a more vertical structure. Prices like operations in general are value-driven.

Early Spring:

Chaotic fluctuations slowly come to an end. This is the time to decide which one of the several "mutations" in process is the one that will become the workhorse for the next growth phase.

Late Spring:

Competition is relatively low and there is no more chaos. You should begin the search for (or development of) leaders in anticipation of the upcoming summer.

Season of Negative Summer:

In most respects it resembles an ordinary Summer. The system becomes centralized and disciplined. Stove-pipe operations come back into fashion. Good leadership is highly sought after. Process agents are also in demand. You have taken control in your own hands and are now in the process of getting rid of what you do not want. Buzz words include: new image, restructuring, vision, excellence, and rebirth. On the product side:

- Kill loser products
- Sell only what you are strong in
- Try to increase profits from the existing client base

Early Part:
Design the company's new image. Despite the hardship, your vision should be long-term. You act dictatorially, like a political leader during a national emergency.

Late Part:
Advertising become a key way to communicate your new image. It is high time to start paying attention to products again.

Season of Negative Fall:

In many ways it resembles an ordinary Spring. It is a period of continuous improvement, hard work, learning, and investments. You are trying to reassure everyone and get back to normal. A certain wise wastefulness is permitted. On the product side:

- Product innovation
- Value-based pricing
- Launch new products

Early Part:
You are at the turning point. Centralization is weakening. The aim changes from **restructuring** to **constructing**.

Late Part:
You are evolving toward a decentralized structure. Recruit generalists. The dark days are coming to an end. You are in a position to teach what you have learned.

Season of Negative Winter:

In many respects it resembles an ordinary Winter. It is a time of turbulence, innovation, and entrepreneurship. The organization becomes decentralized, segmented and horizontal. Fashionable buzz words are:

empowerment, culture-driven, BPR, SBUs, niche markets. Strategies become short-term. The workforce is being retrained and re-skilled. On the product side:

- Prices are customer-driven (may be at a loss)
- Promote recently launched products
- Opportunistic sales force

Early Part:
Encourage risk taking, new ways of thinking and new lines of business. The more new initiatives, the better. Concentrate on increasing the customer base, even if profits suffer.

Late Part:
Now is the time to choose among the new directions set or proposed. A key criterion is which one will have gone beyond infant mortality by the end of this season?

Season of Negative Spring:
   In many ways it resembles an ordinary Fall. The season is characterized by a negative *and* declining growth rate. You are stuck with a situation you do not want. You must transform the organization and change its mindset. You ask for information, data, studies on how others have done it. Cutting costs has become a fact of life. Processes are under examination. Buzz words include: back to basics, strategic accounts, core competencies. Concerning products:

- Improve productivity & efficiency of operations on phasing-out products
- Set prices according to costs
- Do R&D on follow-up products

Early Part:
It is not clear what must be done, but it is clear that it must be big. The organization progressively abandons the decentralized entrepreneurial model with SBUs.

Late Part:
Major reductions become inevitable (e.g. a factor of 2 on the number of employees?) You hire or subcontract specialists to help you do this. You are evolving toward a centralized structure.

IN CLOSING

So far we have seen in this chapter five different ways of determining where we are on the S-curve. It goes without saying that these five ways can be confronted and contrasted with one another. Whenever, and to the extent that there is agreement, we can raise questions concerning the validity of the method that disagrees. We may question, for example, our very first spontaneous answer while pinning the tail on the donkey. Or we may now have a reason to distrust our instinctive or our rational decision-making as the case may be. Accordingly we can pass judgment on strategic-management decisions whether they were based on rational or gut feeling.

Finally, there is a sixth way to estimate our position on the curve quantitatively by fitting an S-curve on historical data be it on sales of units, on revenue turnover, on the evolution of the number of employees, or some other performance metric documented as a function of time. How to do this in detail is described explicitly in Section 10.2 later on.

We may not always have access to all six methods of finding our position on the curve. For some situations data may not exist or it may prove too difficult to get the executive team together for half a day to run the workshop using *Where Are You on the Curve and What to Do about It*. In any case, the consultant should strive to get as many as possible alternative estimations of the position on the curve before tackling the question of setting strategy.

9.5 – CASE STUDIES

The case studies discussed below have been selected because they employ the panoply of tools and methods presented in this book. On each case I recount my engagement from the very beginning as it exemplifies different ways the subject of S-curves can enter the world of business.

Appleton Papers

Three years following the publication of my first book *Predictions* I received a long email from Ken H. a manager of Appleton Papers in Appleton, Wisconsin. After explaining to me how much he was impressed with the book, he proceeded to ask me a dozen detailed technical questions on how to fit S-curves on his company's data. I responded saying that I would be glad to tackle his questions one by one, but that this is what I did for living and that there would be charges. Without hesitation he offered to hire me for two weeks to go and work together with his group on their premises toward answering some of their burning questions.

Appleton, Wisconsin is a small remote Midwestern town, shockingly different from the image of America portrayed by large cities on the east and west coast of the country. My trip from Geneva involved three progressively smaller airplanes and brought me to a flat sparsely populated countryside. Appleton Papers is a major paper manufacturer and an effective *raison d'être* for the town, providing employment and influencing the town's population and culture. For example, my hotel was bustling with activity at 6:00 am while the favorite tease among Appleton employees, some of whom get to work as early as 4:30 am, is "It was me who turned on the lights in your office this morning!"

Appleton Papers produces paper in general but in particular it had been the world's largest manufacturer of carbonless copy paper. This is a multi-part form paper system coated to transmit images from one ply to subsequent plies, with manual or mechanical pressure, without using carbon paper. Carbonless copy paper can be used to create a multitude of multi-part forms, such as: production orders, expense reports, packing slips, credit-card payments, purchase requisitions, medical forms, delivery receipts, parking tickets, and the like. But all these uses have progressively seen the replacement of carbonless copy paper with alternatives such as Xerox, Fax, computer printing, or purely-electronic data storage. Appleton Papers saw sales of their cash-cow product decline and it became obvious

SUBSTITUTION OF NON-IMPACT FOR IMPACT PRINTERS

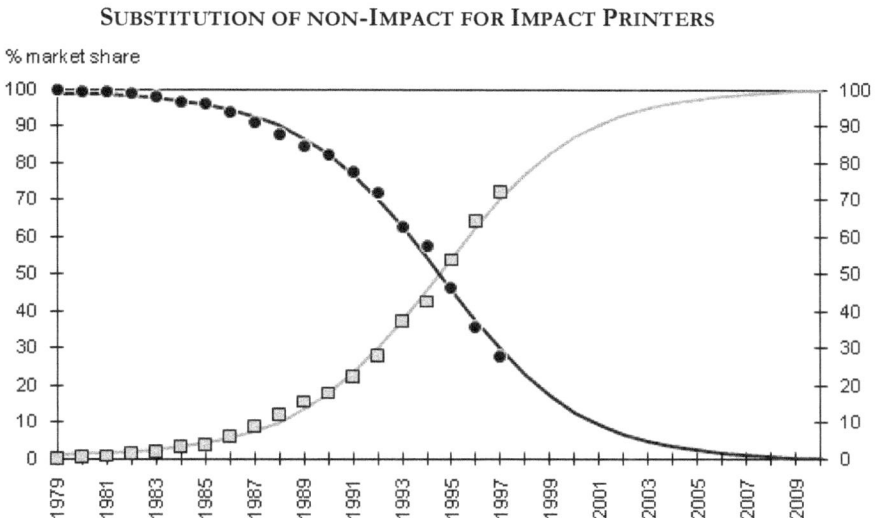

Figure 9.5.1 Impact-printer data (dots) and non-impact printer data (squares).

THE GROWTH OF IMPACT + NON-IMPACT PRINTERS

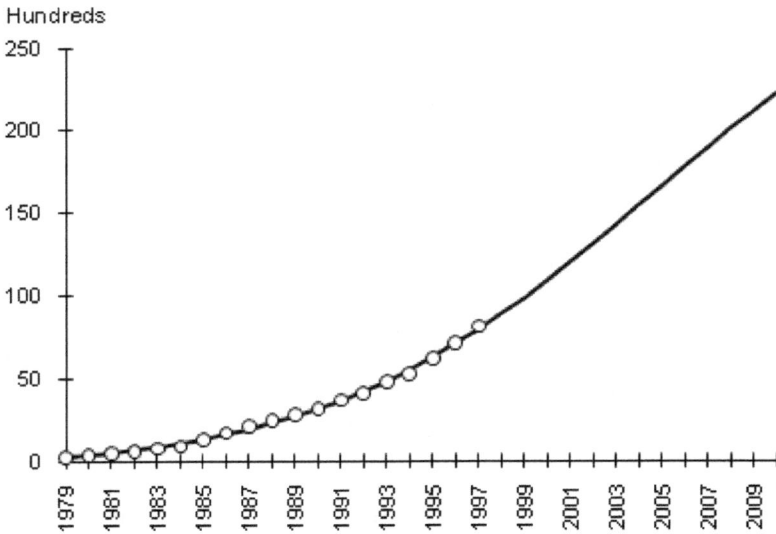

Figure 9.5.2 Annual sales of all printers (impact plus non-impact) and S-curve fit. A natural-growth process penetrated only to 24% by 1997.

that this decline would continue far into the future. That is when their need for accurate long-term forecasts of the decline of carbonless sales became imperative: they needed to correctly anticipate and timely plan for the long-term shrinking of their business. They asked me to consider a 12-year future horizon and make as accurate forecasts as possible.

Their problem became immediately obvious when I looked at the data they gave me on the diffusion of non-impact printers that cannot use the multiform carbonless copy paper, such as laser and inkjet printers. The new "species" was replacing the old one in a classic one-to-one substitution process that was 75% completed at the time, see Figure 9.5.1.

The fitted S-curves left no doubt when they forecasted a smooth decline to zero for the impact-printer population by 2010. The sales of carbonless would necessarily follow suit despite the fact that printers in general had a bright future. As we see in Figure 9.5.2 the overall number of printers—impact plus non-impact—was still in its early stages of its S-shaped growth process.

In fact, the problems of the carbonless business were worse than that. Besides non-impact printing people were beginning to eliminate printing altogether by saving copies of documents only in electronic form. The new competitor loomed ominously as microchip technologies diffused unstoppably in society and not only Appleton managers disposed of no data for this diffusion process but it seemed that such data would probably be impossible to produce.

To begin with I decided to study the diffusion of carbonless as a single species. They had given me detailed data from 1975 onward so I fitted an S-curve on the cumulative data and I obtained a well-defined S-curve that was 60% completed, see top graph in Figure 9.5.3. From that I deduced the product's life cycle shown in the bottom graph of Figure 9.5.3. The intermittent lines indicate a confidence level of 80% estimated as described in Appendix A.1.

The product was entering its fall business season but had a considerable market left. This gave the company, which depended heavily on this product, time to put seeds in the ground for new business lines. At this time diversification should take precedence over vertical integration, something that was not very clear in the minds of the executive team.

Their main concern was the reliability of my forecast because they were planning to base their future needs for personnel and raw materials on it. So I needed to corroborate and confirm my forecast in several ways. One such way was to consider an application of the Volterra-Lotka system of equations for a two-species niche in which competed carbonless with the older one-time carbon (OTC) multiform system that had been phasing out.

They gave me annual sales data for carbonless and OTC from 1975 onward. I applied the Volterra-Lotka Equations 8.1.1 as described in Chapter 8. The relationship turned out to be a predator-prey one with carbonless the predator and OTC the prey. In fact the coupling constants came out -0.3 and 1.0 meaning that for each carbonless sale OTC lost 0.3 sales whereas for each OTC sale carbonless gained 1 sale. The end result was the phasing-out of OTC followed by the phasing-out of carbonless a number of years later, see Figure 9.5.4. The trajectory of carbonless was quite similar to that of Figure 9.5.3 when we considered only one species, but the uncertainties now—not shown in the figure—were expected to be larger because of the difficulties inherent in Volterra-Lotka fits, see discussion in Section 10.4 below, and the fact that the population of one of the species, OTC, had been diminished to very small numbers. Still, it was a first corroboration of the earlier carbonless-sales forecast.

The main unknown and primary concern of Appleton Papers executives was the evolution of their main competitor, which they called NIT (non-impact technologies) and included electronic data interchange. It became imperative to somehow evaluate this "species" quantitatively. I could think of one way of doing this using the software *Where You Are on the Curve and What to Do about It*. I scheduled a half-day meeting with senior executives and I asked them to play the role of top management in NIT a fictitious company providing services in data storage and exchange via all possible non-impact technologies.

CARBONLESS CUMULATIVE

CARBONLESS ANNUAL

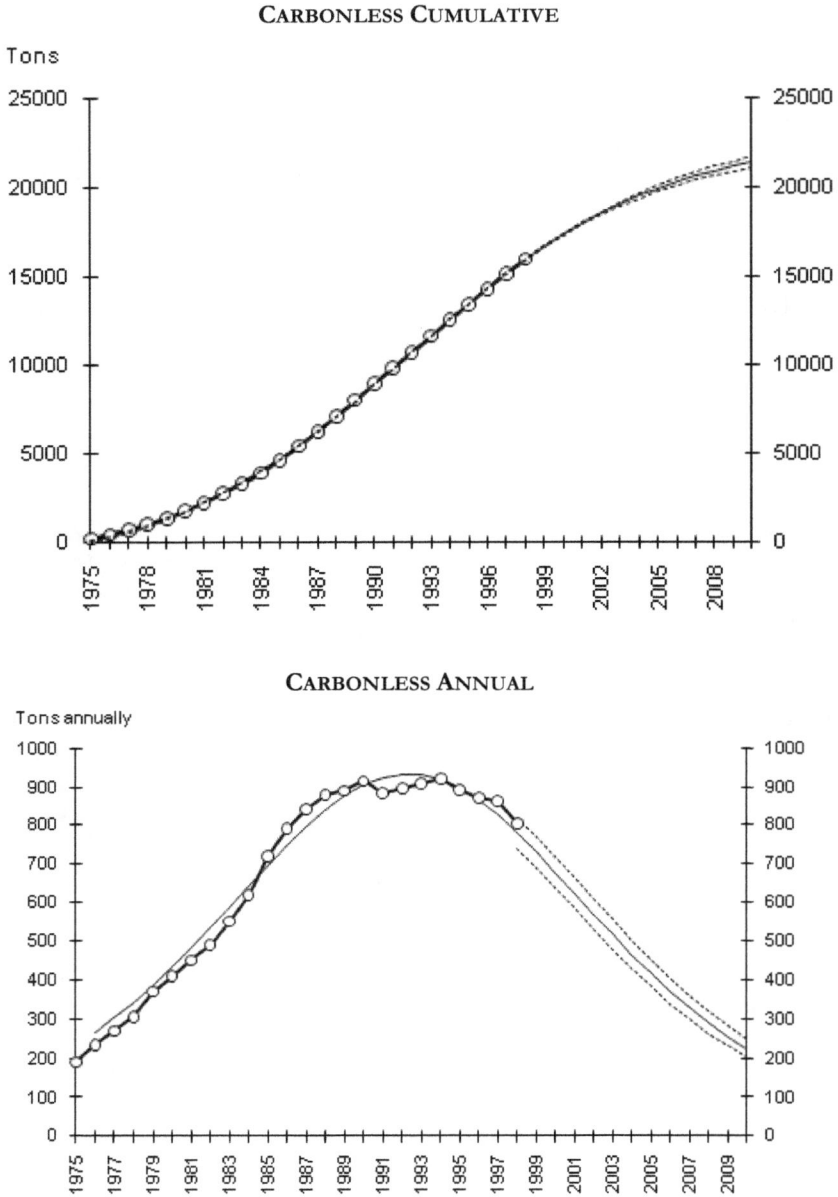

Figure 9.5.3 An S-curve fit on cumulative data (above) and the corresponding life cycle (below). The dotted lines delimit a confidence level of 80%.

CARBONLESS AND OTC: A 2-SPECIES NICHE

Tons annually

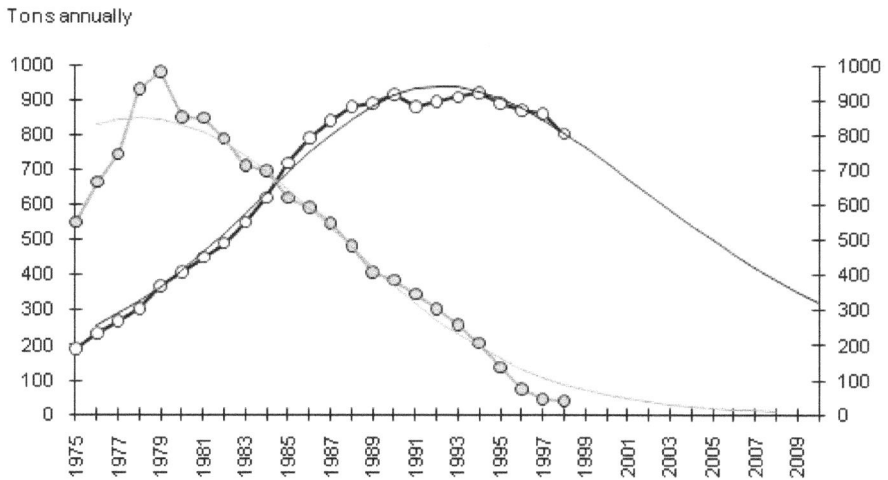

Figure 9.5.4 Volterra-Lotka fits for a 2-species niche: Carbonless (black line) and OTC (gray line).

Following a pin-the-tail-on-the-donkey session and an optimism-versus-pessimism positioning each participant answered the turquoise (rationale) and purple (instinctive) questionnaire described earlier in Section 9.2. I analyzed the answers overnight and obtained a coherent picture. There was much agreement between the seven executives for what concerned the position on the curve, be it via rationale or instinctive decision making. The position on the curve was determined to be at a penetration level of 24%.

The nominal beginning of NIT—the 1% level of the S-curve—was agreed upon as 1985 when Appleton Papers first felt the existence of non-impact technologies. Their annual sales had been rather stable at 0.28 tons per billion dollars of GDP for more than 7 years but began declining in 1985. That year also coincides with the time computer use began making inroads in at all levels of business. The Appleton Papers sales declined to 0.11 tons per billion of GDP in 1998 with all losses were attributed to NIT. This way we had a normalization for our S-curve with a nominal beginning (1%) in 1985 and 24% in 1998. We could thus "fabricate" annual data points for NIT in units of tons of carbonless equivalent, see Figure 9.5.5. Thus quantified the new species in the market could now be analyzed as one of three competitors in a market niche. The Volterra-Lotka system of equations was adapted for three species (the mathematics for this is described in Appendix A.3).

NON-IMPACT TECHNOLOGIES

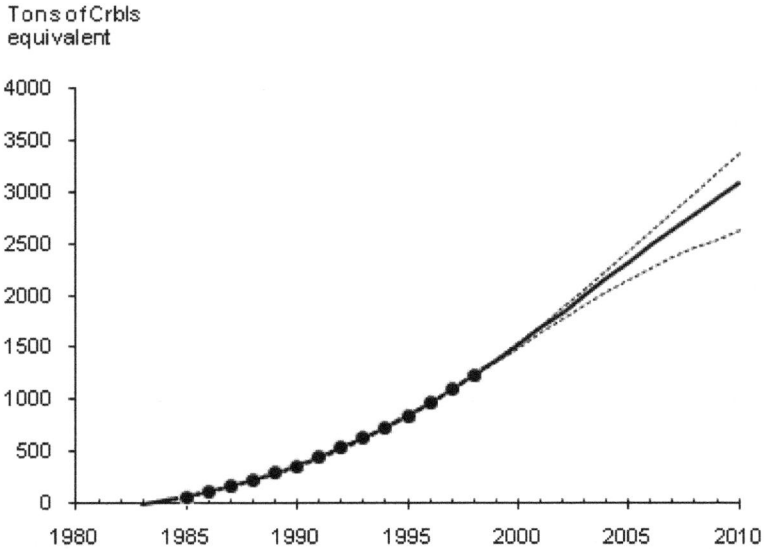

Figure 9.5.5 Brainstormed data on the growth of NIT. The intermittent lines indicate a confidence level of 90% assuming optimistically 10% uncertainty per data point.

The Volterra-Lotka analysis was more elaborate than for the 2-competitor case. It yielded coupling constants for all three pairs possible, see Figure 9.5.6 and Table 9.5.1. The coupling parameters show three kinds of competition. A predator-prey relationship between OTC and carbonless with carbonless the predator (coupling constants -0.7 and 0.2), not unlike the relationship we encountered in the 2-competitor picture of Figure 9.5.4. But also an amensal relationship between carbonless and NIT (coupling constants -0.3 and 0.0) with NIT being impervious to the existence of carbonless while carbonless suffers from the existence of NIT. Finally, pure competition was found between OTC and NIT (coupling constants -0.9 and -3.0) with each one suffering, if unequally, from the other's existence.

The three-way analysis corroborated once again our first carbonless forecast of Figure 9.5.3. In my final presentation to the executive team a summary slide showed all forecasts including the one made by Appleton Papers marketers. Even though they were more pessimistic—see Figure-9.5.7—the differences were small, which made them feel good because they now had increased confidence on what to expect.

OTC, CARBONLESS, AND NIT

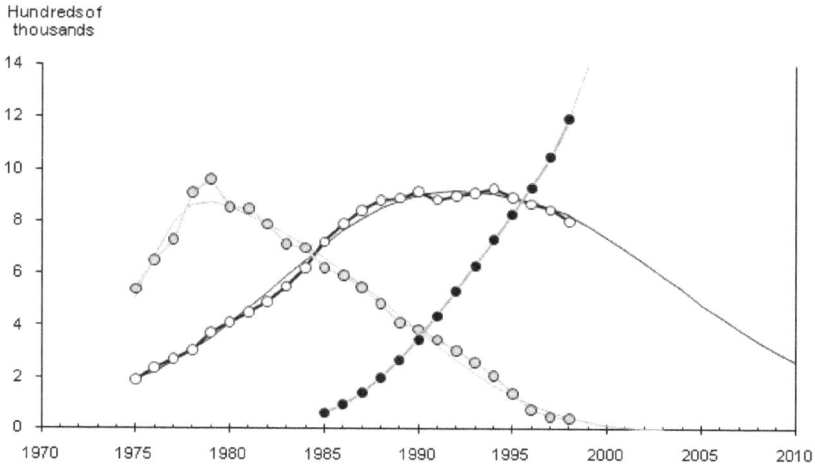

Figure 9.5.6 A 3-way competition in the same niche analyzed by Volterra-Lotka equations.

TABLE 9.5.1 THE 3-WAY COMPETITION COUPLING CONSTANTS

	from OTC	from Cbls	from NIT
OTC		-0.7	-0.9
Cbls	0.2		-0.3
NIT	-3.0	0.0	

SUMMARY SLIDE

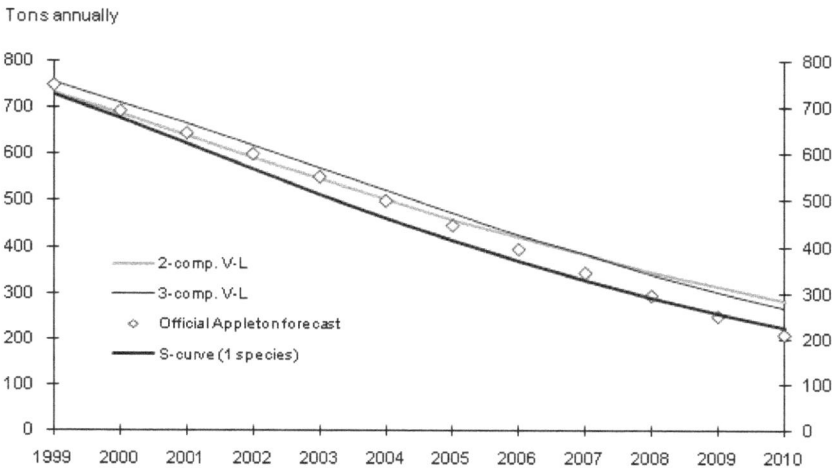

Figure 9.5.7 The final result of the Appleton Papers forecasting project.

In fact I had tried two more approaches, which I did not include in my final presentation to avoid diluting its punch. I had studied the market-share evolutions of the 2-competitor and the 3-competitor niches as described in Chapter 4. Then combining with S-curve fits on the envelopes of the two niches I obtained two more forecasts for carbonless, all in the same ballpark.

Besides customer satisfaction the Appleton Papers case study demonstrates the valuable use of the questionnaire methodology to quantitatively estimate "data" in situations where real data are either unavailable or impossible to get.

Prudential plc

Prudential plc (PRU) is an international financial services company with a product range including personal banking, insurance, pensions and retail investments, institutional fund management and property investments. In the UK it is a leading provider of life insurance and pensions with around seven million customers.

The company's human resource department had adopted my book *Conquering Uncertainty* as reading material in some of their extensive in-house training courses. In September 2003 they invited me to give a talk during a reunion of "alumni" from their "university". While waiting for my turn to speak I came across a circulating 4-page document. It was the CEO's vision for the next 1000 days. I took some notes on what I found to be inconsistent strategic initiatives and when later during my talk I came to the seasons section of my presentation I mentioned that the CEO's vision was not clear as far as the company's business season was concerned. Cost cutting would be appropriate for fall, reducing the error rate for summer, and quarter-by-quarter planning implied winter. What season was Prudential traversing? I did not know at that moment that the CEO was sitting among the audience. He came to me afterward and scheduled a positioning-on-the-curve session with a group of executives and other alumni.

The group consisted of 15 people, 8 executives and 7 alumni. Ahead of the event I sent each one a copy of STRATEST.xls and asked them to answer all the questions and send it back to me. This way I could prepare the analysis results ahead of time.

In the meeting I briefly reviewed S-curves and business seasons and went into presentation of the results as if it were a survey. The underlying assumption was that everyone had been thinking about PRU's current growth cycle when they filled out the questionnaire. Moreover, I made it clear that the results were to be understood as *relative* to the outside environment, in other words, if everyone is seriously ill, having a simple cold is considered being "healthy".

The overall estimate for a position on the business cycle (as indicated by 60% of the participants) turned out to be *late winter* but there was a spread, see Figure 9.5.8. Executives on the average were in a later season and with more disagreement between them than Alumni. In fact, considering only the highest-importance answers (those indicated by weight 4 in the questionnaire) put executives on an early spring. Interestingly, it also gave identical results for instinct as for rationale among executives! It could be that executives were more prone to be influenced by their own plans for action and/or more "jumpy" about world events, but when it came to important things, they were consistent. With their answers the participants had determined their position on the curve in three different ways (including the flowchart way up front in STRATEST.xls). Each way has its merits and weaknesses but each opinion counts. So I concluded by combining all results thus obtaining 3 x 15 = 45 opinions. The overall average positioning turned out to be *early spring* and the error (calculated as the standard deviation of the distribution's spread) was ± ½ season, see Figure 9.5.9. I also showed the position pictorially on an S-curve as in Figure 9.5.10.

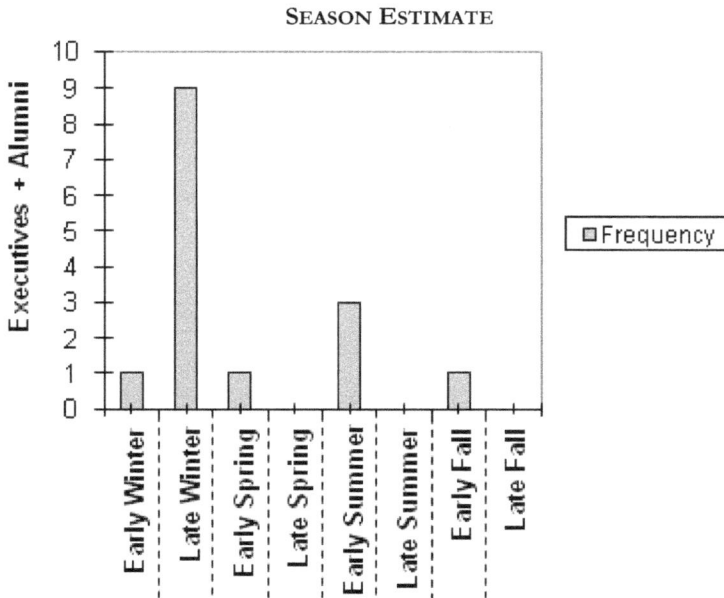

Figure 9.5.8 Based on the answers of the 15 participants (executives plus alumni).

Lively discussions were triggered by my presentation and were funneled by my pointing out that some points of view expressed were in tune while others at odds with being in a business season of early spring.

In tune were:

- 5 executives who put top priority on product innovation, focus on strategic accounts, and value-based pricing (only 1 Alumnus)
- 4 executives (1 Alumnus) who put top priority on opening up, considering new lines of business.
- 11 participants thought little of hiring entrepreneurs while ten people thought little of going liquid.

At odds with being in early spring were:

- Only 1 executive and 1 alumnus voted for continuous improvement; in fact 2 executives gave it least priority.
- Only 2 executives and 1 alumnus gave priority to learning; in fact 5 participants gave it least priority.
- 7 participants found back to basics most important and only 1 participant found it least important.
- 5 participants thought tightening the belt is most important.

OVERALL ESTIMATE

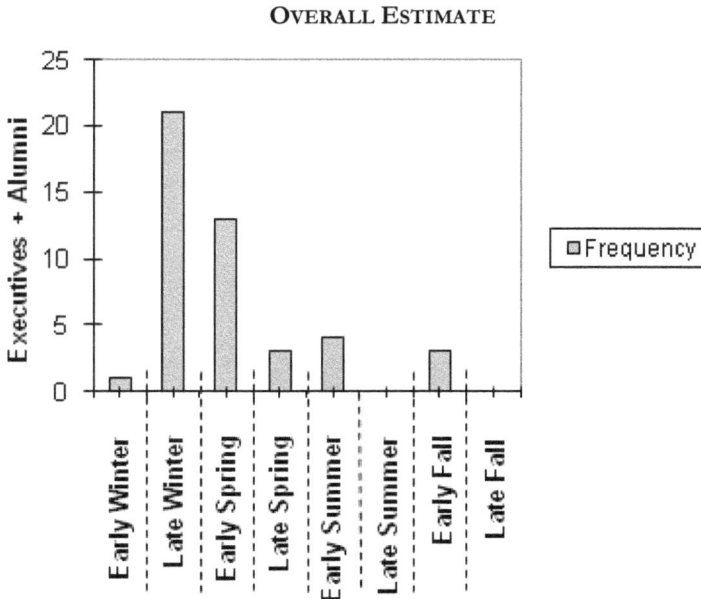

Figure 9.5.9 Averaging all three estimates by all fifteen participants.

PRUDENTIAL ON THE CURVE IN SEPTEMBER 2003

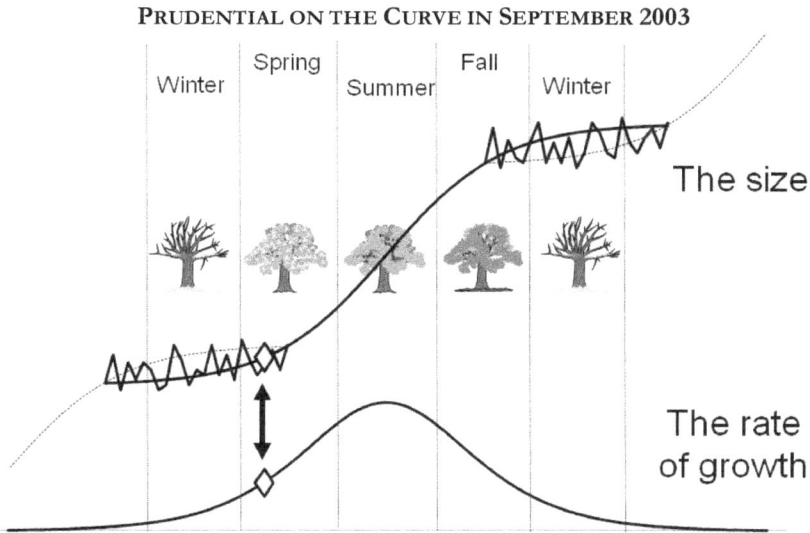

Figure 9.5.10 The position on the S-curve and on the business cycle.

It is noteworthy that there was overwhelming agreement on the importance of centralization. There was also much agreement on the non-importance of: delegation/empowerment, entrepreneurship, and horizontal segmentation, but no desire for vertical integration either.

Two years later Prudential managers contacted me again asking for a short check-up session involving only the executives that had participated in the original work. This time I prepared a stripped down one-page questionnaire that consisted of selective highlights from the elaborate procedure we had previously followed shown in Figure 9.5.11. In particular, it included a pin-the-tail-on-the-donkey exercise, shown at the top of the figure, and five representative multiple-choice questions shown at the bottom. Three of the questions addressed business decisions made rationally, i.e. strategic initiatives, vision, and focus. Two questions addressed the executive's emotional disposition, i.e. whether they had or had not what they wanted and whether they were preoccupied with the *what* or with the *how*. They were asked to fill out the questionnaires and return them to me before our meeting.

This time the analysis was done pictorially showing the participants' positions on S-curves as in Figure 9.5.12. During the presentation-of-results session I assigned numbers to each participant so as to avoid over-influencing the ensuing discussions considering that the CEO was also one of the participants. Of course, upon demand I would reveal a participant's identity.

THE STRIPPED-DOWN QUESTIONNAIRE

Enter one clear dot in the little square that best represents where you think you are, and write an estimate for the duration ΔT in years.

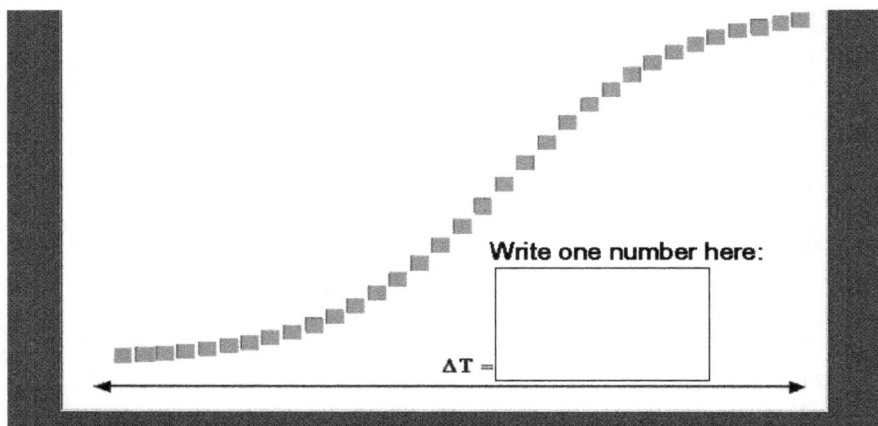

Write one number here:

ΔT =

Enter only one clear dot for each question (only your highest priority):

1. What kind of strategic initiative are you advocating?
   - Business Process Redesign
   - T.Q.M. and Excellence
   - Back to basics, core competencies
   - Continuous improvemen

2. Your vision is:
   - Strategic (long-term)
   - Next quarter only
   - Open up, consider new lines of business
   - Close down, reconsider, have second thoughts

3. You focus on:
   - Learning
   - Not deviating from successful practices
   - Tightening the belt, face-lifting
   - Innovation and entrepreneurship

4. Are you preoccupied with:
   - WHAT to do
   - HOW to do it
   - WHY are you doing what you are doing
   - Try to keep things from changing

5. What best describes your situation:
   - You have what you want
   - You do not have what you want
   - You have what you do not want
   - You do not have what you do not want

Figure 9.5.11 Representative questions chosen for a check-up session.

There was relative agreement among the participants' answers. The conclusion now was that the position on the cycle was an early summer, possibly very close to middle summer. This was not incompatible with having being in early spring in the previous exercise of September 2003. But

POSITION IN THE SEASON

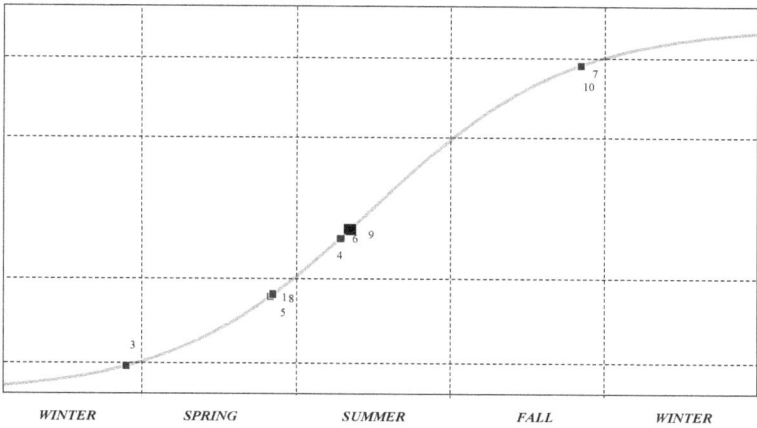

STRATEGIC PROGRAMS
(1st Priorities only)

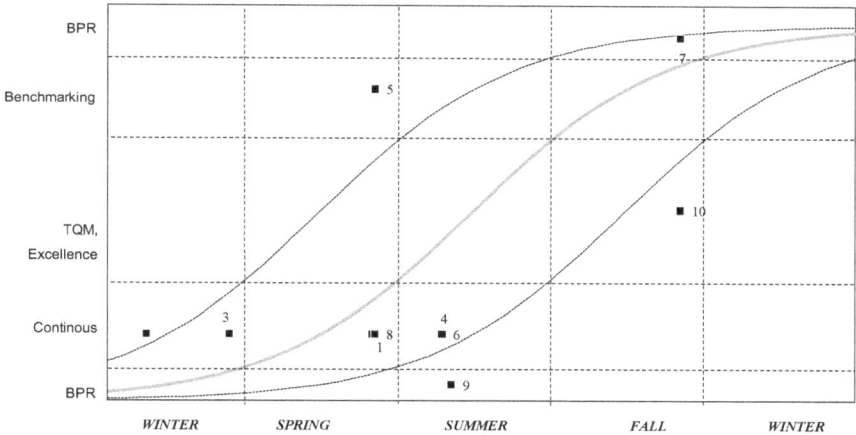

Figure 9.5.12 The positioning in the season resulting from the pin-the-tail-on-the-donkey exercise (top); the large square is the average. Answers for the strategic-initiatives question (bottom); only three executives were significantly off, i.e. more than a season. One-season bands are delimited by the thin gray S-curves.

the season length had gotten shorter, now it was close to 0.67 years whereas two years earlier it had been closer to 0.8 years.

The Prudential case study described in detail here demonstrates how S-curve related consulting activity at the highest level can help determine a company's position on the curve for which there is eventually agreement among the executive team. But the consultant's main added value is in stimulating and facilitating fruitful discussions. Such discussions usually begin with arguments about where exactly on the curve they are and who is right or wrong. But then attention naturally turns to what to do next. Here again S-curves provide rich material to draw from, namely Chapter 3.

NEOSET

In late 1995 I met by chance the CEO of a fast-growing ready-to-assemble furniture manufacturing firm in Greece called NEOSET. When I asked him about his life, he replied: "To be the head of a large successful business is like having mounted a lion. You simply have to go where it wants." To me it was obvious that his business was doing well (summer season), which is why his choices were limited. Later in our discussion he told me that he had recently taken a stroll in the market and realized that their prices were too high following which he ordered a 25% price cut across the board. He was pleasantly surprised but puzzled to see his gross sales jump at places by as much as 100%. He could not understand how price elasticity could be so high. I told him that it was possible to get a deeper understanding of the market competitive dynamics via the Volterra-Lotka formulations that I was utilizing. He was very perceptive and wanted a meeting with me. In our meeting two days later he expressed two more wishes. Early signs for sales in 1996 indicated a loss of momentum in turnover gains. Was the price-cut effect evaporating? If the 1st quarter of 1996 turned out to be only 25% up with respect to previous year, how would the rest of 1996 evolve? And his second concern was what would be the appropriate behavior in the market for NEOSET now, differentiation or aggressiveness? The following week I received the company and market data I had asked for.

At that time the manufacturing of home and business furniture in Greece was largely in the hands of small artisanal enterprises. NEOSET was by far the market leader commanding a share between 5 and 10%. In my mind it was justifiable to treat the Greek furniture market as a duopoly where there were only two competitors NEOSET and All Others grouped together. I could then apply the Volterra-Lotka equations for a two-species niche.

The data were turnover sales in drachmas. To eliminate speculative factors and thus better approximate physical variables I corrected all numbers for inflation. It quickly became clear that the historical horizon should be divided into three separate periods for which the Equations 8.1.1 would be successfully fitted, see Figure 9.5.13. The first period between 1984 and 1991 revealed predator-prey type of competition with

NEOSET prey. The second period between 1991 and 1995 revealed pure competition with both coupling constants negative, and the third period from mid 1995 onward revealed also pure competition but with enhanced attractiveness for NEOSET. The change in trend direction in mid 1995 was obviously related to the price cut. But the change in direction in 1991 puzzled me. It seemed to puzzle NEOSET executives less.

My forecast spelled out a slowdown in the rise of sales following the price cut with overall growth of 26% in 1996 and 25% in 1997. The introduction of the estimated data point for the 1st quarter of 1996 resulted in a small reduction of the attractiveness for NEOSET and to a lesser extent in a reduction of NEOSET's attacker's advantage (the coupling parameter in the growth equation of All Others).

Investigating the sensitivity of each one of the six parameters involved in the Volterra-Lotka equations I was able to make recommendations for corrective actions if desired. They would be more effective when directed toward differentiation and increasing the attractiveness of the products rather than toward counterattack. It would be more profitable for NEOSET to try to limit its losses caused by the gains of All Others rather than increase the damage to All Others whenever it gained. An advertizing campaign with a slogan "we are unique with very good products" would be more effective than "we are much better than the others".

As for the size of the budget for such a corrective action, the model told me (assuming an ideal price elasticity of 1, see Appendix A.3) that a budget matching the losses from dropping prices by 2-3 % would bring the turnover forecasts back to what they were at the end of 1995 indicated by the dotted-line trajectory in Figure 9.5.13.

The presentation of these results triggered lively discussion among the members of the executive team. As I had prepared an interactive version of the Volterra-Lotka fitting procedure, I offered to play more online scenarios with them. Their main concern was what if the competition responded by also dropping prices aggressively in the near future. The scenario I suggested was that All Others drop their prices across the board by 25% in mid 1996.

The Volterra-Lotka result, shown in Figure 9.5.14, had NEOSET enter a declining trajectory from next quarter similar to that of the period 1991-1995, and the turnover of All Others jump up by about 20%; more vivid discussions in the executive team. One marketer remarked we would be witnessing a sizeable increase of the furniture market in Greece. "Where would all the money come from? Would Greek stop eating in order to buy furniture," he asked sarcastically.

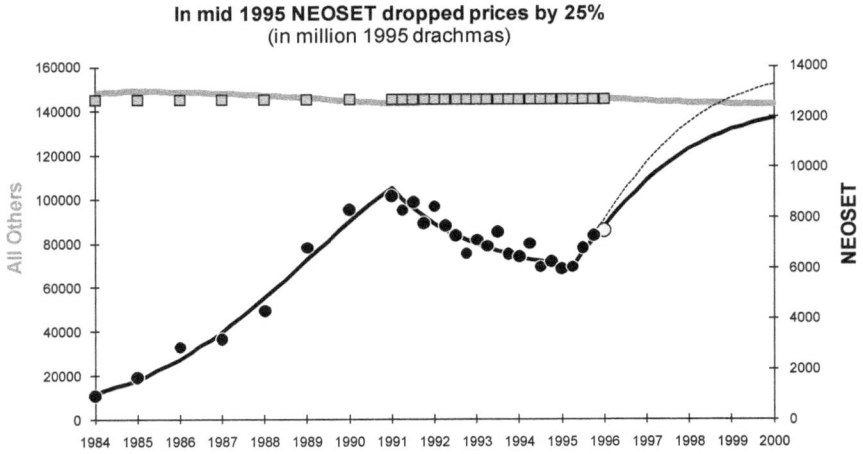

Figure 9.5.13 Inflation-corrected data (NEOSET in black dots, All Others in gray squares) and Volterra-Lotka fits for three different periods. The last NEOSET data point (light gray dot) was estimated from early sales and participates in the black-line fit but does not participate in the fit indicated by the dotted line.

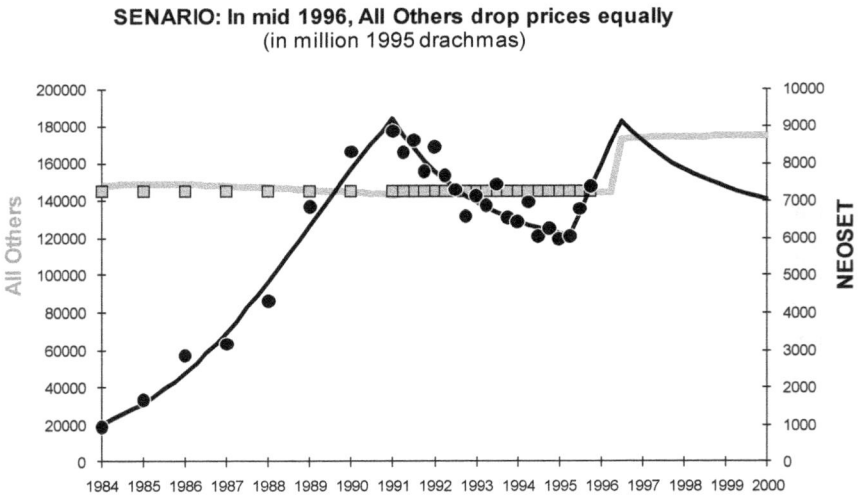

Figure 9.5.14 The scenario played online according to which All Others drop prices by 25% in mid 1996 resulting in a jump of their turnover and a declining trajectory for NEOSET from next quarter onward.

I paused for a minute preparing my answer but the CEO beat me to it by saying, "It is not unreasonable that our price war triggers a rush toward furniture for a while at the detriment of other products in the overall Greek market."

The NEOSET case study demonstrates the impact a Volterra-Lotka analysis can have on managing competition and shaping market image. It also points out the usefulness of being able to play what-if scenarios interactively during executive meetings.

QUALCOMM

In 1985, a group of visionary telecom-industry veterans came together to build "Quality Communications" a plan that has evolved into one of the telecommunications industry's greatest start-up success stories: Qualcomm Incorporated.

Qualcomm began by providing contract research and development services for the wireless telecommunications market. One of the team's first goals was to develop a commercial product. This effort resulted in OmniTRACS®. Since its introduction in 1988, OmniTRACS grew into the largest satellite-based commercial mobile system for the transportation industry by 2000.

This early success led the company to take a daring departure from conventional wireless wisdom. In 1989, the Telecommunications Industry Association (TIA) endorsed a digital technology called Time Division Multiple Access (TDMA). Just three months later, Qualcomm introduced Code Division Multiple Access (CDMA), a superior technology for wireless and data products that changed the global face of wireless communications forever.

Toward the end of 1999, in the wake of the publication of my book *Conquering Uncertainty*, I received an e-mail from a senior manager in the company's executive-education services asking me to lecture their executives on how to adapt their management during the different stages of business and in particular the start-up phase and the maturity phase. "I am not looking for any economic models, but rather business practices, organizational design, and management practices that companies need to implement during each business cycle", she wrote and later continued, "For the past 14 years our company has been focused on growth. Now that the growth has slowed down a bit, we need to focus on managing the business." I replied with, "You have come to the right person", and proposed a one-day event in their premises with the company's concerned executives. I suggested an event agenda as follows:

AGENDA

9:00 – 9:05 a.m. Introductions
9:05 – 9:30 a.m. Overview and historical perspective—Issues
    QUALCOMM is concerned with (by a QUALCOMM executive)
9:30 – 10:30 a.m. The S-Shaped Adventure—New ways of looking at old
    business problems (by T.M.)
10:30 – 10: 45 a.m. Break
10:45 – 12:00 a.m. Workshop: Where are you on the curve? (All)

12:00 – 1:00 p.m. Lunch

1:00 – 2:00 p.m. Success in All Seasons (by T.M.)
2:00 – 2:15 p.m. Break
2:15 – 3:30 p.m. Workshop: Is QUALCOMM appropriately dressed for
    the season it is traversing? (All)
3:30 – 3:45 p.m. Break
3:45 – 5:00 p.m. Workshop: Examine one or two of QUALCOMM's
    products, services or market segments (All)

The event was realized as suggested. During the historical overview
they talked about how speed and bandwidth were key to giving people the
data and Internet applications they want. They proudly presented
QUALCOMM's High Data Rate (HDR) technology and the digital
wireless technology "3G", which at the time was poised as the promising
next generation. In a qualitative graph depicting an artist's view of the
evolution of these technologies the pattern consisted of two step increases
between 10 kbps and 2 + Mbps in what seemed to be three cascading
S-curves (or parts of). Before making my presentation I was able to
borrow that slide and superimpose an approximate time axis (vertically),
see Figure 9.5.15, which smoothly led me into the cascading-S-curves
discussion. It also provided meaningful background for the positioning-
on-the-curve session that followed.

The workshop using STRATEST.xls was carried out collectively by
asking participants to openly vote on a given question, and registering
their average response. The flow-chart positioning resulted in an early
summer season in full agreement with an S-curve fit I had prepared on
historical revenue data from company reports, see Figure 9.5.16. As for
the rational-vs.-instinct questionnaire it became once again source of
discussions and constituted the prime value added. After all, the aim of
the organizers was to sensitize executives about their stage of growth and
the ramifications thereof.

DATA-TRANSMISSION TECHNOLOGIES

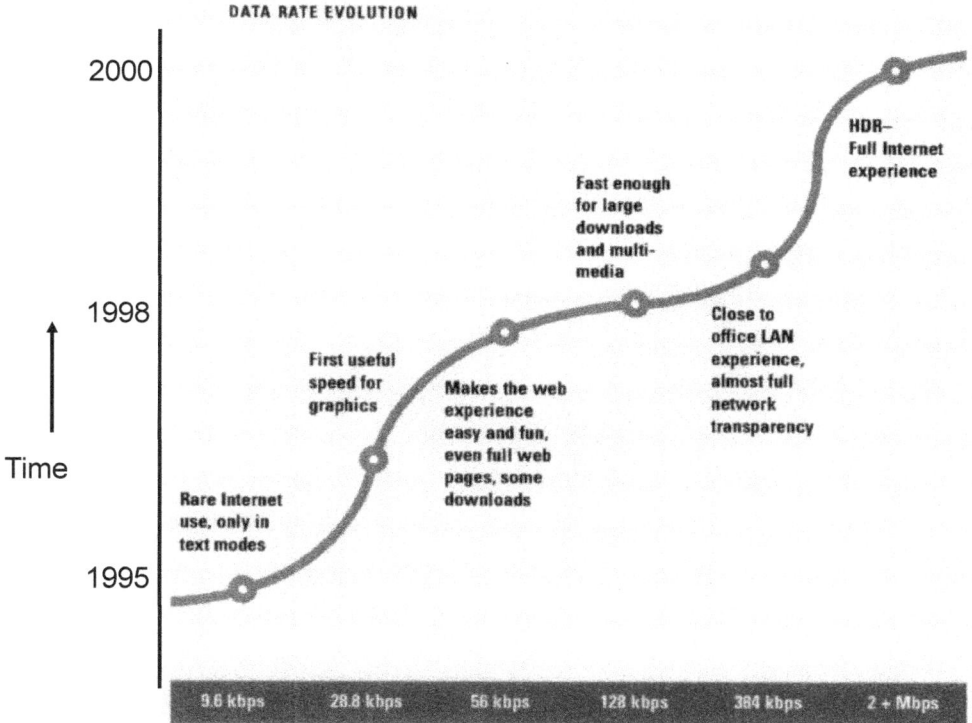

Figure 9.5.15 We discern three cascading S-curves (or parts of) as a function of time (plotted vertically).

QUALCOMM TURNOVER

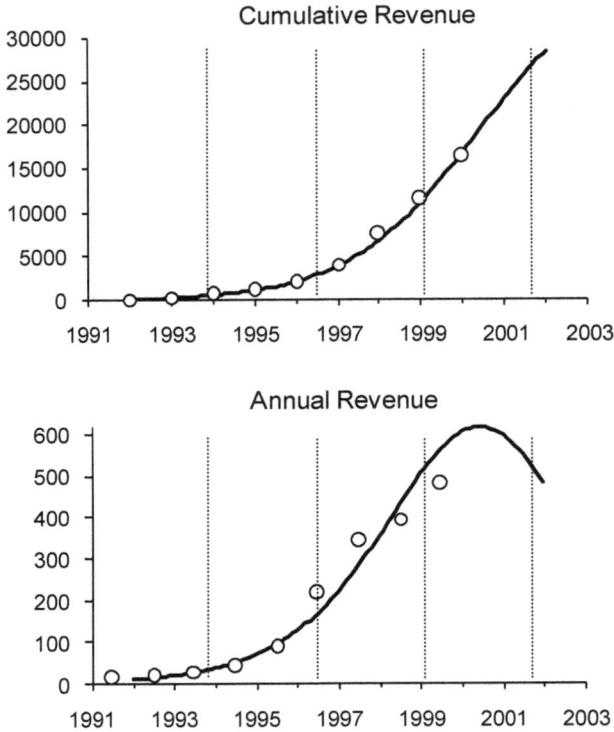

Figure 9.5.16   The position on the curve as determined from data in the company's annual reports. Also in agreement with the position as determined from the flow-chart section of STATEST.xls. The vertical intermittent lines delimit the company's seasons.

The QUALCOMM case study demonstrates a suitable use of S-curves for a business that has no particular problems but has been going through well-pronounced cycles of growth. These people are both perceptive to and ready to take advantage of new ways of thinking and associated insights.

10 – EXCEL-BASED TOOLS

Having written software programs in Fortran, Basic, and other programming languages during my career I have finally resigned to mostly using Microsoft Excel for my S-curve needs. In this chapter I describe how I do this in all the applications of S-curves mentioned in this book. Invariably they invoke the use of the SOLVER.

10.1 – USING THE EXCEL SOLVER TO FIT CURVES ON DATA

The Solver Add-in is a Microsoft Office Excel add-in program that is available when you install Microsoft Office or Excel. To use it, however, you first need to load it in Excel. The Solver can be used to perform what-if analyses, optimization, financial planning, and other functions but here we will invoke only its function-minimization capability, namely to minimize the contents of a cell (invariably a formula) by varying a number of other cells, (the parameters).

We will begin by a simple example fitting a straight line in order to demonstrate the use of the Solver. Suppose we have a sequence of 8 numbers (typically a time-series data) on which we want to fit, let us say, a straight line. We enter the data in two columns (or rows) one representing time and the other our numbers. In Figure 10.1.1 time is entered in cells A5:A12 and the data in cells B5:B12.[*] The fitted curve, in this case the straight line $\alpha x + \beta$, will be in cells C5:C12 with the parameters α and β in cells C1 and C2 respectively. It is useful to introduce a graph—a scatter plot—right from the beginning so as to have an immediate visual feedback on the distribution of the data and the theoretical line we are trying to fit on them.

On column D we will enter the square of the difference between data and line on a cell-by-cell basis. The sum of all these differences, entered in D4 (highlighted in gray in Figure 10.1.1), is what needs to be minimized. This sum is directly related to the Chi Square but is rigorously equal to it only in the special case when all errors on the data are equal to 1 (see discussion at the end of this section).

---

[*] If your data consist of numbers smaller than 1 or greater than 100,000 introduce an appropriate multiplicative factor to end up with data in the range 1 – 100,000. This will reduce the chances for the Solver to misbehave.

Fitting a Straight Line on 8 Data Points

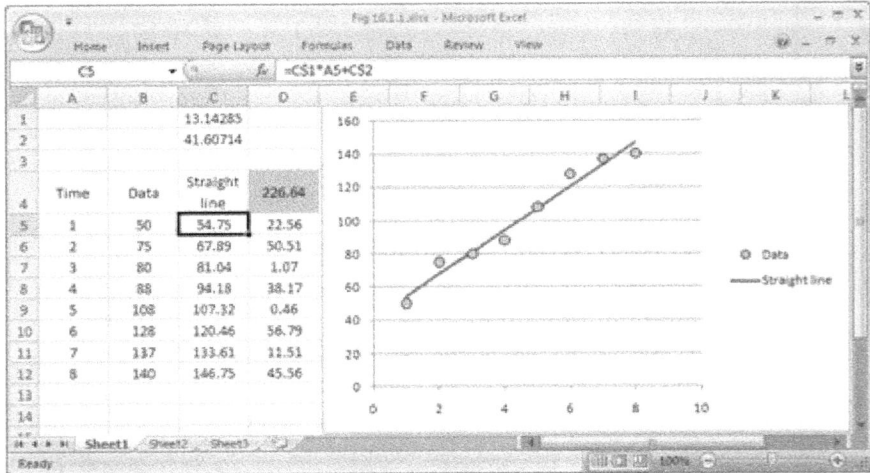

Figure 10.1.1 The setup for a straight-line fit on 8 equally spaced data points. The gray cell D4 is the sum of the differences squared. The theoretical straight-line expression is shown in the content of cell C5.

Invoking the Solver opens a dialogue box where the Solver needs to be told what to minimize by varying what. In Figure 10.1.2 the target cell $D$4 contains the formula (sum related to Chi Square) that must be minimized (notice the black dot in Min) by varying the parameters in cells

Invoking the Solver

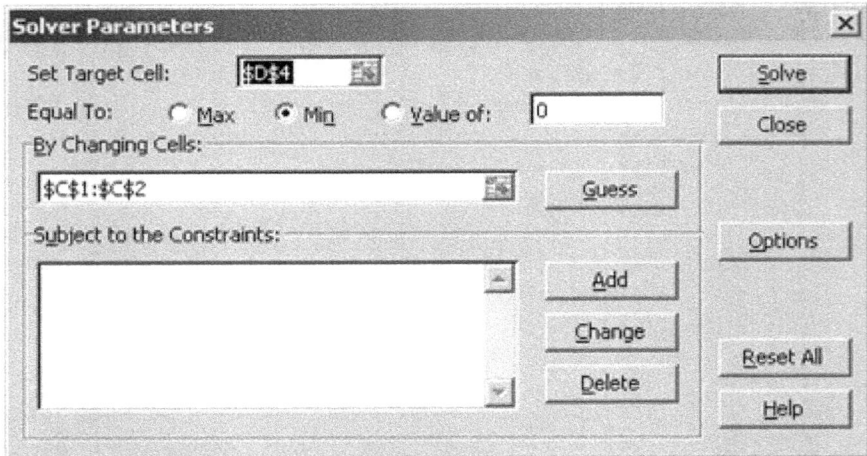

Figure 10.1.2 The Solver dialogue box.

$C$1:$C$2. There are many other buttons in Figure 10.1.2 and the interested user is invited to try to understand their use via Excel's help. By and large, however, the default settings of all these buttons will be suitable for 95% of our needs in fitting S-curves.

Before hitting the button "Solve" in Figure 10.1.2 we must set the parameter values in cells C1 and C2 to some *reasonable* starting values. This helps eliminate erratic behavior by the solver. Here is when feedback from the graph comes in handy (it is obvious for example that a good starting value for parameter β is 50). A measure of the answer's robustness is witnessing no more improvement of the fit by repeated calls to the Solver (value in cell D4 remains unchanged).

By construction, the smaller the sum of the differences squared in cell D4, the better the agreement of the data with the fitted line. Further to a good visual agreement between data points and theoretical line, we show in the section below how rigorous confidence levels can be determined for those rare cases where the uncertainties of the data (error on each data point) are known.

For the majority of cases, however, one should be content with having achieved the best fit Solver can provide and avoid risking incorrect estimates of the confidence level.

The Use of Chi Square

The best technique for fitting an S-curve on data points involves the minimization of a rigorously constructed Chi-Square function. This procedure permits the estimation of confidence levels. Unfortunately, the construction of such a function requires knowledge of the complete and correct uncertainty for each data point. Had we been studying outcomes in casino roulettes, this uncertainty would simply be the statistical error. But for such cases as product sales, annual revenues, discovery of oil reserves, and the productivity of artists as measured by their cumulative artistic achievement, there is always more fluctuation than that due to statistics alone. It then becomes unrealistic to rigorously determine an uncertainty for each data point. When I went back to make an update of the AIDS-victims curve in the US ten years later, I found my old data restated with values that differed up to 80%!

One may think that there exist data sets with no uncertainties whatsoever, for example, the data on Nobel laureates. But the uncertainties needed for the Chi-Square do not concern documentation and reporting but the evolution of a natural law. During World War II there were no Nobel prizes given at all. There is no uncertainty about this fact; nevertheless it constitutes a large fluctuation below the trend in the evolution of the number of Nobel laureates. Also, sometimes there were many laureates who share one prize and other times few. It is the deviations (fluctuations) from the natural-growth pattern that reflect the size of the uncertainty on the data points. For the calculation of the Chi-Square one can generally make only rough estimates for such uncertainties.

Another aspect overlooked by those forecasters who take the trouble to quote an error on their forecasts is the confidence level. A ±10% error on a prediction may sound good until we realize that it usually refers to a confidence level of 68%. In other words, our result is 10% accurate in less than 7 out of 10 times. In physics research a one-standard-deviation "discovery" is considered worthless.

In our Monte Carlo study we give tables that link the expected forecasting error to the uncertainties of the data points, to the confidence levels, and to the range of the S-curve that the data point cover. For example, if the data cover about half of the fitted S-curve and the uncertainty on each data point is of the order of ±10%, then the error on the forecasted ceiling will be ±20% with a confidence level of 95% [1].

A rigorous definition of Chi Square is given below and it involves knowledge of the error σ_i on each data point i.

$$\chi^2 = \sum_{i}^{i=n} \left(\frac{Y_i - Y_{curve}}{\sigma_i} \right)^2$$

where Y_i are the data, Y_{curve} the theoretical expression (e.g. $= ax + b$) and n the total number of data points.

It is rare that we have good knowledge of the errors σ_i as is the case when the fluctuations on the data are of a purely statistical nature—Poisson statistics. I this case the statistical error σ_i is equal to the square root of the number, in other words, $\sigma_i^2 = Y_i$ (another acceptable formulation is $\sigma_i^2 = Y_{curve}$ but the difference has no real bearing). But as we mentioned earlier this is the smallest possible error and is encountered rarely in real-life situations; most of the time the error per data point is larger.

Now dividing the χ^2 by the number of degrees of freedom (i.e., the total number of data points minus the number of parameters in our theoretical expression) yields the *reduced* Chi Square. The *reduced* Chi Square can be used to test the goodness of a fit in a rigorous way, in other words to quantify the probability that a hypothesis is true (in the above case the hypothesis that a straight line should fit well the data is correct). If the *reduced* Chi Square is large, i.e. much larger than 1, then the hypothesis is probably wrong. If on the other hand the *reduced* Chi Square is too small, i.e. much less than 1, then we may conclude only one of the following three alternatives:[2,3,4,5,6]

- The hypothesis is correct but *very improbable* statistical fluctuations of the data value have occurred.
- The values of the uncertainties σ_i have been over-estimated.
- We are dealing with fraudulent data, that is, the data are "too good to be true".

In the example of Figure 10.1.1 the construction of the Chi Square (sum in cell D4) assumed $\sigma_i = 1$ for all i. This comes nowhere near a realistic estimate of the errors as can be evidenced by the value of the *reduced* Chi Square. That is with a 2-parameter theoretical line the number of degrees of freedom is equal to $8 - 2 = 6$ and the *reduced* Chi Square would be $226.64/6 = 37.8$, which is much larger than 1, and yet the graph shows that the hypothesis of a straight line does not seems all that wrong, hence the conclusion that the errors σ_i must have been $>> 1$.

10.2 – HOW TO FIT S-CURVES

We could try to fit a different line on the data set of Figure 10.1.1 and possibly improve the fit with a parabola, hyperbola, or other polynomial. We can even try to fit an S-curve but to do this reasonably well we must ignore the first data point (at time=1). Then we need to replace the formula for a straight-line expression in cells C5:C12 with the following formula for an S-curve:

C$1/(1+EXP(-C$2*(A6-C$3)))+C$4

This expression is basically Equation 2.2.2 plus a constant C$4 representing the pedestal C on which the S-curve sits. It is obvious by inspection of the data pattern that the S-curve in this case will be described by four parameters instead of three because it will be sitting on a pedestal. Inspection also helps us decide on appropriate starting value for the Solver's four-parameters search, namely 140 for the ceiling M, 5 for the midpoint t_o, and 1 for the slope α even if the Solver is generally not very sensitive to staring values. The fit result is shown in Figure 10.1.3. The fit may seem much better than for the straight-line case (sum of differences squared now equal to 2.26) but we must remember that we are fitting with 4 parameters instead of 2 and only 7 data points instead of 8.

FITTING AN S-CURVE ON 7 DATA POINTS

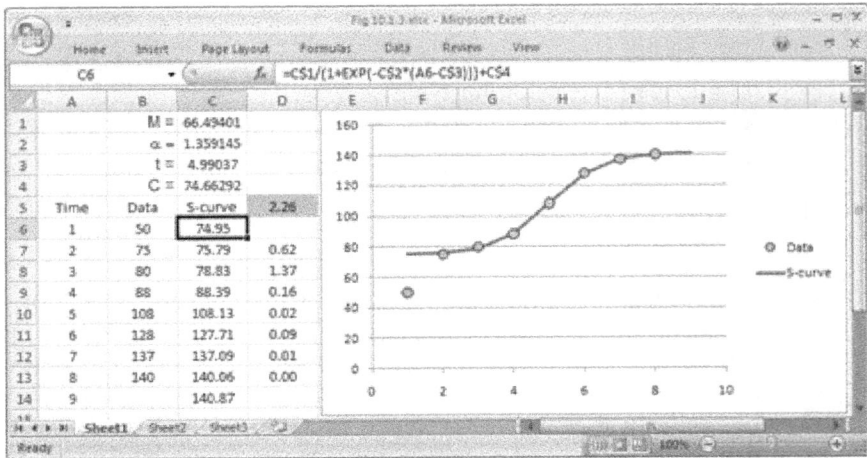

Figure 10.1.3 The setup for an S-curve fit on 7 equally spaced data points (the first data point at t=1 does not participate in the fitting procedure). The theoretical S-curve expression is shown in the content of cell C6.

The above S-curve example was rather simplistic in that it dealt with very few data points and a rather complete growth process. More frequently we are faced with many data points that spread over only part of an S-curve. Such an example was the VAX 11/750 sales described in Section 2.3. The data in the lower graph of Figure 2.3.1 represent quarterly sales and constitute a typical business data set. To fit an S-curve to these data one needs to first construct the cumulative variable shown in column C of Figure 10.1.4.

Choosing starting values for this example was mostly straightforward: 9000 for the ceiling M, 1985 for the mid-point t_0, and 0 for the pedestal C. The only difficulty is in choosing a starting value for the slope α, the range of which is typically between 0.1 and 1. Here some visual feedback from the graph can be very useful. This example hardly needed the fourth parameter C because the S-curve as outlined by the data did not seem to sit on a pedestal. Indeed, the Solver found a small negative value for the pedestal, probably compatible with zero within the expected uncertainties.

This example illustrates the use of weights. Notice that the in the formula of the difference squared in Cell F6 there is a multiplication by the corresponding data point Cell C6. This procedure emphasizes recent data during the fitting procedure (alternatively, division instead of multiplication would have emphasized early data). The advantage in putting emphasis on recent data is double. First, it ensures a smooth

THE SALES OF VAX 11/750

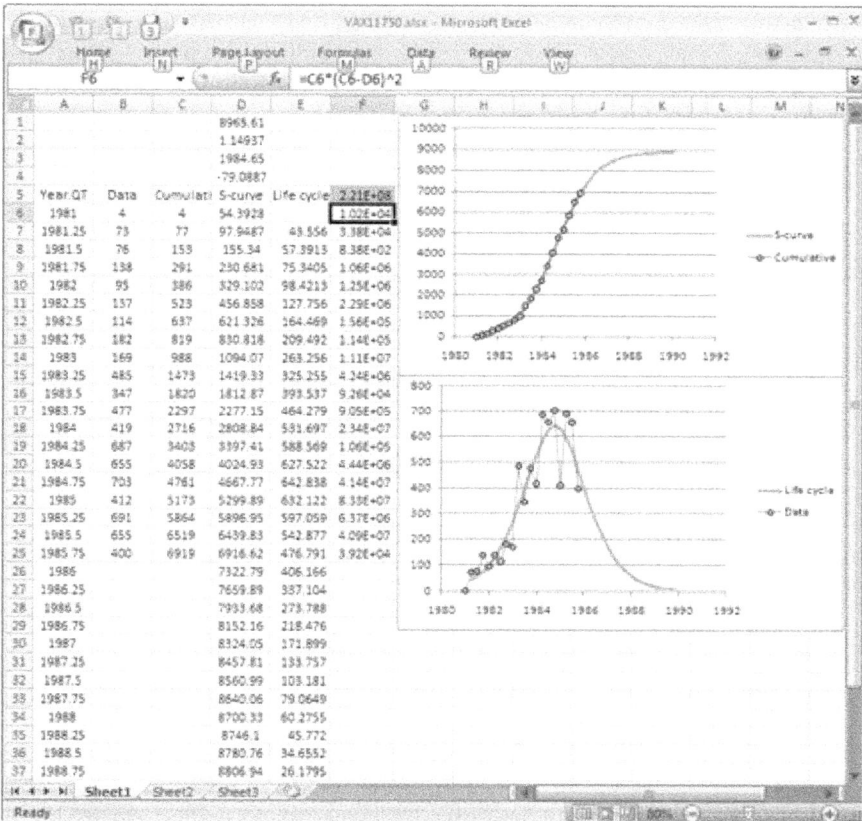

Year.QT	Data	Cumulati	S-curve	Life cycle	
			8963.61		
			1.14937		
			1984.65		
			-79.0887		
					2.21E+08
1981	4	4	54.3928		1.02E+04
1981.25	73	77	97.9487	43.556	3.38E+04
1981.5	76	153	155.34	57.3913	8.38E+02
1981.75	138	291	230.681	75.3405	1.06E+06
1982	95	386	329.102	98.4215	1.25E+06
1982.25	137	523	456.858	127.756	2.29E+06
1982.5	114	637	621.326	164.469	1.56E+05
1982.75	182	819	830.818	209.492	1.14E+05
1983	169	988	1094.07	263.256	1.11E+07
1983.25	485	1473	1419.33	325.255	4.24E+06
1983.5	347	1820	1812.87	393.537	9.26E+04
1983.75	477	2297	2277.15	464.279	9.05E+05
1984	419	2716	2808.84	531.697	2.34E+07
1984.25	687	3403	3397.41	588.569	1.06E+06
1984.5	655	4058	4024.93	627.522	4.44E+06
1984.75	703	4761	4667.77	642.838	4.14E+07
1985	412	5173	5299.89	632.122	8.33E+07
1985.25	691	5864	5896.95	597.059	6.37E+06
1985.5	655	6519	6439.83	542.877	4.09E+07
1985.75	400	6919	6916.62	476.791	3.92E+04
1986			7322.79	406.166	
1986.25			7659.89	337.104	
1986.5			7933.68	273.788	
1986.75			8152.16	218.476	
1987			8324.05	171.899	
1987.25			8457.81	133.757	
1987.5			8560.99	103.181	
1987.75			8640.06	79.0649	
1988			8700.33	60.2755	
1988.25			8746.1	45.772	
1988.5			8780.76	34.6552	
1988.75			8806.94	26.1795	

Figure 10.1.4 The bell-shaped life-cycle curve below (in red) has been calculated via successive subtractions from the S-curve above (in red), which has been fit on the cumulative data of Column C. The sum of the differences squared in Cell F5 (highlighted in gray) is weighted by Column C.

transition to the forecasting trajectory, and second it generally results in a higher ceiling for the S-curve thus neutralizing to some extent the natural tendency of S-curve fits to underestimate the ceiling (see discussion in Section 2.6).

The life cycle in Column E is calculated by successive differences from the cells in Column D. Once the life cycle is determined, seasonality can be calculated by averaging the corresponding-quarter deviations from the data values. The software package *A Second Lease on Life* from Growth Dynamics (also incorporated in the package *Where Are You on the Curve*), is built around the fitting procedure described here. Besides a calculation of seasonality it offers a number of additional features.

The fitting procedure discussed so far can be used to fit any theoretical expression (analytic function), for example two S-curves cascading, the bell-shaped mathematical derivative of the S-curve Equation 2.2.2 (see mathematical expression given in Appendix A.3), or even the elaborate expression for the cycle of services also presented in Appendix A3. In each case the analytical function must be coded in a worksheet column and all of the parameters involved must be given to the Solver. For two cascading S-curves, there will be a total of 6 or 7 parameters depending whether there is a pedestal or not. For the bell-shaped mathematical derivative of the S-curve there will be only 3 parameters even if the corresponding S-curve sits on a pedestal!

Non-equal spacing of the data points presents no particular problem provided the graph is of the "Scatter" type. But special attention must be paid when constructing the life-cycle curve from the S-curve.

The Software Package "A Second Lease on Life"

A Second Lease on Life is a do-it-yourself S-curve fitting program built on Visual Basic and Microsoft Excel. You can fit an S-curve to a given set of data and consequently determine the position on the corresponding life-cycle curve. The program delimits the four equal-duration seasons as defined in Chapter 3. The delimitation of season is done so as to divide the S-curve span—from penetration level of 1% to 99%—into five equal periods (winter, spring, summer, fall, winter). For this it suffices to calculate the time "summer" begins (penetration level of 30%) and the time it ends (70%) from Equation 2.2.2 as follows:

Summer begins at $t_{30\%} = \frac{1}{a}\left[\ln\frac{0.3}{0.7} + at_o\right]$

Summer ends at $t_{70\%} = \frac{1}{a}\left[\ln\frac{0.7}{0.3} + at_o\right]$

The Solver is used to minimize the sum of differences squared. The data can be weighted in four different ways depending on what section of the historical period needs to be emphasized: "Flat", "Early" history, "Recent" history, or "Custom". For most practical purposes the first three choices of weights suffice. For the choice "Custom" one needs to adjust the weights on a point-by-point basis. The greater the weight, the closer the fitted S-curve will pass from the data point in question. It is recommended that all three weights are tried. The different answers one obtains give some indication of the robustness of the answer. But preference is generally given to the weights emphasizing recent history.

Following a successful fit the program calculates seasonal indexes for each quarter by averaging deviations between the sales data and the life-cycle curve. This enables correcting the forecasts for seasonality.

Finally, the program enables what-if scenario playing. This capability addresses a frequent concern of business planners, namely how probable is that a set target will be surpassed or otherwise not quite reached. Alternatively, the feature can be used to gauge the probability (and by inference the difficulty that will be encountered) in exceeding a certain target by say 10%. Such what-if capabilities are valuable to marketers and strategic planners.

The calculation of the probability that a certain ceiling will be reached is done via the *reduced* Chi Square distribution (see earlier discussion in Section 10.1) for which knowledge of the error per data point is needed. This error has been approximated as equal to the average deviation between data and life-cycle curve in the lower graph of Figure 10.1.4. From look-up tables steps have been defined matching ranges of the *reduced* Chi Square with ranges of confidence levels (probability). Thus probabilities can be estimated for ceiling values above or below the optimum value determined by the Solver.

In the program the button "Explore Possibilities" triggers the appearance of a green pad on which movements of the cursor translate into variations of the value of the ceiling M (vertical displacements) and the value of the pedestal C (horizontal displacements). In every new cursor position, the other two parameters a and t_o are automatically calculated via a linear regression on the data. In this way there is a continuous "morphing" of the S-curve in the graph on the M and C values dictated by the position of the cursor on the pad; simultaneously the size of error and the corresponding probability of occurrence are displaced. The percentage displayed on top of the red error column is the probability of realization of the S-curve shown in the graph.

It must be said that this probability of achieving a certain target (value for M) is only indicative. The scientific rigor in the quantitative calculation of the confidence levels has been compromised by the approximation of the errors on the data points and by the stepwise matching of *reduced* Chi Square values to confidence levels mentioned earlier. Still, this feature constitutes a unique user-friendly tool for obtaining quantitative science-based feedback on the probability to achieve a certain growth target. It should also be noted that because of the way it was constructed this probability estimate is meaningful only for the "Recent" weights and should not be compared between different weights.

10.3 – HOW TO FIT S-CURVES WITH A VARIABLE CEILING

It is often encountered that the niche into which species are growing does not remain constant over time but increases, if gently. This typically happens when the niche in question consists of a market, a population, or a living organism that itself grows with time. In such cases M is not a constant in Equation 2.2.1, which now can no longer be solved analytically but must be approximated with iterative numerical techniques. M may be increasing with time or with X, to a first approximation linearly as follows:

$$M = at + b \qquad \text{or}$$
$$M = aX + b$$

we will choose here the second case because it results in a finite growth of M over time (in fact it can be shown that it is S-shaped like X.

Equation 2.2.1 can then be rewritten as:

$$\frac{dX}{dt} = \alpha X \left(1 - \frac{X}{M}\right) = \alpha X \left[1 - \frac{X}{(aX + b)}\right] \qquad 10.3.1$$

where α is not the same constant as in Equation 2.2.1 and certainly different than a.

By the definition of a mathematical derivative, the centered discrete derivative for equally-spaced data points can be approximated as:

$$\frac{dX}{dt} \cong \frac{\Delta X}{\Delta t} = \frac{X_{n+1} - X_{n-1}}{2\Delta t}$$

which for $\Delta t = 1$ can transform Equation 10.3.1 to the following:

$$X_{n+1} = 2 \left[\alpha X_n - \frac{\alpha X_n^2}{(aX_n + b)}\right] + X_{n-1} \qquad 10.3.2$$

This equation can easily be programmed into the column of an Excel worksheet. Subsequently the sum of differences squared can be calculated with the values X_{n+1} subtracted from the corresponding data point. The Solver can then be invoked to minimize this sum by varying a total of four parameters, namely α, a, b, and X_o, the last being the starting values for the iteration of Equation 10.3.2.

The fitting procedure here encounters two new difficulties when compared with fitting simple S-curves. The first is that the expression for X_1 cannot be calculated according to Equation 10.3.2 because there is no X_{-1}. We therefore approximate it according to the one-sided discrete derivative as follows:

$$\frac{dX}{dt} \cong \frac{\Delta X}{\Delta t} = \frac{X_{n+1} - X_n}{\Delta t} \qquad \text{and}$$

$$X_1 = (1 + \alpha)X_o - \frac{\alpha X_o^{\,2}}{(aX_o + b)}$$

The second difficulty is choosing a good starting value for α. This slope, whose starting value is not obvious even in the simple S-curve fit, plays a more crucial role here. A poorly chosen starting value can easily result in solutions with chaotic behavior because of the discrete nature of the expressions that are being iterated. In Appendix A3 there is a mathematical procedure involving the minimization of a Chi Square that permits an analytic determination of α, which can then be used as an excellent starting value.

Example: US Nobel Laureates

An analysis of the US Nobel Laureates with a variable-ceiling S-curve was discussed in Section 2.6 and the results were compared with the classic S-curve approach in Figure 2.6.1. Here will go into the technical details on how it was done.

Figure 10.3.1 shows US Nobel laureates per capita, annual and cumulative data in Columns C and B respectively. The expression for an S-curve with variable ceiling is entered in Column F as follows:

Cell F7 =(1+F$1)*F6-(F$1/(F$2*F6+F$3))*F6^2

and from the 8th row onward:

Cell F8 =2*(F$1*F7-F$1*F7^2/(F$2*F7+F$3))+F6

The target to be minimized by the Solver is Cell G5 and represents the sum of the differences squared between Columns B and F on a cell-by-cell basis. There are no particular weights applied (i.e. flat weights assumed).

The results (α, a, b, and X_o) are displayed in Cells F1:F4 respectively. These are the four parameters that were varied by the Solver in order to minimize the sum in Cell G5. Furthermore, indirect calculations yield values for the final M (Cell D3), and the timing and penetration level of the curve's inflection point in Cells D1 and C2 respectively. The timing of the inflection point is given simply by the maximum of the life-cycle curve in Column D. The relevant mathematical derivations described in Appendix A3:

Cell D3 = F3/(1-F2)
Cell C2 =(-B2-SQRT(B2^2-4*B1*B3))/(2*B1)/D3

where B1 = F2^2-F2, B2 =2*F2*F3-2*F3, and B3 = F3^2

To choose starting values we begin by assuming that the ceiling of the S-curve is not varying, i.e. $a = 0$ and $b = M$. The starting value for X_o is the first data point. The starting value for α—Cell I3—can be chosen rather precisely here thanks to the mathematical derivation described in Appendix A3 [Cell I3 = (H4+I4)/J4 where H4, I4, and J4 represent the sums of the respective columns].

The existence of a pedestal demands a straight-forward generalization with the introduction of an additive constant (5th parameter to be varied) in the expressions of Column F8.

US NOBEL LAUREATE S PER CAPITA

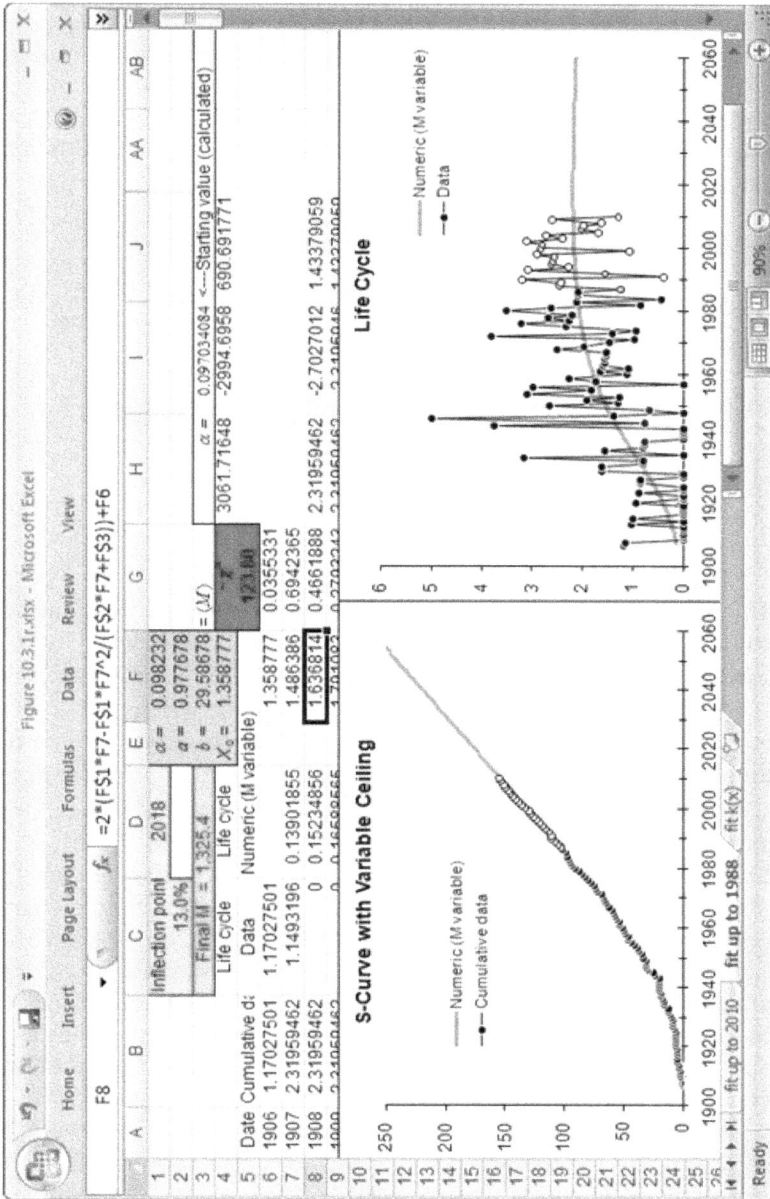

Figure 10.3.1 The gray line is an S-curve fit with variable ceiling (*M*). Open circles are recent data not considered in the fit.

10.4 – HOW TO FIT THE VOLTERRA-LOTKA EQUATIONS

Just like the case of the S-curve with a variable ceiling, the Volterra-Lotka system of equations is also not amenable to an analytic solution. Therefore solving Equations 8.1.1, and the more complicated expressions for a three-species niche presented in Appendix A3, needs to be approached numerically and to do that we need to transform differential equations to difference equations.

By the definition of a mathematical derivative:

$$\frac{dX}{dt} \cong \frac{\Delta X}{\Delta t} = \frac{X_{n+1} - X_n}{\Delta t}$$

which for $\Delta t = 1$ can transform Equations 8.1.1 to the following:

$$X_{n+1} = (1 + a_x)X_n - b_x X_n^2 + c_{xy} X_n Y_n$$

$$Y_{n+1} = (1 + a_y)Y_n - b_y Y_n^2 + c_{yx} X_n Y_n$$

10.4.1

This set of equations can easily be programmed into two adjacent columns of an Excel worksheet. Subsequently the overall sum of differences squared can be calculated with the values X_n subtracted from the corresponding data of species No. 1 while the values Y_n from the corresponding data of species No. 2. The Solver can then be invoked to minimize this sum by varying a total of eight parameters, namely a_x, b_x, c_{xy}, a_y, b_y, c_{yx}, X_o, and Y_o, the last two being starting values for the iteration of Equations 10.4.1.

The particular difficulty with fitting equations 10.4.1 comes from the discrete nature of the formulae, which can cause a chaotic state to appear (the link between S-curves and the chaos equation is briefly discussed in Appendix A3). A simultaneous variation of eight parameters by the Solver more often than not breaks into oscillatory (read chaotic) solutions. The user may need to vary few parameters at a time and come back to the same parameters in different combinations several times before the Solver indicates no more improvement. But here good starting values play a primordial role. Good starting values for X_o, and Y_o are trivial; they are the first data points of the two species. The challenge is finding good starting value for the other six parameters.

In Appendix A3 there is a mathematical procedure describing an analytic minimization of the Chi Square that results in six equations for our six unknowns (the Solver parameters). Solving the six equations we find a first answer for the six parameters, which constitute excellent starting values for the Solver minimization.

Example: Nobel Laureates as a 2-Species Niche

A Volterra-Lotka analysis of the US Nobel Laureates was discussed in Section 8.5. Here will go into the technical details on how it was done. Figure 10.4.1 shows the data in Columns C and D for American and Other Nobel laureates respectively. The following theoretical expressions, modeled on Equations 10.4.1, were entered in Columns K and L respectively:

Cell K8 = (1+$K$2)*K7+$K$3*K7^2+$K$4*L7*K7
Cell L8 = (1+$L$2)*L7+$L$4*L7^2+$L$3*K7*L7

For the calculation of the two constituent Chi Squares in Cells M6 and N6 the errors on the data were assumed to be purely statistical. Therefore, the expressions in Columns M and N were:

Cell M7 = (C7-K7)^2/K7
Cell N7 = (D7-L7)^2/L7

The overall Chi Square, i.e. the sum of the two constituent Chi Squares was in Cell M4 and the *reduced* Chi Square in Cell O4.

The Solver was asked to minimize the overall Chi Square by varying the total of eight parameters in Cells K2:L4 and K7:L7. The results shown in Figure 10.4.1 are also presented in terms of the user-friendly variables **attractiveness**, **niche size**, and **competition constants** defined in terms of the constants a, b, and c in the Volterra-Lotka Equations 8.1.1 of the form:

$$\frac{dX}{dt} = aX - bX^2 + cXY$$

Following trivial algebraic manipulations this equation can be cast in the following form:

$$\frac{dX}{dt} = bX\left[\left(\frac{a}{b} + \frac{c}{b}Y\right) - X\right]$$

which can now be directly compared to the S-curve equation repeated here:

$$\frac{dX}{dt} = \alpha X(M - X)$$

(please note that $\alpha \neq a$).

Comparing the two equations we can understand why:

Attractiveness is defined as e^a and measures how many new sales will be triggered by one sale (this becomes obvious when X and Y are *very* small).

The **niche size** is defined as a/b and represents the virtual ceiling M of an S-curve in the hypothetical case in which the competitor would grow alone in the absence of competition (for $Y = 0$ the two equations become identical).

The **competition constant** is defined as c/b and represents what happens to one's potential sales (niche size) when the competitor wins one sale ($Y = 1$).

The values of the user-friendly variables are displayed in the boxed Cells S1:V3. More specifically and considering that the theoretical expressions in Columns K and L had a + sign in front of the b parameter, the expressions used are:

Cell T2 = EXP(K2)	Cell U2 = K2/(-K3)	Cell V2 = K4/(-K3)
Cell T3 = EXP(L2)	Cell U3 = L2/(-L4)	Cell V3 = L3/(-L4)

In running the Solver the crucial choices of starting values were made as follows: the first data points in Cells C7, D7 were taken as starting values for K7, L7 respectively. As for the other six parameters to be varied, as mentioned earlier, their starting values were taken from the matrix B20:D21 and transposed into Cells K2:L4. The subsequent running of the Solver was more or less straightforward but it necessitated two additional requirements: Cell K2 >= 0 and L4 <= 0 in order to eliminate solutions with nonphysical (negative) niche sizes.

HOW TO USE THE VOLTERRA-LOTKA EQUATIONS IN A 2-SPECIES NICHE

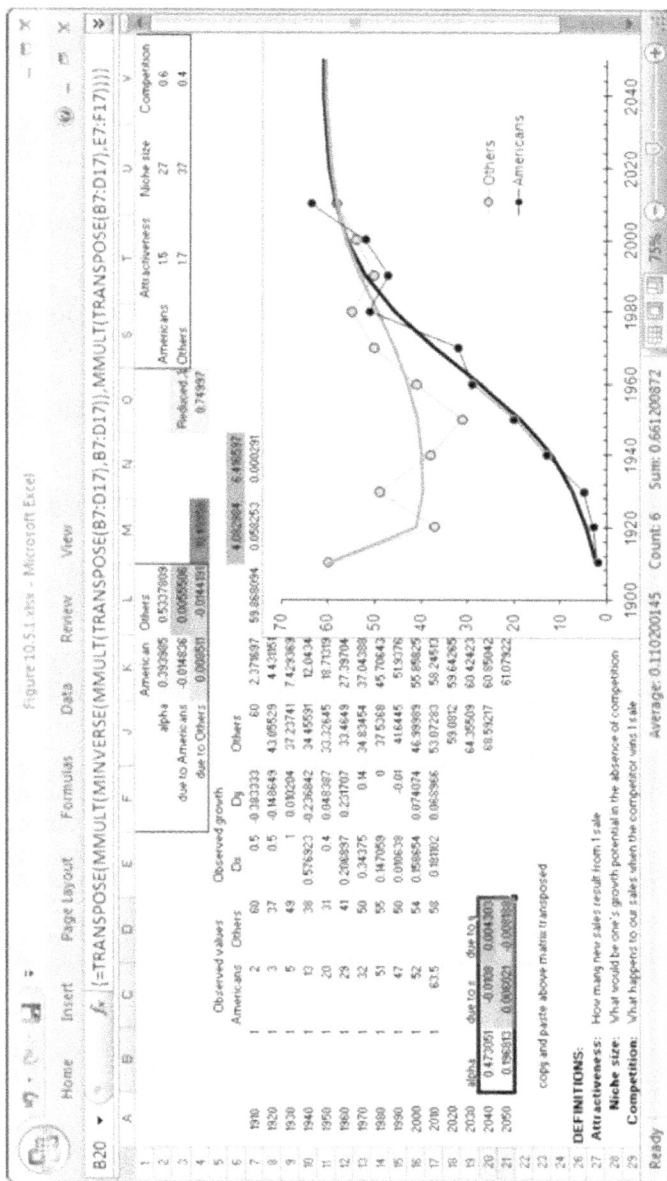

Figure 10.4.1 The Excel worksheet applying the Volterra-Lotka model to a 2-species niche for Nobel-prize awards. The 2010 data points are projections based on data from years 2001-2009. The formula bar shows the intricate array in Cells B20:D21.

IN CLOSING

In this chapter there is adequate instruction on how to use Excel to fit curves on data and in particular S-curves and Volterra-Lotka equations. The former deals with single-species niches whereas the latter can handle niches with two or more species. The example of US Nobel laureates has demonstrated how to tackle a competitive situation in progressively increasing sophistication, complexity, and accuracy of results. This example was first taken up in Chapter 2 by fitting a single S-curve on the data. It was then improved by fitting an S-curve with a varying ceiling. Finally in Chapter 8 the example demonstrated the use of the Volterra-Lotka equations, which threw light on how the very first attempt could have been less inadequate had the S-curve been fit on annual instead of cumulative data. In this chapter we explained all the technical details, which included the use of the *reduced* Chi Square to evaluate confidence levels.

Of course, fitting eight parameters (for the two-species niche) is more complicated than fitting only three or four for a single S-curve, particularly given the fact that the former involves iterative discrete manipulations that may result in solution of chaotic nature. To avoid meaningless solutions good starting values for the Solver are essential and can be obtained analytically. The difficulties become more serious for a three-species niche, which would involve 15 parameters, see mathematical generalization of the many-species problem in Appendix A3.

But given long time series-data of good quality it is possible to obtain significant and surprising insights on how "species" behave in the market-place. For example, in the case of US Nobel laureates the coupling constants indicated that the ability of Nobel laureates to "multiply", i.e. the extent to which a Nobel laureate incubates more laureates, is lower for Americans than it is for other nationalities. This type of understanding could not have been obtained by simple S-curve fits or other traditional forecasting techniques for that matter.

EPILOGUE

"Predictions helped me think much more clearly about the world around me."
    Thomas Dorsey, Author of *Point & Figure Charting*

"I feel there is much wisdom in the book about life in general in a variety of ways…it provided some profound insights to me."
    Ken Ferlic, Physicist

"[Modis'] contributions will help me become an even better dad and husband."
    Hamilton Lewis II, Market Analyst

There have been many endorsements of my work on S-curves, some by renowned scientists and others by businesspersons who pointed out the usefulness of the subject be it on forecasting, strategy setting, or competition management. But the above three have been singled out here because they attest to the added value the ubiquitous S-curves can bring on a gut level. The tools and methodologies I have described earlier can help the practicing executive enrich his or her daily work in different ways as shown in the various case studies presented earlier. But they can probably provide the decision maker with fruitful insights early on in *all* his or her endeavors. I cannot think of a project, in which competition and growth play an important role, that would not benefit during its early stages in some way from employing one of the approaches described in this book.

An analysis involving S-curves is less meant to replace traditional business practices and more to enrich them with complementary understanding. It is like lateral thinking, an independent second opinion, so frequently solicited from the medical corps concerning serious health problems. Moreover, science-based conclusions and advice are always appreciated for their objectiveness, that is, the lack of human bias.

The most respected scientific laws are the simple ones. The simpler the law, the more fundamental it is, and the broader its domain of application. This is the case with natural growth in competition, the law that follows the S-shaped pattern. The pattern has an associated life cycle—namely a beginning, a growth phase, a maturity phase, a declining phase, and an end. Moreover, these phases match the seasons metaphor in many respects, with the end corresponding to a second winter.

Fundamental laws are not forgiving. It is unwise to try to fight a well-established natural-growth process. It is far more efficient to anticipate, prepare, and tune in with what is happening by following least-resistance paths. A company's turnaround is effectively tantamount to the death of the old company in favor of the birth of a new one. This is a necessary condition, creating the possibility but not a guarantee for new growth. By contrast, a long life cycle can be secured by identifying and supporting the company's various business units one by one and in accordance with the season of each. For example, invest in those in spring season, and replace those in fall season.

Winter is the season when changes are easiest to implement. Yet even in winter, the biggest resistance to change should be expected from the human element, the company's culture. Culture is the collective programming of the mind that distinguishes human communities into "species." It is responsible for wars. People are the only animals that destroy their own through war, an act that is basically an expression of intercultural competition. Cultural forces influence the rate of most social change. Culture represents the inertia (mass) that resists the implementation of leaders' visions. Rich cultures, often stemming from long traditions, tend to be non-innovating. Cultural changes are so slow that long-term thinking is essential, and perseverance is more important than argument.

One way to deal with resistive cultural forces is to involve the people in the decision-making process. This approach works well with small groups such as executive teams and management boards. Computer-based tools like *Where Are You on the Curve and What to Do about It* aid decision making in three ways:

- They extract conscious and subconscious knowledge from informed and experienced executives. Combining intelligent people with intelligent tools produces results that neither could produce separately.
- They ensure the participants' buy-in, involving them in the conclusion-arriving process.
- They achieve quick results. Looking at the big picture helps participants arrive at difficult decisions within a short time.

But perhaps the S-curve approach can be of even greater help in a qualitative way, without the use of computers, curve-fitting programs, and mathematical calculations. When the S-curve and its life cycle are grasped more than just intellectually, they give rise to a better understanding of the most probable evolution of a process and how much of it still lies ahead. Such understanding goes well beyond the supertanker analogy, which claims that supertankers cannot make sharp turns, and therefore their immediate course is predictable. The life cycle of natural growth is to a first approximation symmetric, so that there is as much to be expected from the time the maximum rate of growth is reached to the end of the cycle as was obtained from the beginning of the cycle to the time of the maximum rate of growth. From half of a growth process one can intuitively visualize the other half.

Invariably there is change, some of it imposed, some of it provoked. For one reason or another, transitions always take place. Change may be inevitable, but if it follows a natural course, it can be anticipated and planned for. Timing is important. In the world of business there is a time to be conservative—the phase of steep growth when things work well and the best strategy is to change nothing. There is also the time of saturation when the growth curve starts flattening out. What is needed then is innovation and encouragement to explore new directions. Our leaders may not be able to do much about changing an established trend, but they can do a lot in preparing, adapting, and being in harmony with it. The same is true for individuals. During periods of growth or transition our attitude needs to be a function of where we are on the S-curve. The flat parts of the curve in the beginning and toward the end of the process call for action and entrepreneurship, but the steeply-rising part in the middle calls for noninterference, letting things happen under their own momentum.

S-curves enable us to see more clearly further into the future and make predictions, but they also enable us to obtain a better understanding of the past. Fundamental natural laws such as competition between species and survival of the fittest can reveal unique insights into what the future has in store for us. But also into what the past may hide. After all, the past is not immune to the passage of time. More than once we have witnessed popular world leaders and successful political systems regress into dishonor and oblivion. The way we think and act undergoes continuous transformation. Naïve (e.g. linear) extrapolations may be recipes for disaster whereas a grasping of natural laws can yield enhanced intuitive farsightedness. Moreover, when quantitatively employed via such methodologies as S-curves and the Volterra-Lotka equations, they can provide practical and unique day-to-day decision support.

APPENDIXES

A.1 - ESTIMATION OF THE UNCERTAINTIES IN S-CURVE FITS

Alain Debecker and I undertook an extensive computer simulation, (a Monte Carlo study) to quantify the uncertainties on the parameters determined by S-curve fits.[1] We carried out a large number of fits, (around forty thousand), on simulated data randomly deviated around theoretical S-curves and covering a variety of time spans across the width of the life cycle. We fitted the smeared data using Equation 2.2.2 from Section 2.2. Each fit yielded values for the three parameters M, a, and t_o. With many fits for every set of conditions, we were able to make distributions of the fitted values and compare their average to the theoretical value used in generating the scattered data. The width of the distributions allowed us to estimate the errors in terms of confidence levels.

The results of our study showed that the more precise the data and the bigger the section of the S-curve they cover, the more accurately the parameters can be recovered. I give below three representative look-up tables. From Table A.1.2 we can see that historical data covering the first half of the S-curve with 10% error per data point will yield a value for the final maximum accurate to within 21%, with a 95% confidence level.

As an example, let us consider the sales of the minicomputer VAX 11/750 shown in Figure 2.3.1. At the time of the fit, there had been 6,500 units sold and M was estimated at 8,600 units. Consequently, the S-curve section covered by the data was $6,500/8,600 = 76\%$. From the scattering of the quarterly sales, the statistical error per point, after accounting for seasonal variations, was evaluated as 5%. From Table A.1.3, then, we obtained the uncertainty on M as somewhat higher than 4% for a confidence level of 95%. The final ceiling of 8,200 fell within the estimated uncertainty.

Finally, we were able to establish correlations between the uncertainties on the parameters determined. One interesting conclusion, for example, was that among the S-curves that can all fit a set of data, with comparable statistical validity, the curves with smaller values for a have bigger values for M. In other words, a slower rate of growth correlates to a larger niche size and vice-versa. This implies that accelerated growth is associated with a lower ceiling, bringing to mind such folkloric images as short life spans for candles burning at both ends.

TABLE A.1.1

Expected uncertainties on *M* fitted from data covering the range 1% to 30% of the total S-curve. The confidence level is marked vertically, while the error on the historical data points is marked horizontally. All numbers are in percentages.

	1	*5*	*10*	*15*	*20*	*25*
70	2.7	13	28	47	69	120
75	3.2	15	32	53	81	190
80	3.9	17	36	62	110	240
85	4.8	19	41	81	130	370
90	5.9	22	48	110	210	470
95	8.5	29	66	140	350	820
99	48.5	49	180	350	690	

TABLE A.1.2

Expected uncertainties on *M* fitted from data covering the range 1% to 50% of the total S-curve. The confidence level is marked vertically, while the error on the historical data points is marked horizontally. All numbers are in percentages.

	1	*5*	*10*	*15*	*20*	*25*
70	1.2	5.1	11	17	23	23
75	1.4	5.5	12	19	26	32
80	1.8	6.4	14	22	29	36
85	2.1	7.3	16	25	36	42
90	2.6	8.8	18	29	42	48
95	3.1	11.0	21	39	56	66
99	4.6	22.0	30	55	150	110

TABLE A.1.3

Expected uncertainties on *M* fitted from data covering the range 1% to 80% of the total S-curve. The confidence level is marked vertically, while the error on the historical data points is marked horizontally. All numbers are in percentages.

	1	5	10	15	20	25
70	0.5	1.9	3.9	5.1	8.1	8.9
75	0.6	2.1	4.4	5.5	9.0	9.6
80	0.7	2.4	4.8	6.2	9.8	11.0
85	0.8	2.8	5.5	7.1	12.0	13.0
90	1.1	3.3	6.3	9.1	13.0	16.0
95	1.3	4.0	7.6	11.0	16.0	18.0
99	2.2	5.6	9.1	15.0	21.0	31.0

A.2 - DEVIATION BETWEEN S-CURVE AND CORRESPONDING EXPONENTIAL

Here we will examine at what time the S-curve deviates from an exponential pattern in a significant way, see Figure A.2.1. Table A.2.1 below quantifies the deviation between a logistic and the corresponding exponential pattern as a fraction of the S-curve's final ceiling. By "corresponding" exponential we mean the limit of Equation 2.2.2 from Section 2.2 as $t \to -\infty$.

Divergence of Exponential from S-curve

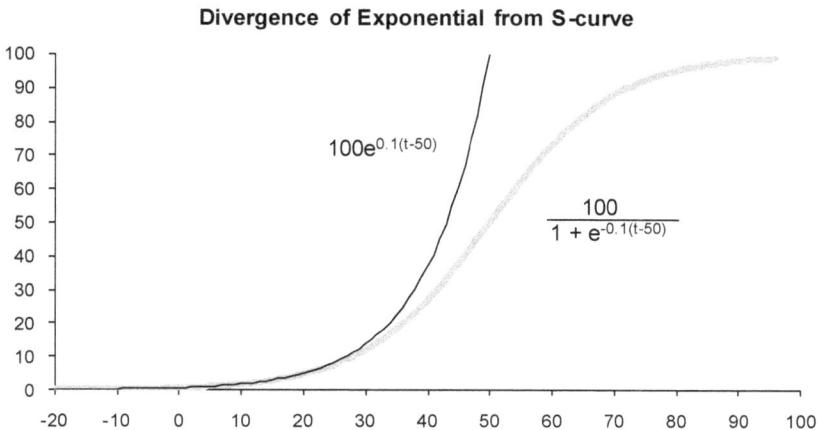

$$100e^{0.1(t-50)}$$

$$\frac{100}{1 + e^{-0.1(t-50)}}$$

Figure A.2.1. A theoretical S-curve (gray line) and the exponential (thin black line) it reduces to as time goes backward. The formulae used are shown in the graph.

Table A.2.1: The Deviation: (Exponential – S-Curve)/S-Curve

Deviation	Penetration
11.1%	10.0%
12.2%	10.9%
13.5%	11.9%
15.0%	13.0%
16.5%	14.2%
18.3%	15.4%
20.2%	16.8%
22.3%	18.2%
24.7%	19.8%
27.3%	21.4%
30.1%	23.1%
33.3%	25.0%
36.8%	26.9%
40.7%	28.9%
44.9%	31.0%
49.7%	33.2%
54.9%	35.4%
60.7%	37.8%
67.0%	40.1%
74.1%	42.6%
81.9%	45.0%
90.5%	47.5%
100.0%	50.0%

When the S-curve pattern reaches 10% of its ceiling, the exponential reads 11.1% above the S-curve level. When the S-curve is half way completed, the exponential pattern reads 100% above the S-curve level. Considering that a 15% deviation between exponential and S-curve patterns cannot go easily unnoticed, we can safely say that by the time an S-curve reaches a penetration level of 13% there can be little ambiguity as to whether the pattern is still compatible with a pure exponential. Alternatively said, a data pattern that unquestionably begins deviating from an exponential (i.e. lags behind) should not reach a ceiling before at least 7 times the present level.

A3 – MATHEMATICAL FORMULATIONS

In Part I of this book we saw how S-curves and related methodologies can be used in business situations whereas in Part II we saw the technical details, and in particular the Excel setups, on how exactly to do that.

Below we go into the mathematics that supports the tools and methodologies in Parts I and II. This mathematics may look complicated at times; moreover it is not indispensable because one can use the formulations in Part II as such trusting they are correct. Nevertheless, this book would not be complete without rigorous mathematical expressions and derivations for what is being offered. This way the scientific-minded user has the option of not only checking the applications presented in Part II but also programming his or her own applications for Excel or other software platforms.

The Logistic Life Cycle

The logistic equation that gives rise to the S-curve pattern was formulated as in Equation 2.2.2 the first mathematical derivative of which gives rise to the bell-shaped pattern of the life cycle. The expression in detail is:

$$\frac{dX(t)}{dt} = \frac{\alpha M}{(1 + e^{\alpha(t-t_o)})(1 + e^{-\alpha(t-t_o)})} \qquad \text{A. 3.1}$$

This is what has to be coded into the Excel worksheet in order to fit a bell-shaped curve on a given set of data. The parameters to be varied by the Solver are M, α, and t_o.

Experience has demonstrated, however, that most of the time it is preferable to fit and S-curve on the cumulative data and then deduce the life cycle by successive subtractions.

The Chaos Equation

The logistic-growth equation is intimately related to the equation that gives rise to states of chaos.[1] Equation 2.2.1 is repeated here for convenience:

$$\frac{dX}{dt} = \alpha X(M - X) \qquad \text{A. 3.2}$$

where α and M constants.

By the definition of a mathematical derivative:

$$\frac{dX}{dt} \equiv \frac{\Delta X}{\Delta t}\bigg|_{\Delta t \to 0}$$

if Δt is small but does not tend to 0, we can replace $\dfrac{dX}{dt}$ by $\dfrac{\Delta X}{\Delta t}$

and obtain $\left(\Delta X\right)_n = aX_n\left(M - X_n\right)\Delta t$

and because $(\Delta X)_n \equiv X_{n+1} - X_n$ we obtain

$$X_{n+1} = X_n + \left(\Delta X\right)_n \Delta t = X_n + aX_n\left(M - X_n\right)\Delta t$$

Now $\Delta t = 1$ corresponds to time steps of size 1 and concords with incrementing n by 1 at a time. A trivial algebraic manipulation then yields:

$$X_{n+1} = aX_n(C - X_n) \quad \text{where } C = \frac{1 + aM}{a}$$

which is the *chaos equation*, otherwise known as the *logistic discrete equation*:

$$X_{n+1} = rX_n(1 - X_n) \tag{A.3.3}$$

where r is a constant .

The two equations A.3.2 and A.3.3 are strikingly similar but the former is solved via integration and its solution gives rise to the smooth S-shaped logistic pattern (Equation 2.2.2), whereas the latter is solved via iteration and its solution gives rise to states of chaos for $r > 3.7$. The former emphasizes the presence of a trend and has become the tool to describe natural growth. The latter emphasizes the lack of trend and has become the tool to describe chaos. The chaotic fluctuations appear on what corresponds to the ceiling of the logistic after the upward trend has died down, as shown in Figure A.3.1.

GENERATION OF STATES OF CHAOS

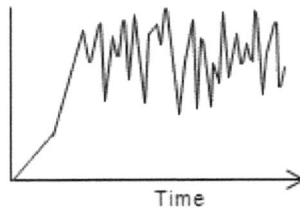

Time

Figure A.3.1 A typical graph of Equation A.3.3 and values of $r > 3.7$.

It has also been shown that if Equation A.3.2 is first solved and then made discrete, chaotic-type fluctuations can be expected before *as well as* after the curve's steep rise.[2] The pattern thus obtained is comparable to a cascade of steps like the one shown in Figure A.3.1 (corresponds to cascading S-curves).

Price Elasticity

Price elasticity relates the volume of sales to the price. Obviously, the lower the price, the higher the number of transactions. Therefore the volume must be inversely proportional to the price. In order not to lose any generality, we assume:

$$V = \frac{C}{P^n} \qquad\qquad A.3.4$$

where C is a constant, V is the volume of sales in dollars, and P is the price.[3]

Taking the mathematical derivative and for small ΔV and ΔP we have:

$$\frac{dV}{dP} = -\frac{nC}{P^{n+1}} \cong \frac{\Delta V}{\Delta P} = -n\frac{V}{P}$$

or expressed otherwise:

$$\frac{\Delta V}{\Delta V} = -n\frac{\Delta P}{P} \qquad\qquad A.3.5$$

which defines n as price elasticity, relating a change in volume ΔV to a change in price ΔP.

Typical values of n turn out to be around 1, which makes sense because a certain budget can in principle yield twice as many transactions at half the price.

Equation A.3.5 constitutes a quantitative definition of price elasticity. It relates volume changes to price changes. The determination of price elasticity n is straightforward for all cases where there exist sales data on a large spectrum of price range. It suffices to make a histogram of sales turnover as a function of price bucket and then fit Equation A.3.4 to this curve by asking Solver to vary the two parameters C and n.

If the elasticity in a given situation is determined as $n = 1.09$, then a 10% drop (rise) in price will increase (decrease) in the revenue by 10.9%. Needless to say that the changes ΔV and ΔP must be small as required by the derivative approximation mentioned earlier. Large changes are likely to result to non-elastic i.e. irreversible behavior. For example, a 50% drop in price may yield a certain rise in sales volume, but a subsequent rise in price to the level before the drop will most probably fall short of restoring the volume to its level before the drop.

Learning and Economies of Scale

Economies of scale—and much of the success of the industrial revolution can be demystified—as follows.[4] Manufacturing costs grow like an area variable but the utility produced like a volume variable. To understand this, think of manufacturing a container. Costs will be proportional to the total surface ($\propto r^2$), but the container's usefulness—what customers pay for—is the volume it encloses ($\propto r^3$). Consequently, costs and volumes between State 1 and State 2 are related as follows:

$$\left(\frac{V_2}{V_1}\right)^{\frac{1}{3}} = \frac{r_2}{r_1} = \left(\frac{C_1}{C_2}\right)^{\frac{1}{2}} \qquad \text{and}$$

$$\frac{V_2}{V_1} = \left(\frac{C_1}{C_2}\right)^{\frac{3}{2}} \qquad\qquad \text{A.3.6}$$

The exponent 3/2 agrees well with the value 1.6 experimentally established, and quoted in Chemical Engineering Handbooks for process industries.

If all prices were cut in half, the money available would suffice for twice the volume of transactions. But doubling the volume would incur only 26% more manufacturing costs (from Equation A.3.6)—hence the profit!

Obviously reality is not that simple, but Equation A.3.5 implies more important rewards for bigger volumes. The moral of the story is along the lines of "bigness is goodness"—that is, the greater the volume, the greater the profit. This is not the entire story, however.

We saw in Section 2.7 that the S-shape learning process is intimately related to economies of scale. The reasoning was different there. We simply invoked the similarity between the experimental industry curve, and the inverse of the S-curve expression:

$$\frac{1}{X(t)} = \frac{1 + e^{-\alpha(t-t_o)}}{M} = \frac{1}{M} + \frac{e^{-\alpha(t-t_o)}}{M}$$

When graphed this expression depicts an exponential decaying toward a constant final value $(1/M)$, which is how the industry curve has been experimentally evidenced. The implication is that learning alone could have accounted for the reduction of costs with volume. The truth probably involves both phenomena, i.e. voluminous production and learning.

S-Curves with Variable Ceiling

In Section 10.3 we discussed the case of a species growing into a niche that does not remain constant during the growth process; in particular we assumed that M increases according to: $M = aX + b$.

We also talked about the importance of the starting value for α and gave the expressions for the final ceiling M and α to be entered in the designated worksheet cells without explaining how these expressions were be derived. Below we give the two derivations.

The ceiling M is the maximum value reached by the variable X. It can be analytically determined by setting the variable's first derivative to zero:

$$\frac{dX}{dt} = \alpha X \left[1 - \frac{X}{(aX + b)} \right] = 0$$

which occurs for $X = \frac{b}{a-1}$ (other than the degenerate solution $X = 0$). The reader should not confuse α with a.

The starting value for α can be obtained via the method of minimizing the least-squares error.[5,6] The quantity F below is akin to the Chi Square and is function of α, a, and b.

$$F = \sum_i (X_i - Q_i)^2$$

where X_i are the data points and Q_i the theoretical calculation form Equation 10.3.2, namely:

$$Q_i = 2 \left[\alpha X_{i-1} - \frac{\alpha X_{i-1}^2}{(aX_{i-1} + b)} \right] + X_{i-2}$$

we can look for a minimum for F by setting its first partial derivative with respect to α equal to zero:

$$\frac{\vartheta F}{\vartheta \alpha} = 0 = 2 \sum_{i} (X_i - Q_i)\left(-\frac{\vartheta Q_i}{\vartheta \alpha}\right)$$

which implies:

$$\sum_{i} (X_i - Q_i) = 0$$

or

$$\sum_{i} \left(X_i - 2\left[\alpha X_{i-1} - \frac{\alpha X_{i-1}^2}{(aX_{i-1} + b)}\right] - X_{i-2}\right) = 0$$

This last expression is linear in α and therefore can be solved to determine a value for α—shown below—in terms of the sums of X_i, X_{i-1}, X_{i-2}, and the constants a, and b. The reader is warned not to confuse a with α.

$$\alpha = \frac{1}{2}\left(\frac{\sum X_i - \sum X_{i-2}}{\sum X_{i-1} - \sum \frac{X_{i-1}^2}{aX_i + b}}\right)$$

The Life Cycle of Services

In Chapter 7 we discussed the life cycle of services in terms of two types of mortality parameterization.[7] The simplest possible assumption was a constant percentage decay rate, in other words an exponential decay of the form:

$$\frac{1}{R(u)}\frac{dR(u)}{du} = -k$$

where $R(u)$ is the remaining population of age u, and k is a constant.

The convolution function below folds mortality into the product life cycle as expressed by Equation A.3.1:

$$Q(t) = \int_{0}^{\infty} \frac{\alpha M e^{-ku}}{(1 + e^{\alpha(t-u-t_o)})(1 + e^{-\alpha(t-u-t_o)})}\,du$$

and this is the expression that is fitted on the data and graphed in Figure 7.2.

A slightly more sophisticated expression for mortality is a linear function for the percentage decay rate:

$$\frac{1}{R(u)}\frac{dR(u)}{du} = aR(u) + b$$

where a and b are constants. It is worth pointing out that this equation is the same as the logistic Equation 2.2.1. The mortality function here is an S-curve, which becomes obvious by setting $N = -a/b$:

$$\frac{dR}{du} = -bR(N - R)$$

Furthermore, we can eliminate one of the constants by setting $N = 1.0$ because the mortality ceiling is at 100%.

The new convolution function below involves five parameters, three from the logistic growth Equation A.3.1 and two from the logistic mortality:

$$Q(t) = \int_0^\infty \frac{\alpha M}{(1 + e^{\alpha(t-u-t_o)})(1 + e^{-\alpha(t-u-t_o)})(1 + e^{a(u-u_o)})} du$$

this last expression was used for the graph in Figure 7.3 and is valid for young as well as older products. It can be coded into an Excel worksheet and fitted to a set of historical data via the Solver by varying the five parameters: M, α, a, t_o, and u_o.

Volterra-Lotka Equations for More than Two Species

Whenever there are more than two species in a niche, the Volterra-Lotka system of equations becomes increasingly complicated.[8] For example, three species in a niche require a total of 15 parameters to be varied (including three starting values X_o, Y_o, Z_o). The equations are the following:

$$\frac{dX}{dt} = a_x X - b_x X^2 + c_{xy} XY + c_{xz} XZ$$

$$\frac{dY}{dt} = a_y Y - b_y Y^2 + c_{yx} YX + c_{yz} YZ$$

$$\frac{dZ}{dt} = a_z Z - b_z Z^2 + c_{zx} ZX + c_{zy} ZY$$

For the general case of n species the number of parameters to be varied would be equal to $n(n + 1) + n$.

Finding Good Starting Values for the Solver in Volterra-Lotka Applications

It was pointed out earlier that solving the Volterra-Lotka equations via the Solver may result in meaningless/chaotic behavior of the solution particularly when the starting values have not been carefully chosen. Here we present a method for choosing appropriate starting values by again using the method of least squares to solve a set of linear equations having more equations than unknowns.[9]

We will present the two-species case, which can be trivially generalized to more species.

The Volterra-Lotka system of equations for two species, Equations 8.1.1, can be rewritten as:

$$\frac{1}{X}\frac{dX}{dt} = a_x + b_x X + c_{xy} Y$$

$$\frac{1}{Y}\frac{dY}{dt} = a_y + b_y Y + c_{yx} Y$$

Going now to the discrete case and centered derivatives we have:

$$\frac{\Delta X_i}{X_i} = \frac{X_{i+1} - X_{i-1}}{2X_i} = a_x + b_x X_i + c_{xy} Y_i$$

$$\frac{\Delta Y_i}{Y_i} = \frac{Y_{i+1} - Y_{i-1}}{2Y_i} = a_y + b_y Y_i + c_{yx} X_i$$

A.3.7

We want to minimize the square of the differences between data points D_i^X, D_i^Y and respective theoretical expression, namely:

$$\chi^2 = \sum_i (D_i^X - a_x - b_x X_i - c_{xy} Y_i)^2 + \left(D_i^Y - a_y - b_y Y_i - c_{yx} X_i\right)^2$$

This is equivalent to performing the least-squares process using the equations:

$$F_i = a + b X_i + c Y_i = 0 \qquad\qquad \text{A.3.8}$$

with the unknown array **A** and the residual array **K** defined as follows:

$$\mathbf{A} = \begin{bmatrix} a_x & a_y \\ b_x & b_y \\ c_{xy} & c_{yx} \end{bmatrix} \qquad \text{and} \qquad \mathbf{K} = \begin{bmatrix} \Delta X_1 & \Delta Y_1 \\ \Delta X_2 & \Delta Y_2 \\ \Delta X_3 & \Delta Y_3 \\ \vdots & \vdots \\ \vdots & \vdots \\ \vdots & \vdots \end{bmatrix}$$

Using Equations A.3.8 the Jacobian matrix is:

$$\mathbf{J} = \begin{bmatrix} \dfrac{\vartheta F_1}{\vartheta a} & \dfrac{\vartheta F_1}{\vartheta b} & \dfrac{\vartheta F_1}{\vartheta c} \\ \dfrac{\vartheta F_2}{\vartheta a} & \dfrac{\vartheta F_2}{\vartheta b} & \dfrac{\vartheta F_2}{\vartheta c} \\ \dfrac{\vartheta F_3}{\vartheta a} & \dfrac{\vartheta F_3}{\vartheta b} & \dfrac{\vartheta F_3}{\vartheta c} \\ \vdots & \vdots & \vdots \\ \vdots & \vdots & \vdots \\ \vdots & \vdots & \vdots \end{bmatrix} = \begin{bmatrix} 1 & X_1 & Y_1 \\ 1 & X_2 & Y_2 \\ 1 & X_3 & Y_3 \\ \vdots & \vdots & \vdots \\ \vdots & \vdots & \vdots \\ \vdots & \vdots & \vdots \end{bmatrix}$$

Lacking other information, the weighting matrix, **W**, is the identity matrix, that is:

$$\mathbf{W} = \mathbf{I}$$

And the unknowns $a_x, b_x, c_{xy}, a_y, b_y, c_{yx}$ can be solved for using the equation:

$$\mathbf{A} = (\mathbf{J}^t \mathbf{W} \mathbf{J})^{-1} \mathbf{J}^t \mathbf{W} \mathbf{K} = (\mathbf{J}^t \mathbf{J})^{-1} \mathbf{J}^t \mathbf{K}$$

which can be programmed directly into Excel cells using an array and the built-in functions TRANSPOSE, MMULT, and MINVERSE; see for example, the contents of the array B20:D21 in Figure 10.4.1.

The starting values thus determined constitute a first answer. The subsequent use of the Solver aims to fine-tune these values.

NOTES AND SOURCES

PREFACE

1. Theodore Modis, *Predictions – Society's Telltale Signature Reveals the Past and Forecasts the Future*, (New York: Simon & Schuster, 1992).
2. Theodore Modis, *Conquering Uncertainty*, (New York: McGraw-Hill, 1998).
3. http://www.growth- dynamics.com/default.asp?page=articles

1 – INTRODUCTION

1. *Statistical Abstract of the United States*, US Department of Commerce, Bureau of the Census; also from the *Historical Statistics of the United States, Colonial Times to 1970*, vols. 1 and 2 (Washington DC: Bureau of the Census, 1976).
2. John D. Williams, "The Nonsense about Safe Driving," *Fortune*, vol. LVIII, no. 3 (September 1958): 118–19.
3. Ralph Nader, *Unsafe at Any Speed*, (New York: Grossman Publishers, 1965).
4. For the data source see Note 1 above.
5. Isaac Asimov, *Exploring the Earth and the Cosmos*, (New York: Crown Publishers, 1982).
6. *Good News Bible, Today's English Version*, The Bible Society, Collins/Fontana.
7. La santé sans la médecine, est-ce prévisible? by T. Modis, *Médecine & Hygiène*, No 2083, 1995.

2 – NATURAL GROWTH IN COMPETITION

1. J.C. Fisher and R.H. Pry, "A Simple Substitution Model of *Technological Change,*" *Technological Forecasting and Social Change*, vol. 3, no 1 (1971): 75-88.
2. As presented in T. Modis, *Predictions*, (New York: Simon & Schuster, 1992).
3. A. Debecker and T. Modis, Determination of the Uncertainties in S-Curve Logistic Fits, *Technological Forecasting & Social Change*, 46 (1994) 153-173.

4. T. Modis, Strengths and Weaknesses of S-Curves, *Technological Forecasting & Social Change*, 74, No 6 (2007) 866-872.

5. Benjamin Gompertz, On the Nature of the Function Expressive of the Law of Human Mortality, and on a New Mode of Determining the Value of Life Contingencies, *Philosophical Transactions of the Royal Society of London*, 115, (1825):513–585.

6. Frank Bass, A New-Product Growth Model for Consumer Durables, *Management Science*, 15, (1969):215-227.

7. Among other models are: Vijay Mahajan and Milton E.F. Schoeman, Generalized Model for the Time Pattern of the Diffusion Process. *IEEE Transactions on Engineering Management EM-24*, 12-18, (1977). Nigel Meade, Forecasting Using Growth Curves - an Adaptive Approach, *Journal of Operational Research Society*, 36, (1985):1103-1116.

8. Data source: US Geological Survey at: http://minerals.usgs.gov/ds/2005/140/gold.pdf

9. The classic work on economic cycles by Russian economist Nikolai D. Kondratieff in 1926 resulted in his name being associated with this phenomenon: N. D. Kondratieff, "The Long Wave in Economic Life," *The Review of Economic Statistics*, vol. 17 (1935):105–115.

10. The data come from Stanley Sadie, ed. *New Grove Dictionary of Music and Musicians*, (London: Macmillan, 1980). The S-curve fit is discussed more extensively in *Predictions*, see Note 2 above.

11. C. Marchetti, La Saga dei Nobel, *Technology Review* (Italian edition) 13 (1989) 8-11.

12. T. Modis, Competition and Forecasts for Nobel Prize Awards, *Technological Forecasting & Social Change* 34 (2) (1988) 95-102.

13. T. Modis, *Predictions – 10 Years Later*, (Geneva Switzerland: Growth Dynamics, 2002).

14. B.L. Golden, P.F. Zantek, Inaccurate Forecasts of the Logistic Growth Model for Nobel Prizes, *Technological Forecasting & Social Change* 71 (4) (2004) 417-422.

15. T. Modis, US Nobel Laureates: Logistic Growth versus Volterra-Lotka, *Technological Forecasting & Social Change*, 78 (2011) 559–564.

16. It was Frank Lulei at MZSG at that time who suggested to me to fit S-curves with variable ceilings.

3 – SEASONS OF GROWTH

1. Alfred J. Lotka, *Elements of Physical Biology*, (Baltimore, MD: Williams & Wilkins Co., 1925).

2. W. Brian Arthur, "Positive Feedbacks in the Economy," *Scientific American*, February 1990, pp. 80-85.
3. The chaotic fluctuations are discussed in Chapter 5, but for an in-depth study see Theodore Modis, "Fractal Aspects of Natural Growth," *Technological Forecasting & Social Change*, vol. 47 (1994) 63-73.
4. See Theodore Modis and Alain Debecker, "Chaoslike States Can Be Expected before and After Logistic Growth", *Technological Forecasting & Social Change*, vol. 41 (1992) 111-120.
5. See Cesare Marchetti, IIASA, Pervasive Long Waves: Is Human Society Cyclotymic? Prepared for the conference "Offensiv zu Arbeitsplätzen: Weltmärkte 2010". Cologne, 14-15 September 1996.

4 – SUBSTITUTIONS

1. J.C. Fisher and R.H. Pry, "A Simple Substitution Model of *Technological Change,*" *Technological Forecasting and Social Change*, vol. 3, no 1 (1971): 75-88.
2. Steven Schnaars, *Megamistakes: Forecasting and the Myth of Rapid Technological Change*, (New York: The Free Press, 1989).
3. A similar graph was first published by Nebosja Nakicenovic, "The Automobile Road to Technological Change: Diffusion of the Automobile as a Process of Technological Substitution," *Technological Forecasting and Social Change*, vol. 29 (1986) 309–40.
4. See Note 3 above.
5. See Note 1 above.
6. This graph has been adapted from one in Fisher and Pry, see Note 1 above.
7. Adapted from a graph by Nebojsa Nakicenovic in "The Automobile Road to Technological Change: Diffusion of the Automobile as a Process of Technological Substitution," see Note 3 above.
8. Nebojsa Nakicenovic, "Software Package for the Logistic Substitution Model," report RR-79-12, International Institute of Advanced Systems Analysis, Laxenburg, Austria, (1979).
9. See Marchetti's website http://www.cesaremarchetti.org/.
10. C. Marchetti, "Primary Energy Substitution Models: On the Interaction between Energy and Society," *Technological Forecasting and Social Change*, vol. 10 (1977): 345-56.
11. T. Modis, *World Future Review*, 1, No 3, June-July 2009.

12. Data sources: Marchetti, see Note 10 above, and Statistical Review of World Energy 2008 at http://www.bp.com/.
13. Wood is mostly made of cellulose, which is a carbohydrate (carbon plus water). Marchetti has published these molar-ratio estimates in "When Will Hydrogen Come?" *Int. J. Hydrogen Energy*, 10 (1985) 215-219.
14. Data source: Dataquest, June 1992.

5 – CASCADES OF S-CURVES

1. T. Modis, Fractal Aspects of Natural growth, *Technological Forecasting and Social Change*, 47 (1994) 63-73.
2. This idea was first published in H. B. Stewart, *Recollecting the Future*, (Homewood, IL: Dow Jones-Irvin, 1989).
3. T. Modis, The Normal, the Natural, and the Harmonic, *Technological Forecasting & Social Change*, 74, No 3, (2007) 391-399.
4. This figure has been published in Reference 3 above.
5. See Stanley Davis and Bill Davidson, *Vision 2020*, (New York: Simon & Schuster, 1991).
6. See Note 1 above.
7. See Theodore Modis, *Predictions*, (New York: Simon & Schuster, 1992), pp. 178-179.
8. See Note 1 above.
9. T. Modis, Why the Singularity Cannot Happen, in *Singularity Hypotheses*, A. H. Eden et al. (eds.), The Frontiers Collection, Springer-Verlag, Berlin Heidelberg, (2012), pp 311-339.
10. See Note 9 above.
11. See also Note 1 above. The data come from: Laffont, A., and Durieux, F., *Encyclopédie Médico-Chirurgical*, Editions Techniques, Paris, 1985; Kaufmann, Lang, and Rieben, *Croissance de la taille et du poid de 4 à 19.5 ans – Garcons et filles suisses domiciliés dans le canton de Genève en 1972*, Editions Médicine et Hygiène, Geneva, 1976.

6 – EVENT ENHANCEMENT

1. As reported by David Clutterbuck and Stuart Crainer in *Makers of Management*, (London: MacMillan, 1990).

7 – THE LIFE CYCLE OF SERVICES

1. G. W. Potts, "Exploit Your Product's Service Life Cycle," *Harvard Business Review*, vol. 66 (1988) 32-36.
2. T. Modis and A. Debecker, "Determining the Service Life Cycle of Computers," in N. Nakicenovic and A. Grubler, eds., *Diffusion of Technologies and Social Behavior*, (Springer-Verlag, Laxenburg, Austria, 1991).
3. Marchetti, C., Longevity – An operational definition, private communication.

8 – VOLTERRA- LOTKA

1. 1. Alfred J. Lotka, *Elements of Physical Biology*, (Baltimore, MD: Williams & Wilkins Co., 1925).
2. This is based on Verhulst's original description of natural growth for a species population: P. F. Verhulst, "Recherches mathématiques sur la loi d'Accroissement de la Population" ("Mathematical Research on the Law of Population Growth"), *Nouveaux Memoires de l'Académie Royale des Sciences et des Belles-Lettres de Bruxelles*, vol. 18 (1945): 1-40; also in P. F. Verhulst, "Notice sur la loi que la population suit dans son accroissement" (Announcement on the Law Followed by a Population During Its Growth"), *Correspondence Mathématique et physique*, vol. 10: 113–21.
3. Farrell, C., A Theory of Technological Progress. *Technological Forecasting & Social Change* 44, No. 2 (1993) 161-178.
4. Pistorius, C.W.I., and Utterback, J.M., The Death Knells of Mature Technologies, *Technological Forecasting & Social Change*, 50, No. 3 (1995) 133-151.
5. This chapter is based on the article: T. Modis, Genetic Re-Engineering of Corporations, *Technological Forecasting & Social Change*, 56 (1997) 107-118.
6. C. Farrell, Survival of The Fittest Technologies, *New Scientist 137*, 6 February 1993.
7. P.F. Drucker, The Discipline of Innovation, *Harvard Business Review*, May-June (1985) 67-72.
8. Richard N. Foster, *Innovation the Attacker's Advantage*, (New York: Summit Books, 1986).
9. Cooper, R. G., and Kleinschmidt, E. J., *New Products: The Key Factors in Success*, (American Marketing Association, Chicago, 1990).
10. Smitalova, Kristina, and Sujan, Stefan, *A Mathematical Treatment of Dynamical Models in Biological Science*, (Ellis Horwood, West Sussex,

England, 1991). Actually, credit for the original classification must be given to Odum, E., *Fundamentals of Ecology*, (Saunders, London, 1971), and to Williamson, M., *The Analysis of Biological Populations*, (Edward Arnold, London, 1972).

11. Frank Sulloway, *Born to Rebel*, (Boston: Pantheon, Harvard University Press, 1996).
12. See Note 3 above.
13. T. Modis, US Nobel Laureates: Logistic Growth versus Volterra-Lotka, *Technological Forecasting & Social Change*, 78, 2011, 559–564.
14. T. Modis, Strengths and Weaknesses of S-curves, *Technological Forecasting & Social Change*, 74, No 6 (2007) 866-872.

9 – COMPLETING THE PANOPLY

1. D. Robert Buzzell, and T. Beadley Gale, *The PIMS Principles: Linking Strategy to Performance*, (New York: The Free Press, 1987).
2. Theodore Modis, *Conquering Uncertainty*, (New York: McGraw-Hill, 1998).
3. See Note 2 above.

10 – EXCEL-BASED TOOLS

1. A. Debecker and T. Modis, "Determination of the Uncertainties in S-curve Logistic Fits," *Technological Forecasting & Social Change*, 46 (1994) 153-173.
2. Taylor, John R., *An Introduction to Error Analysis*, 2nd Ed., (University Science Books, 1997).
3. Bevington, Philip R., and Robinson, D. Keith, *Data Reduction and Error Analysis for the Physical Sciences*, 2nd Ed., (McGraw-Hill, 1992).
4. Evans, Robley D., *The Atomic Nucleus*, (McGraw-Hill, 1969).
5. Bennett, Carl A., and Franklin, Norman L., *Statistical Analysis in Chemistry and the Chemical Industry*, (Wiley, 1954).
6. To translate *reduced* Chi-Square values to confidence levels one may also use interactive calculators found in the Internet, for example: http://www.danielsoper.com/statcalc/calc12.aspx and http://www.hostsrv.com/webmaa/app1/MSP/webm1010/chi2.msp

APPENDIX A1

1. A. Debecker, and T. Modis, Determination of the Uncertainties in S-curve Logistic Fits, *Technological Forecasting & Social Change*, 46 (1994) 153-173.

APPENDIX A3

1. T. Modis, Reply to Martino's comments on "The normal, the natural, and the harmonic," *Technological Forecasting & Social Change*, 74, No 3 (2007) 402-404.
2. T. Modis, and A. Debecker, Chaoslike States Can Be Expected Before and After Logistic Growth, *Technological Forecasting & Social Change*, 41 (1992) 111-120.
3. Theodore Modis, *Conquering Uncertainty*, (New York: McGraw-Hill, 1998).
4. See Note 3 above.
5. Nash, Stephan G. and Sofer, Ariela, *Linear and Nonlinear Programming*, (New York: McGraw-Hill, 1996).
6. Wolf, Paul R. and Ghilani, Charles D., *Adjustment Computations*, (John Wiley, New York, 1997).
7. T. Modis and A. Debecker, "Determining the Service Life Cycle of Computers," in N. Nakicenovic and A. Grubler, eds., *Diffusion of Technologies and Social Behavior*, (Laxenburg, Austria: Springer-Verlag, 1991) 511-522.
8. Odum, E., *Fundamentals of Ecology*, (London: Saunders, 1971); and Leslie, P. H., A Stochastic Model for Studying the Properties of Certain Biological Systems by Numerical Methods, *Biometrika* 45 (1957) 16-31.
9. See the website: http://www.orbitals.com/self/least/least.htm, and also see Notes 5-6 above.

ACKNOWLEDGEMENTS

I am gratefully indebted to the work of Cesare Marchetti who has contributed enormously to making the formulation of natural growth a general vehicle for understanding society. I draw extensively on his ideas, ranging from the concept of invariants (Chapter One) to the productivity of Mozart (Chapter Three) and the evolution of nuclear energy (Chapter Four). This book could not have come into existence had it not been for the work of Cesare Marchetti and of his collaborators, Nebojsa Nakicenovic and Arnulf Grubler, at the International Institute for Applied Systems Analysis in Laxenburg, Austria. I am grateful to them for keeping me abreast of their latest work and for all the fruitful discussions we have had together.

Of great importance has been the contribution of my colleague and friend, Alain Debecker. His competences in mathematics and computer sciences reflect on many aspects of this book and in particular the entire Chapter Seven.

Chapter Six, the methodology of Event Enhancement, owes its existence to the arduous work of Susanne Seror whose ideas and Excel skills contributed to shaping this consultancy offering from the very beginning. She was involved in the data collection and analysis of both conferences discussed under case studies in this chapter.

I want to thank Frank Lulei, who was at the MZSG at the time, for the many fruitful discussions we had, which lead to the development of the methodology fitting S-curves with a variable ceiling.

My colleague and friend of old times, Phil Bagwell, taught me the intricacies of economies of scale and price elasticity, which I was then able to connected to S-curves.

Finally, I want to thank my wife, Maria, who gave me continuous moral as well as physical support.

Theodore Modis
Lugano, Switzerland
June 2013

INDEX

Page numbers in **bold** refer to principal discussions
Page numbers in *italics* refer to figures.

64-bit technology, 57, 90,*90*
A Second Lease on Life
   software, 5, 197-199
A Second Lease on Life, 3, 62, 64
accidents,
   car, 14-17, *16, 22*
   nuclear, 86
adaptation, 50
advertising, 4, 8, **139-145**, 168
African
   Zulus, 18
aggressiveness, 184
amensalism, 136
Appleton, 4, 170-178, *171-172, 174-178*
attack, 4, **133-134**, *138*, 139-140,
   145, 185, 231
attractiveness, **132**, 140-143, 144-
   148, 185, 205-206
aviation, 56-57
   industry, 101

backcasting, 3, 37
ballpoint
   pens, 61, **136-138**, *138*
Bass model, 34
BCG matrix, **109-111**, *111*, 116
bell curve, **23**, *23*, 26, *26,* 28, 47
benchmarking, 8, 52, 116, 120, 166,
   183
bias, 41-42, 53, 154, 161, 164-165,
   209
bottom-up, 61, 167
   forces, 62, 87
BPR, 52, 116, *119,* 167, 169, *183*
bureaucracy, 49

cannibalization, 34, 93
cascading
   careers, 64
   S-curves, **93**, *94,* 198
ceiling, 25, 27-30, *30*, 31, 37, *40*, 41-
   43, *44*, 47, 55, 68, 73, 90, 98, 100-
   101, 103, *103,* 120, 122, 127, 147,
   194-197, 199, 213, 215, 217, 219,
   223
   variable, 3, 5, 9, *16*, 41, 200-204,
   203, 206, 208, **221**, 228
centralization, 67, 168, *181*
change management, 167
chaos, 3, 5, 7, 52, **54-55**, 62, 96, 120,
   131, 167, 204, 218, *219*, 229, 233
character displacement, 137-138
Chi Square, 5, 31, 41, 94, 125, 146,
   191-195, 199, 201, 204, 205, 221,
   232
   reduced, **194-195**, 205, 208
children, 139
cirrhosis, 22
classical music, *69*
commensalism, 136-137
competition, 7, 13, 22, 28, 30, 35,
   36, 43, 46, 49, 51, 54, 65, 69, 72,
   71, 74, 76, 77, 79, 85, 93, 110,
   122, 128, 131, 132, 134, 135, 136,
   137, 138, 139, *141*, 144, 146, 147,
   148, 149, 150, 167, 180, 181, 190,
   192, 217, 218, 223, 224, 227
   management, 137
competitors, 7, 35, 46, 52, 74, 75,
   83, 131, 133, *135*, 149, 175, 184
complexity, 20, 23, 208

confidence level, 42, *58*, 146, 148, 173, *174, 176,* 193-194, 199, 208, 213, 232
conservative, 32, 70, 139, 166, 211
core competencies, 49, 166, 169
correlation, 36, 136, 213
counterattack, 8, 133-134, 137, *138*, **139-141**, 185
coupling constants, 134, 137 143, 147, 148, 173, 176-177, 183, 208
cross-discipline, *23*, 51, 166
culture, 18, 33, 62, 96, *119*, 148, 167, 171, 210
  driven, 169
cumulative, 69
  data, 32, 34, *35*, 36, 39, 42, *44, 58, 58,* 63, 66, 93-94, 121, *122,* 129, 147, 149, 173, *174,* 193, *197,* 201, 208, 217
  growth, 3, 25, *26,* 28, 47
  cumulative variable, 30, 196, 204

Darwin, 49, 71, 137-138
Debecker, Alain, 31, 121, 213, 227, 229, 213-233
derivative, **65-66**, *65,* 154, 155, 156, 200, 202, 203, 206, 219, 220, 221, 222, 223, 224
differentiation, **141**, 1*44,* 145, 184-185
diffusion, 28, 71, **84-85**, 91, 101, 121, 172-173, 228-229, 231, 233
Digital Equipment Corporation (DEC), 7, 13, 101
displacement, 82, 107, 140, 199
  daily, **17-18**, 56
  character, 137-138
diversification, 173
downward-pointing S-curve, 3, **67**, 154-155
Drucker, Peter, 134, 231

economies of scale, 3, 5, **45**, 109
  and learning, 220
economy, 53, 66, 74, **97-98**, 101, 111, 229
  US, 111
  world, 45, 49, 51, 59, 61,

energy consumption, 59, *60*, 61-62, 84, *86*, 93
energy sources, 84-87, 89
  renewable, 77
entrepreneurship, 7, 49, 167-168, 181, 211
equilibrium, 7, 14-15, 18-19, 22, 30, 54
event enhancement, 2, **109**, 112-113, 230

feedback, 7, 53, 110, 116, 127, 191, 193, 196, 199,
  positive, 52, 229
flow-chart, 188, 190
fluctuation, 31, 41, 47, 51, 52, **54-54**, 59, 77, 81, 96, 146, 161, 167, 193-195, 218-219, 229
Fourier analysis, 108
fractal, 2, 54, **96-97**, *97,* 103, 229-230
future, 7, 21, 32, 37, 45-46, 51, 56, 60, 67-70, 72, 77, 81, 86, 99, 101, 110-111, 113, 121, 140, *144*, 148, 154-156, 172, 185, 211, 227, 229-230

Gaussian, 24, *24*, 35
GNP, 66
Gompertz, 34, 228
Greek, 29, 134, *135*, 143, 153, 184-185
growth
  function, 27, 45, 49
  human, 4, 105, 106
  logistic, 29, 33, 121-123, 121-123, 125, 131, 149, 153, 157, 223, 228-229, 232-233
  natural, 3, 21-23, 25, *25*, 27-28, 33, 46-47, 50, 54, *65,* 71, 75, 78, 93, 97, *97,* 209, 211, 218, 227, 229-231

harmonic motion, 49, 93, 107
heartbeat , 19-20
historical data, 32, 37, 41, 125, 170, 213-215, 224
Hitchcock, Alfred, 62-64, *63*

HLB, 4, 110-115, *111, 114-115*
homeostasis, 14, 19, 26, 30
horizontal segmentation, 181
hyperbola, 45, 195

image building, 139, 145
inflation, 66
in-hospital infections, 22
innovation, 7, 49, 51, 54, 61, 69, 91,
   98, 107, 167-168, 180, 211
instinct, 8, 156, **160-165**, 179, 188
integral, 25-26, 34
invariants, 13, 18, 21-22, 30
investment, 7, 66, 141-142

just-in-time replacement, 93

Kondratieff, 36, 49, 59, 93, 96, 98,
   228

learning, 21, 29, 45, 51, 62, 68, 70,
   167, 168, 180, 221
life cycle, 7, 8, **23-25**, *23, 24,* 27, 28,
   32, 34, 35, 46, 51, 58, 64, 66, 70,
   84, 96, 97, 98, 100, 101, 102, 104,
   105, 109, 121, 122, 123, 124, 128,
   153, 155, 159, 161, 173, 174, 197,
   209, 210, 211, 213, 217, 222, 223
   of services, 4, 5, **121**, 222, 231
life expectancy, 19, 20
limited resource, 33, 36, 41, 145
limiting factors, 9
logarithm, 75, 80
logistic function, 28, 34, 37, 47, 75
Lotka, Alfred J., 49, 131, 228, 231

Magic, 13
Marchetti, Cesare, 13, 14, 20, 41, 84,
   91, 125, 228-231
market
   microorocessor, 89
   penetration, 7
   Personal "Vehicle", *74*
   share, 52, 75, 78, 84, 90, *90*, 91,
      101, 103, *103*, 109-110, 134, 137,
      143-144, 148, 166
   transportation, 17
   trends, 4, 89

Michele parameter, 42
Microsoft, 3, 4, **58-59**, *58*, 93, 104,
   105, 195, 202
Monte Carlo, 4, 198, 223
Moore's law, 4, 105
mortality, 30, 121, 122, 123, 124,
   125, 126, 127, 128, 129, 172, 235
   infant, 19-20, 50, 57, 77, 89, 169
Mozart, 64
mutation, 108
mutualism, 136

Naisbitt, John, 56
negative correlation, 37, 136
NEOSET, 4, 184-187, *186*
nested S-curves, 97, 101
neutralism, 136, 138
niche, 13,
   capacity, 27, 30-33,
   market-, 7, 28, 32, 34, 54, 66, 93,
      101, 103, 122, 132, 138, 140, 148,
      175
   micro-, 22, 75
Nobel, 41-43, *44-45*, 46, 145-
   146,*146*,**147-149**, 193-194, 201,
   203, 205, *207*, 208, 228, 232
nominal beginning, **38**, 40, 41, 154,
   175
nylon, 61, 140-143, *141*

obsolescence, 73, 122, 128
Oedipus, 153, *154*
optimization, 46, 162, 195
optimism, 70, 156, 175
oscillation, 55, 96
overshoot, 31, 55, 57

particle accelerator, 7, 39
pedestal, 37, 104, 106, 199, 200,
   202, 203, 206
penetration level, 31, 104, 177, 202,
   206, 221
pent-up demand, 39, 55, 57, 99,
   103, 104
PIMS, 162, 236
pin-the-tail-on-the-donkey, 154,
   177, 184, 186

population, 15, 16, 22, 27-28, 30,
    31-32, 38-39, 43, 44, 70-72, 97,
    131-133, 136, 147-148, 173-175,
    204, 227, 235
precursor, **55**, 57-58, 101, 102
predator-prey, 137, 175, 178, 187
predictive power, 26-27, 29, 32
price, 7, 22, 34, 36, 46, 66, 67, 70,
    102, 104, 111, 128, 134, 137, 139,
    143, 187-188, 190, 223,
    elasticity, 5, 80, 142, 184-185,
    219-220
product
    computer, 34-35, *35*
    innovation, 51, 98, 168, 180
    life cycle, 93, 99-100, 102, 121,
    223
    portfolio, 109, 110
    replacement, 7, 93, 98
    sales, 31, 66, 93, 98, 121, 193
    substitution, 7
productivity, 40, 56-57, 60, 63, 149,
    162, 168, 171, 197
projections, 34, 72, 86, 89-91, 148,
    211
proportional, 27-29, 41, 45, 66, 72,
    107, 132, 219220
Prudential, 4, 178-184, *179-183*

QUALCOMM, 4, 187-190, *189-
    190*

rapid-growth phase, 26, 107
rationale, 4, 8, 160, **163-166**, *162,
    164,* 179, 182
raw data, 32
replacement product, 93, 169
restructuring, 171
returns on investment, 66
rheostasis, 26
riddle, 153, *154*
ROI, 66

saturation, 27, 84, 99, 100, 103, 132,
    221
Schumpeter, Joseph, A., 61

S-curves, 46, **93-94**, *94,* 96, 188,
    189, 198, 219
S-curves, 3, 8-9, 28, 30, *30,* **31-34**,
    44, 45-46, 59, *73, 83,* 120, 134,
    148-149, 170, 178, 181, *183,* 188,
    189, 190-191, 209, 211, 228, 230,
    and competitive substitutions, 71
    and chaos, 204, *219*
    and economies of scale, 45
    73, 78
    and human growth, 106, *106*
    and the shortening of life cycles,
    99, *99*
    cascades of, 93, *94,* 198
    deviations from, 39-40
    downward-pointing, 67
    fractals of, 96-98
    how to fit, 195, 200
    intuitive use of, 68
    nested, 101
    uncertainties of, 213,
    with variable ceiling, 41, 221
seasonal, 7-8, 34, 49-50, *53,* 59,
    160, 197-199, 213
seasons, 8, **49-51**, *52,* 54, 60-61, 66-
    68, *69,* 70, *95,* 96-97, 107, 110,
    119, 120, 153-155, 165, 178, 188,
    190, 198, 209, 228
    business, 7, 61-62, 64, 95-96, 109,
    111, 153, 173, 178, 180
segmentation, 50, *52,* 61-62
    horizontal, 181
self-regulation, 15
semiconductors, 4, 89
sensitivity analysis, 142, 145
sigmoid function, 34
Solver, 5, **191-192**, *192,* 193, 195,
    198, 199, 201, 202, 204-206, 208,
    217, 224, 226
species, 5, 7, 14, 20, 28-29, 32-36,
    35, 56, 58-59, 64, 71-72, 104, 125,
    131-133, 136-137, 140, 143, 146-
    149, 172-173, *175,* 200, 204-205,
    207, 207-208, 210-211, 220-221,
    224, 231
speed, 7, 14-18, 56, 57, 65, 66, 72,
    91, 128, 137, 188, 227

cars, 66
sphinx, *153*
starting value, 9, 193, 195, 196, **201-206**, 221, 224, 226
stock rating, 66
strategy, 4, 8, 64, 87, 93, 102, 110, 111, 134, 138, 153, 154, 156, 160, 165, 209, 211, 232
STRATEST1.xls, 155
substitution, 3, 4, 7, 22, 57, **71-78**, *79,* 80-85, 87, 89-91, 109, 131, 137, 140, 171, 172, 227, 229
survival of the fittest, 7, 9, 34, 49, 67, 211, 231
symbiosis, 136
symmetry, 27

top-down forces, 61
TQM, 116, 120
trial and error, 31
turnover, 170, 184-186, *190*, 220

uncertainty, 154, 155, 160, 176, 193, 194, 213

conquering, **8**, 53, 77, 165, 166, 227, 232-233
unification, 20, 62
grand, 21
up-and-down-and-up, 70
USA, 33
USSR, 33

vertical integration, 49, 166, 173, 181
Volterra-Lotka, 4, 5, 8, 9, 43, **131**, 134, 137-139, 143-149, *144*, 173, *175,* 175-176, *177,* 184-187, 204-205, *207*, 208, 211, 224, 228, 232

Where Are You on the Curve and What to Do about It, 8, 65, 112-113, *153*, **154**, 161, 164-166, 170, 210
wool, *141*, 140-143